GEORGE FOX
&
THE QUAKERS

East Midlands HOME AREA

To Lincoln

Mansfield
Skegby
Scotland
Newark on Trent
Alfreton
Ripley
Sleaford
Ashbourne
DERBY
NOTTINGHAM
GRANTHAM
Uttoxeter
BURTON ON TRENT
Loughborough
Melton Mowbray
N
Ashby de la Zouche
Swannington
WATLING STREET
LICHFIELD
Tamworth
TO CHESTER, IRELAND N.W.
Atherstone
Fenny Drayton
LEICESTER
(30 May 1645: Sack of Leicester by Royalists)
Oakham
STAMFORD
Baddesley Ensor
Mancetter
Hartshill
Whetstone
Broughton Astley
Uppingham
Sutton Coldfield
Nuneaton
BIRMINGHAM
Lutterworth
Market Harborough
Oundle
Scale in Miles
1 2 3 4 5 6 7 8   12   16
COVENTRY
TO LONDON
R. Naseby (14 June, 1645)
Kettering
To LONDON
THE GREAT NORTH ROAD

The 1652 Country

Windermere
Grayrigg
R. Rawthey
KENDAL
Firbank Fell
Draw Well Farm
SEDBERGH
Underbarrow
Garsdale
Tullythwaite Hall
Brigflatts
Dentdale
Colton
Bouth
Staveley
Crosslands
Dent
High Newton
Preston Patrick
Camsgill
From Pendle Hill, George Fox's possible route through the Dales to Swarthmoor Hall.
Lindale
KIRKBY LONSDALE
ULVERSTON
Cartmel
SWARTHMOOR HALL
Yealand Conyers
+ Sunbreck Burial Ground
CARNFORTH
N
The Bay
R. Lune
R. Kent
Scale
1 2 3
MILES
Further S.E. near Clitheroe
PENDLE HILL

E. Makins. delt.
LANCASTER

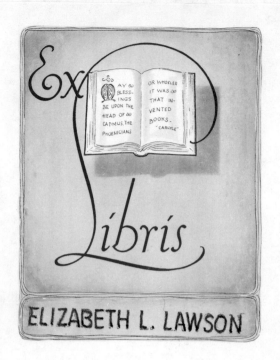

Ex Libris

MAY & BLESS-INGS BE UPON THE HEAD OF CADMUS, THE PHOENICIANS OR WHOEVER IT WAS THAT IN-VENTED BOOKS. "CARLYLE"

ELIZABETH L. LAWSON

GEORGE FOX & THE QUAKERS

CECIL W. SHARMAN

Quaker Home Service · London

Friends United Press · Richmond, Indiana

First published March 1991
by Quaker Home Service, London, U.K.
and Friends United Press, Richmond,U.S.A.

ISBN 0 85245 230 6
ISBN 0944350   14 3

Cover design by John Blamires
based on a photograph by Simon Warner

Printed in Great Britain in Palatino Roman 11/12 pt
by Headley Brothers Ltd The Invicta Press
Ashford Kent and London

CONTENTS

ILLUSTRATIONS

Maps and Family Tree

Plates

PICTURE CREDITS

PREFACE

George Fox took on the religious and political establishments of his day in the name of a purer Christianity and a juster social system. This led to a remarkably strenuous, varied and dangerous career. As he went on, his life expanded from its first private level, with its family ties and his own devotional exploration, to a second, the communal, as others joined with him to form an active movement or society, and then to a third level, the political, as he came up against the attempts of the state to destroy his movement and avoid the challenge of its ideas. To make sense of Fox's life we have to look at the interactions between these three levels.

It may seem odd today that religion could generate so many controversies, and that everyone used concepts drawn from the Bible. Yet their story of dissent and persecution, of civil disobedience and protest, was remarkably like much that happens now, with political slogans and manifestoes as sacred texts, and causes that include the natural world and the environment. The Seventeenth Century, despite all its differences, often seems like a prototype for our own. For such reasons alone the story of Fox and the Quakers, arch-protesters in an age of protest, deserves attention.

Both Fox and the people who worked with him felt that they were doing something of lasting importance. They defied censors and licensers to publish innumerable books and pamphlets. They put their experiences into journals; they kept their correspondence, and every record they could, of their lives and deliberations. Much of the story can therefore be told in their own words, the strangeness of which, like an unfamiliar accent, should soon pass. In an outline such as this, brevity and accuracy are hard to keep together, and it is only too likely that one or the other may have suffered. Yet I grieve for the topics and the lively stories which had to be left out. Fox's message itself is given here mainly from his point of view. A critical study of his teachings, and a comparison with conventional theologies, needs books and essays of its own.

Any general study of this kind is deeply in debt to the schol-

1

ars who do the hard labour of examining the original material. I am grateful to those who have read and commented on the manuscript, to the Librarians at Friends House, London, and Woodbrooke College, Birmingham, and to St Deiniol's Library, Hawarden, Clwyd. The staff at the local branch of Cheshire County Library also deserve thanks for their patient hunting out of books from around the country.

A little of the material was used in a paper called *George Fox and his Family* which appeared in *Quaker History*, the Bulletin of the Friends Historical Association, Philadelphia, in 1985 and 1986.

★   ★   ★

Quakers use no titles, simply first names and surnames. Often, in Fox's time, for brevity, they used initials, Fox's own being often written 'G.ff'. Because the same few first names come round frequently, here the surnames alone are mostly used. Margaret Fell, later Fox, is easily recognized simply as Margaret, and her daughter as Margaret junior, or, after her marriage, as Margaret Rous. Fox had two companions called Whitehead, not related, the major one was named George, the other John.

Until our own time Cumbria was divided into three counties, Cumberland, Westmorland, and the Furness area of Lancashire. Here only the present day 'Cumbria' is used, in the belief that the old names would not convey any more distinct meaning.

All dates are given with the year beginning on January 1st, and not, as it then did, on March 25th. Spellings and punctuations are modernised. Most quotations are abridged. Although this brings in the risk that the meaning may become distorted, to do differently would lengthen the book enormously, and lead to a confusing mass of side issues.

Measurements and money values are accompanied by their metric equivalents. To give a present day equivalent for money values is difficult, if only because the costs of different things or services have not increased equally, and because of the frequent adjustments made necessary by inflation. Labour, for example, was relatively very cheap, but some other costs, including transport, were very high. A very rough guide is to multiply any sum by a hundred, and to think on from there.

To avoid footnotes, whilst making it possible to follow up quotations, initials of titles, or author's names, are included in the text, as unobtrusively as possible. These refer to the list given at the end. Quotations without a source are either often used phrases, or close to another from the same work. 'Q' at the beginning of a reference means 'Quoted in'.

FOREWORD

George Fox first gathered Friends 340 years ago by 'opening to them the way'; for our time also, his life has become part of his message. His *Journal* told his own life-story fully and vividly, so that efforts to improve on it have recently been few. Modern readers, however, find Fox's *Journal* so detailed, and so quick to assume his readers' familiarity with situations, events and outlooks of his time that though we constantly quote it we rarely read or grasp it as a whole. Here Cecil Sharman has done us important service, placing all the key events of Fox's life within their historical setting, and bringing out Fox's warmth of personality and his intense sense of mission, mirrored in what his friends like John Banks and William Penn told of him. These sides of Fox stand out also in Sharman's edition of Fox's Epistles, *No More But My Love*.

Fox's warm compassion and dry wit were often hidden behind his earnestness. He compared the pompous 'new clothes' claimed by 'reborn' but spiritually naked 'Christians' around him to Adam's and Eve's fig leaves 'A sunshine day might dry their aprons to powder' (EQW p.505). Sharman shows us that the moral sensitivity linked to Fox's warmth made his early years more agonizing than modern readers imagine who merely delight that Fox did not, like John Bunyan, bewail himself as 'the chief of sinners.' Ten or twelve times in his years of youthful searching, Fox found himself helpless before 'temptations and despair.' Repeatedly, when he found evil or hypocrisy in professing Christians he 'was afraid of all company' and would 'forsake all.' Few were 'tender' enough to appreciate his sense of guilt. This is the meaning of Fox's early discoveries that 'Jesus Christ had been tempted and had overcome'; therefore 'one Jesus Christ can speak to thy condition'. This did not end Fox's despair over temptations. His 'Yo-yo' relationship to his proud but strictly Puritan father, which several times drove him from home and then made him return 'afraid they would say I was disobedient to my parents' (N p.189) deserves a psychologist's insight such as Erik Erikson gave to Gandhi, as does Fox's stern Epistle to his parents (#5 in Ellwood's and Canby

4

Jones' editions), calling them to follow what he had found. Fox's most decisive 'opening' came out of his own inner awareness, in contrast to John Bunyan's 'openings' of Bible verses: Fox had fled from outward temptations in vain because the sources of evil, 'the natures of swine, dogs, vipers . . . Sodom and Egypt' (all intense symbols in his day) were within himself. He cried out 'why must I be thus' and found both within and beyond himself 'an ocean of darkness and death, but an infinite ocean of light and love which flowed over the ocean of darkness' (N p.19). After a final struggle by which he 'was altered in countenance and person,' he was freed from despair over temptations. For some months his released joy and love gave him a sense that he could live in 'the state of Adam before he fell' (N p.27). Modern Friends need not cramp Fox's experience into Wesley's forms of Justification and Sanctification, but can let Fox shed light on Wesley's life and our own.

Fox used language of Light more than of Love or Freedom: the Light shows truth, inner and outer reality. Yet truth for Fox was always active and moral: 'speak truth, act truth . . . Do justly, speak truly to all people whatsover. Then are ye a dread and terror to the unjust' (EQW p.435). Fox discerned truth better than do most of us who also may have been freed to live totally dependent on grace. Such folk included in his day both the Ranters who rebelled against Puritan culture, and Puritans like John Cotton who tried to build a New England upon biblical grace. Fox did not let either Calvinists or Ranters 'plead for sin' by ignoring what God empowers humans to do.

Fox saw the Power of God, to which Geoffrey Nuttall points in introducing the Nickalls edition of Fox's *Journal,* as shaping history around him. Fox's boyhood reading included John Foxe's *Book of Martyrs* written a century before to tie into a continuous tradition Stephen and Paul, John Hus and the Lollards and the Protestants burned by Catholic 'Bloody Mary' at Smithfield. This heroic vision of history inspired the Puritan revolution against Charles I. Cromwell had seen God's Providence in military victories. George Fox saw God's Spirit as fulfilling in Quaker 'Children of Light' the work begun in biblical times and the English Reformation. He let his life story echo the setting out of Abraham from home, Jesus' healings by faith, the sending out

of 70 disciples, and the proclaiming of the Day of the Lord from
'a high mountain'. Yet his apocalyptic urgency, of which
Douglas Gwyn has written, was less a return to the 'gospel
order' of the early Church than an opening of the way for the
Spirit's new work, 'primitive Christianity' not 'revived' but
continued.

Fox held to his Testimonies at the cost of repeated jailings and
was thus impatient when Nayler, Perrot, or Wilkinson and Story
challenged his leadings. Yet his mission to 'open' his hearers to
the Light made him reject any permanent power or position.
The patterns of Quaker business meetings he set up in the 1660's
relied on the Spirit's guidance, not of Fox, but of each group's
membership as a whole. Quaker ministry, like Fox's own, was
inherently temporary:

> It is a mighty thing to be in the ministry of the Lord and to go
> forth in that, for it is not as customary preaching, but to bring
> people to the end of all preaching; for [after] your once speak-
> ing to people, then people come into the thing ye speak of
> . . .And take heed of many words, but what reacheth to life
> . . . settles others in the life . . . Friends must be kept in the life
> which is pure . . . . that they may answer the life of God in
> others which is pure . . . So walk in the love of God'
> (N.p.340–41).

Hugh Barbour
Earlham College
April 1990

Chapter One

THE NATIONAL SCENE

The People

The Seventeenth Century has often been compared with our own, as a time of great uncertainty, change and conflict. Disputes about the right way to live, the right way to manage the country and the right form of worship drew in far more people, especially of the 'ordinary' sort, than in any past period, and led to painful upheavals and adjustments. The many strong and lively personalities of the time have almost all been forgotten and we have difficulty in making sense of the issues about which they fought so vigorously. Nor did their radical groups generally leave successors surviving to our own day. One of the few which has done so is the Religious Society of Friends, the Quaker movement which grew directly out of the work and experience of the first Quaker, George Fox. What therefore distinguished this movement from those others which have been lost? What was it about George Fox which led both state and church in his own day to fear and persecute him so fiercely? Why is he, rather than any of those others, still remembered?

Present day Quakers have often seemed so preoccupied with more recent developments that they have ignored both Fox himself and the strange world in which he moved and out of which his witness was shaped. Some writers in his England called it a 'world turned upside down' but what they had in mind was far from our worries about global chaos. The differences between their world and ours are just as relevant as the likenesses. Their motives, their sensitivities, and even the matters they took for granted depended on its conditions. To make sense of the Quakers - of the views and attitudes from which their revolutionary faith had to grow, and of the way they carried on their everyday lives - we need a picture of the England against which Fox and his followers reacted.

Even in its appearance their England was so very unlike the

place we know today that to recognize it we need to make difficult adjustments to our own sympathies and scales of per-
ception. To begin with, in comparison with anything most of us
know, it would have appeared empty. The total population was
rising towards about five million, but most people lived in small
villages, for, apart from London, with its three hundred and fifty
thousand, Norwich and Bristol with their ten thousand or so,
hardly ten towns had over five thousand. Places now huge cities
were small local market centres with two or three thousand
people, or were undistinguished villages, often with only a hundred or so inhabitants. According to our only source of information, the number of communicants in the parish, Fox's
birthplace, the Leicestershire village of Fenny Drayton, was one
of this sort. Computer graphics can show us a group of people
on the screen and then wipe some of them away. We need to
imagine an England in which only one person moves where we
now see ten; and then, with the people not there, we can wipe
out all the buildings, roads, and other equipment which they
might have used. From what is left has then to go everything
requiring any kind of energy but muscle, wind and water. This
difference helps to account for the small scale and the disconcerting intimacy of happenings, despite everyone's great preoccupation with rank and the outward manifestations of status.

Most people then were young in years, though often old in
hardship. Some did reach sixty, but those who survived childhood thought themselves lucky to pass forty, in face of the incessant risks of accident and illness. We hear only of the l665 'Great
Plague', but in fact epidemics of some sort happened somewhere every year or so, along with the endemic smallpox. For
women the prospects were even poorer. Those who survived
the infections of childbirth often died of exhaustion after incessant pregnancies. Another strange feature of the time was the
indifference to injuries, and the brutal punishments, especially
of the weak, such as children and criminals. If we could go there
as time travellers, the effects of strange diseases, especially dis-
figuring eczemas and rotten ulcers, would startle us. We should
be even more dismayed by the stench of long unwashed bodies
and clothing. And of course there would also be the rubbish to
make its contribution, from sewage to slaughterhouse waste. It

appears that hardly anyone even noticed this. Fox himself mentions various stinks so often and with such revulsion that he at least must have had an unusually fastidious nose.

In harsh seasons the poor died of exposure, and, when crops failed, of hunger. No one then could collect the information from which they might have analysed their problems, but all felt the effects: slumps as the price of grain or woollen cloth fell; inflation, as prices rose inexplicably; and the overcrowding and unemployment arising from a population explosion which the farming and manufacturing techniques couldn't cope with. The leader of a Puritan emigration to America in 1630 had written,

> This land grows weary of its inhabitants, so as man who is the most precious of all creatures is here more vile and base than the earth we tread on ... Men spending as much labour and cost to recover or keep sometimes an acre or two of land as would procure them many hundred as good or better in another country. (Edwards p.244)

It is easy to forget that Fox's England was in our terms almost a 'primitive' country where local harvests, floods, and droughts mattered more than the goings on amongst the great folk in London.

The poor were inescapably everywhere, the beggars, - handicapped, aged, and unemployed, - and the labourers, many of whom were little better off than those who had no work at all. After the fighting these were joined by wounded and discharged soldiers, who got very little sympathy when they were no longer useful. In the country were the various grades of farmer, from impoverished tenant smallholders to yeomen, almost as wealthy as some of the squires, who were distinguished by their living mainly off the rents of farms, sometimes in several parishes. In the towns were craftsmen, and some who might be called shopkeepers. Many people lived within households of a master and his wife, with their children and a varying number of workmen, apprentices and servants. In London, and a few other places, were major merchants, wholesalers with various import-export businesses and sometimes money-lending connections. Scattered here and there were professionals, almost too few to count: doctors, better at collecting fees than at curing patients with their strange and brutal treatments; lawyers, skilled at threading the mazes of an antiquated legal system and even better at enriching themselves; but there was hardly anyone who might be called 'civil servant', or any sort of administrator. In the parishes were the clergy. A few of them were well off, if they had the rights to enough tithes or good glebe land, but many were as poor as schoolmasters, struggling to collect ten or twenty pounds a year. Many parsons in fact doubled up as farmers or teachers, coaching the few bright boys around them. The economic and class labels of today cannot be made to fit such a more basic and in some ways more uniform society, where nearly everyone not farming was likely to have begun with a craft or trade, even though sometimes able to end by directing the work of others.

Another consequence of the 'emptiness' of the country was that you could journey for far longer than is possible today with scarcely a sight of house or person. Large tracts were unenclosed, and the big open fields not only had no hedges but often no trees. On the other hand you could find yourself moving through wide stretches of heath and common, as well as much larger areas of forest than today. The roads themselves were very different, usually no more than beaten earth tracks with brushwood or rough stones tossed into the worst holes near a village. Travellers therefore rode or walked. Goods went on packhorse trains. Wheeled carts were coming into use, but away from the area round London were rare. Heavy springless carriages had been invented, but were even rarer until after the middle of the century. Everyone avoided waggon or carriage in any wet season when the tracks were lost in mud so deep that even ridden horses could founder. Nevertheless, somehow, people did move about, and the Quaker preachers were amongst the most incessant travellers. Later in the century, as living standards rose, stage coach services started up, at first in the counties bordering London, where they were widely used and fairly cheap.

The best speed, whether of horse or lumbering waggon, was three or four miles an hour in favourable going. For taking long distance messages, say to the North, or the West country, horses were used in relays so that the post-rider always had a fresh one, and so might therefore average about eight miles an hour. Letters and instructions were sent fairly systematically by carriers and post riders but the time lags meant that the central authorities were very dependant on the goodwill and the initiative of the people out in the counties or, as they often asserted, their 'countries'. Nevertheless, by 1637, the movements of carriers had become regular enough for a timetable to be compiled and printed and in many areas they even kept going through the disturbances of the mid century. Within reach of a few places, like London and Oxford, the first printed news-sheets might be seen, but over most of the country news reached the ordinary people from the peddlars and packhorse men, slowly and often garbled in passage. These slow and erratic communications produced discrepancies in attitude and administration which frustrate our attempts at generalisation.

On the roads where Fox was to spend so much time, apart from the occasional member of the nobility with his entourage, there were craftsmen and traders making their rounds of the markets, a few people exchanging family visits, some others on legal or other business, and some looking for work or going off for apprenticeships to a town, even all the way to London. The wandering unemployed merged into the beggars and thieves who molested travellers along the lonelier stretches, and sometimes beat them to death for very little, as they did the unfortunate Quaker, James Nayler in 1660. Nevertheless even in a lifetime many moved no further from their home parish than could be walked or ridden in a day, a circuit of up to thirty miles. The authorities were suspicious of anyone found apparently wandering far from home unless a very good reason could be given. Most local trade was carried on at the fairs and markets, where, of course, news and opinions also circulated, as people from one centre met others from further afield. Since Fox began his working life attending markets for his employer, he must during that time have been able to pick up information and make contacts which he could use when his own wider travels began.

Those who were in a position to think of learning or public opinion could order books and pamphlets from London or from one of the few provincial booksellers, but they still had to wait for the slow haul of packhorse or waggon to bring them. For most of the time there was a further difficulty. Governments and churches had always taken for granted that publications should be dependent on their approval. Over the past century the licensing system had varied in effectiveness, but in the 1630s King Charles and his Archbishop Laud had begun to enforce the censorship as strictly as they could, until, after about 1640, the increasing political disunity frustrated this. Then for a few years came a great increase in the number of unorthodox and controversial works, up to a thousand titles a year. Nevertheless a truly free press was thought to be so dangerous that the new 'Parliamentary' authorities, as soon as they gained firmer control, re-enforced censorship through licensers of their own. Later on, after the Restoration, the new rulers were even stricter, but with quite different views on what to approve. Quakers, who were amongst the most active of authors, sometimes using small mobile presses, like dissidents in some countries today, fell foul of all of them.

In this sparsely peopled, slow moving country, happenings of the sort which we think must have caused a great stir seem often to have gone by almost unnoticed. Yet during Fox's boyhood events were beginning to develop which for a time were to affect many lives and change the face of the country. From 1637, royal messengers, and then armies, had been moving up the Great North Road, the route to Scotland, as King Charles attempted to impose his English book of church services and his English style bishops on the church of his other kingdom, already committed to a Presbyterian system. That road was too far to the east to affect Fenny Drayton, but the village is only just north of Watling Street, the road to Ireland, by way of Chester, as well as to the troubled north-west. In the five or six years up to 1643, when Fox's own travels began, that road also had seen much unusual and unwelcome movement.

Government

The conflict between King, church and people, and its aftermath, so affected Fox and his Quaker movement that to understand them we need to look at two further differences between that time and ours. First, from the beginning of history everyone in power had agreed that the monarch was the true source of authority. 'May it please your Majesty' was far more than a verbal formula. In practice as well as theory the monarch really did rule the country, and if he failed through tyranny or weakness the likely outcome was anarchy. In normal times Parliament met only for short sessions during which the members discussed proposals from the King and raised a medley of minor and local problems. Judges and magistrates enforced the royal law according to statutes and precedents which by the 1630s had become a labyrinth of the obsolete and the incomprehensible. One curious feature was the great respect paid to the intricacies of documentation. An error in a writ could frustrate a bigoted judge or enable a sympathetic justice to release a defendant. It was a legal wonderland from which almost any conclusion could be drawn, but which could be accepted so long as there were no grounds for serious dispute.

Ministers and officials were men the King appointed for his own reasons, and with little reference to Parliament, even to the Lords. The legal authorities might say 'King in Parliament' but in practice the King was expected to do nearly all the work and to pay for the running of the country out of the income from his own estates and from various traditional dues (mainly those of customs and excise). Only when things seemed not to be going well was any serious opposition likely, when the King's orders upset the customary ways, and especially when people of substance were hurt in their pockets. Even then defiance was usually treated as treason or rebellion, to be answered by force. By 1640 things were going very badly. Inflation, changing needs, and mismanagement had made the king bankrupt and led him to such strange schemes for making ends meet that many felt driven to oppose him.

The second and related difference concerns religion. Everyone was of course expected to accept Christian teaching and belong to the Christian church but, in addition, in England as in every other country, only one form of faith was permitted. All agreed that this was essential. Church and state were indivisible, though sometimes the secular and sometimes the ecclesiastical powers had the upper hand. In theory, if he - or she - had the strength, the form of church was that chosen by the

ruler, and in practice that was usually so. One result was that
England had experienced four changes in the previous hundred
years, a fresh one with each accession, and each leading to a
burst of persecution. Dissent counted as treason, and traitors
were to be got rid of ruthlessly. Having made her own Church
Settlement in 1559, Queen Elizabeth had been determined that
everyone should keep to it, so that Papists on one side and Protestant reformers who wanted to continue the purification of the
church on the other had been repressed. The Pope's Bull, or
order, of 1570, encouraging Catholics to disobey the Queen, the
attempted invasion by the Spanish Armada fleet of 1588, and
various plots, including the much publicised Gunpowder Plot of
1605 against King James, could be used to remind everyone how
much Catholics should be distrusted, even though most of them
were eager only to assert their loyalty and to live quietly. And if
more immediate demonstrations were needed of the sufferings
that could result from religious dissent there were plenty to be
found in the current religious wars on the continent.

One lingering memory was that of the martyrs of the past
hundred years. Each side when in power had destroyed those
who wouldn't acquiesce in its favoured doctrine and church
system. Catholics could revere the three hundred or so Papists,
mostly Jesuit missionaries, destroyed under Elizabeth. Protestants had about as many victims of their faith to recall, a few
who had fallen foul of Elizabeth, but most killed during the brief
reign of her passion-driven sister Mary before her. The descend-
ants of these unfortunates looked on them with pride as people
who had brought honour to their families. Fox took care to say
that his mother was descended from 'the stock of the martyrs'.
According to another, but rather doubtful tradition, Margaret
Fell, who was later to be his wife, was related to an Anne Askew
who had been tortured and burned to death in 1546 'for her
insistence in reading the Bible in Lincoln cathedral'.

To make sure that these Protestant martyrs stayed fresh in
memory, a writer named John Foxe had compiled his enormous
biographical collection of the *Acts and Monuments* in honour of all
who had suffered persecution by Papists, mainly in his own
time and the preceding century. First published in 1563, his
book, later known as Foxe's *Book of Martyrs*, stayed in circulation

right through the conflicts of the Stuart period and the Commonwealth. For good measure it was illustrated with many woodcuts drawing attention to the gruesome ways in which the victims were done to death. It was an openly propagandist work, with what was later to be called a millenarian outlook. Its stories seem to have lingered at the back of people's minds more like nightmares than as tributes to heroic steadfastness in faith. Yet a copy of this book was thought even more likely to be found in a parish church than the Bible.

The Teaching of the Church

Though most people still thought that the state should have only one religious system they could no longer agree about which one. Religious arguments therefore took up much time and energy, because all agreed that one question which had to be answered correctly was that of the right faith to be held. This pre-occupation began to affect the general assumption that good order in the state required everyone to belong to its one church. If wrong beliefs or a wrong form of worship could destroy your body in this world and your eternal soul in the next then finding the right faith could override other ties. The one point everyone accepted was that atheism or agnosticism was not possible. Even though a few extremists did talk of such ideas, to reject belief entirely was a sign of ultimate insanity or depravity. Like the notable church leader Richard Baxter, most could agree that 'Every man that hath a reasonable soul should know God that made him, and know the end for which he should live.' (Watkins p.4)

The work of the reformer Luther, in the early fifteen hundreds, had been followed by that of John Calvin, and a theology based on his teaching was dominant in this country, as in much of northern Europe. With many references to the writings of St Paul, the Calvinists tried to come to terms with the human sense of sin and inadequacy, with the omnipotence of God, with his omniscience and with the conflicting qualities of mercy and justice. Basing themselves on the Bible, which they all agreed was the only valid authority, both religious and historical, they held that all human beings, as descendents of Adam and Eve, the first of sinners, were inherently evil and incapable of achiev-

ing goodness by their own exertions. On the other hand, Jesus
Christ, as son of God, by his death, which they thought of as his
'vicarious sacrifice', had 'paid the price of sin' on behalf of
humanity. Those who in faith accepted this gift, which was not
dependent on human merit or deserving, would receive his
grace, to be 'saved' from Hell and granted the bliss of Heaven.
Luther had taken the doctrine this far. Calvin made a further
step and said that not all humans, nor all Christians, even
though they might call themselves Calvinists, could hope for
this happy outcome, but only those whom God had chosen, or,
as was more often said, 'elected', according to the doctrine of
'predestination'.

This doctrine had arisen from the attempt to account for the
consequences which they thought followed logically from the
omniscience and omnipotence of God. If everything was already
known from the beginning of creation then so was the fate of
every mortal. Voluntary repentance, good works and so on
could not affect the matter. They were appropriate signs that
one might have been chosen for salvation but could not alter
what was already ordained, although their lack could be an
indication that grace was missing and that the prospects for the
future were bleak. Nevertheless no one could ever be sure that
he or she was among the elect. The bitter antagonism to the idea
that salvation could be open to all, or even more that it could be
brought about by 'works' or any humanly willed way of life was
related to earlier campaigns against the Catholic practices of
indulgences or acts of penance. These were thought of as imper-
tinent attempts to strike a bargain by external behaviour.
Quaker assertions that no one need be left out of divine forgiveness, and that God's grace was universal, helped to get
them mixed up with Catholics and generated much fury against
them.

In practice this concept of predestination led some people to
an assurance that they were indeed among the saved, and
tempted them into self-righteous behaviour, sometimes harsh
and domineering. Others misapplied it to excuse self-indulgent
or obviously immoral conduct, on the ground that what was
fore-ordained could not be changed. Some went through their
lives in agonies of self-doubt, but many succeeded in accepting

the ambiguities of their faith in a way that led to deeply earnest lives of quiet devotion and useful work. In their everyday ministry preachers often allowed the parish laity to hold the common-sense and expedient attitude that their eternal future could be influenced by the way they lived now. It is important to appreciate the pervasive influence of the predestination concept, until its decline after the 1660s, both because it dominated many lives and because much early Quaker teaching was directed at it.

Luther believed that all Christians could mediate God's love to others, especially within their families, and had spoken of the 'priesthood of all believers', but neither the Calvinists after him, nor the Episcopalians, had any sympathy for laymen who presumed to preach or take public services. Yet as priests lost their sacred character, as mediators between the human and divine through the eucharist and the other sacraments, they became simply pastors and instructors. The concept of the eucharist as a sacred sacrifice was rejected and replaced by that of a memorial meal at the Lord's table. Consequently ornate stone altars on raised platforms and isolated by their rails at the east end of churches often gave way to plain wooden tables in the body of the church, round which people might sit, sometimes with their hats on as in their own homes. Many rejected not only the old vestments, or even a plain surplice, but any form of word or action which could be seen as ritual, from the sign of the cross in baptism to the use of a ring in marriage.

Much depended on the views of individual bishops or parish clergy. The few churches today which have kept their early seventeenth century interiors look very plain beside the many now full of Victorian refurbishments. Whilst the reformers thought that 'godly and learned ministers' should instruct their congregations in the 'Word of God' through their sermons, the state authorities feared that this could lead to independent thinking and wanted them restricted to the *Prayer Book* and the official homilies. Otherwise the words spoken in church were to be based on the Bible itself, with singing limited to the psalms, in metrical versions whose poetic and musical deficiencies were soon to be ridiculed, although popular and lively ballad tunes were sometimes used.

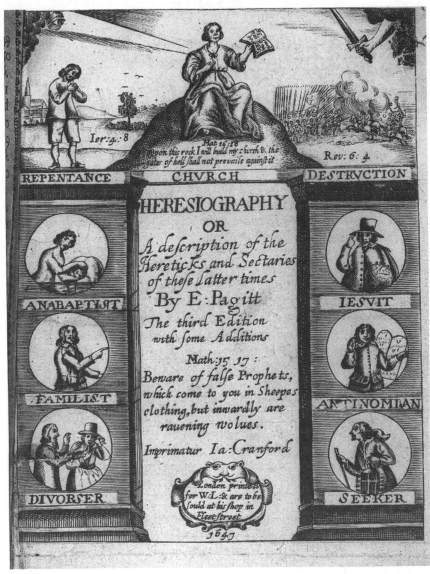

A hostile work on religious sects from the 1640s.

Church and People

If we try to survey the complex set up of the l630s and early 1640s we find a wide and overlapping range of beliefs and practices, very much like the confusion of political factions in our century. At one end were the Catholics who were alleged to long for a return to the old church, with its threat of external domination from the Papacy, as well as to the imposition of Catholic doctrine, liturgy and organisation. In fact it seems likely that most of the actual Catholics would have been quite willing to give their full loyalty to King and Government if only they could have been left quietly to attend Masses and make confessions with Catholic priests. Many avoided penalties by token attendances at the parish church and, given time, they might well be expected to content themselves with it. The handicaps were real enough, except in the north and west countries, to cause only the more resolute to let themselves be identified, so that their numbers are uncertain, and the estimates range from 40,000, to ten times as many secret sympathizers. Much of the antagonism to Catholicism was provoked by the extreme views and aggressive methods of the Jesuits in their enthusiasm for the re-conversion of the country. However irrational, the fear of Catholics persisted throughout the century and provided a pretext for the persecution of quite different dissidents, especially the deeply hated Quakers.

Although, in days before opinion polls, assertions about what people believed are speculative, it does appear that most had grown accustomed to the rather hybrid church which had taken shape through Elizabeth's Church Settlement, where Lutheran and Calvinist doctrines went along with survivals from Catholic practice, although the mixture varied from one parish to another, as can be seen from the records of prosecutions over vestments and so on. After all, most men and women needed their energies for the everyday problems of survival and were willing to go along with what they heard in church, like Fox's father, who, as his son said, 'remained a hearer of the priests all his life'. In his area these were, of course, not Laudians, but advanced Puritans

A generation earlier the Scots had already reached a completely Presbyterian system, with its synods and elders, and

many wanted England to follow their example, or at least to get
rid of the half secular bishops with their great powers as royal
agents, and be free to make further changes. These English Presbyterians were on the whole the most numerous and best organised. They were also the most learned, prosperous, and in most
things but religion the most conservative and authoritarian.
After 1641, with the bishops out of the way, they increased their
efforts in the parish churches, with their their long, scholarly
sermons and their *Directory of Public Worship*, instead of the *Book
of Common Prayer*.

However, by this time a lot of people wanted change of a
different kind, and argued that merely to be a parishioner was
not enough to make one a church member. To these people true
fellowship in a 'gathered church' could be gained only by an
experience of repentance and conversion, followed by the
accepting of a covenant of unity with others in the congregation.
This led to curious arrangements whereby in the same parish
church, and sometimes with the same minister, there could be a
'mixed multitude' of parishioners at the open parish service, and
another group worshipping separately at a different time,
although some of its members might attend both. Hence the
variety of names found, 'Independent' for the covenanted congregation, (from which arose the later name of Congregational-
ist), with 'semi-separatist', and 'Separatist' for those readier to
cut themselves off from the parish, with their own pastors and
meeting places, usually houses.

In detail the scene appears even more complex and more
obscure. Some groups held ideas going back to earlier dissidents
like the Lollards, others had been influenced by thoughtful or
daring pastors. One such pastor, - whose followers naturally
had got the name of Brownists - was Robert Browne (1550 - 1633)
who had gathered congregations in Nottinghamshire and Lin-
colnshire, but who in 1582 had gone into exile in Holland. Aban-
doning the hope of a united national church reform, he
published *Reformation without Tarrying for Any*, a work which
very much influenced later Separatists, though he was no longer
a leader. In the Skipton area, around a village called Grindleton,
not far from Pendle Hill, another preacher, perhaps linked with
yet another group called the Familists, had reached some views

not unlike those of Fox, although any influences remain
uncertain.

One sixteenth century Continental sect with what were
thought to be especially dangerous ideas were the Anabaptists.
They were supposed to refuse to obey rulers or to serve as soldiers, and to hold other strange ideas on freedom of worship
and practice, including their rejection of the politically important rite of infant baptism. Although to insist on adult 'believer's
baptism' seems now an innocuous choice, this stand upset the
authorities because infant baptism was then seen as the process
by which each new child was enrolled by means of the church
into the state. To make baptism wait for adult decision brought
up the most outrageous challenges to kingship and property.
Even without other old and tired allegations that the Anabaptists went in for licentious erotic goings on these would have
been enough to justify crushing them. Yet some Anabaptist
groups did form in England, although less radical in outlook
than those in Holland, and were able to struggle on, at least in
London.

As the country moved towards a crisis in the 1630s these
groups were amongst the first to come out of the shadows.
Whilst they had existed almost as an underground they had to
learn to manage their own affairs and use pastors who had never
been ordained, a practice that got them the contempt of the
scholarly Presbyterians. As is the way of radical movements, the
Baptists, as the name soon became, themselves broke into two,
the Particular Baptists keeping to the Calvinist teaching of limited grace, and the larger group of General Baptists taking up the
view of the Dutch theologian Arminius that grace was universal.
They attracted active and independent minded people who
became leaders in the republican movement and the army.
When Fox left his home, Baptists were amongst the first with
whom he associated, and at least one of his relatives was a
London Baptist.

During Fox's boyhood, in the 1630s, the Elizabethan
balance, or compromise, was finally ruined, because King Charles I, with more conviction but less political sense than his
father, wanted to bring the whole country into an exact conformity with the sort of church he favoured. The supporters of this

kind of church got the label 'Arminian', but although they set
aside election and predestination, opening the grace and mercy
of Christ to many more Christians, what mattered most to them
was their sacramental approach to worship. They wanted to restore some of the order and beauty of ritual, including the use of
the old liturgy and vestments, which had been lost in the course
of the century. To further these changes Charles began to
appoint as bishops active and authoritarian men whose efforts
to bring the whole country into conformity with their own views
stirred up great resentment, which was directed at his Archbishop, William Laud.

To complete the picture we need to recognize that outside
these literate and dominant groups there existed also the
uncounted thousands of the poor. Even if these had wanted to
join in worship the country churches were often too far from
each other to be reached regularly on foot, and in towns the
buildings were too small for the growing populations. Consequently these outsiders held in their heads a jumble of ideas,
from phrases of the Mass to scraps of much more primitive
religions. Although the learned might deride these as magic and
superstition they were all that some people had, and indeed
often lingered on underneath the faith got from the preachers.
Spells seemed useful against disasters and illnesses for which no
other remedies were on offer. Any unusual event or behaviour
could lead to a witchcraft pogrom. We can never safely ignore
the influence of this dark undercurrent of more or less pagan
belief, even in those who seemed most educated or enlightened.

In all this variety, the customary word 'Puritan' sometimes
comes to seem only a convenient label for those who practised
what many others were more or less in favour of, an umbrella
term for all those individuals and congregations who struggled
for the further reform or purification of doctrine and life, and
who expressed their convictions in a strict, sober conduct. Nor
did people rush to call themselves by that name, for it came from
more worldly observers who thought that the Puritans were
going tiresomely far in their objections to harmless moderation.
John Pym, later to be a leading Parliamentarian, was quoted in
1621 as grumbling at 'that odious and factious name of Puritan'.
(Edwards p.259) When the young Fox gathered followers they

came from a wide range of backgrounds, though many had been associated with Independents or Baptists. At first they seemed only a new and more troublesome sort of Puritan, but they were sharply differentiated from them in their interpretation of Christian teaching, in their attitude to the church and the Bible, and in their humanitarian outlook, even if not in their outward behaviour. Almost everyone wanted to suppress them.

The Crisis

If all the people of power and influence in the 1630s had acted as with hindsight we think they should have done, the dangerous tensions might have been dispersed safely, but they were far too trapped in the limitations of their time for such an outcome and drifted into almost half a century of strife. Perhaps we should not regret this, for the confusion of the forties and fifties allowed radical thinkers to survive long enough to publish their messages or to gather followers. Unhappily they were still feeling their way, without experience of social change, in unfavourable conditions, and against fierce opposition, so that almost all were eliminated. It is a fascinating might-have-been of history to speculate how England would have fared if the Levellers and radicals had succeeded in winning wider support and so become the founders of the modern state. Yet without the courage and perseverance of the few who were able to struggle on through the bleak years after the 1660 Restoration even the limited reforms and tolerations of the final years of the century might never have been gained. And in this campaign Quakers were amongst the leaders and the greatest sufferers from repression.

As the dissensions about the right ordering of religion became more threatening those would-be Presbyterians who opposed Charles and his bishops became even more thoroughly convinced that the system they preferred should be the only one authorised and that it should be enforced fiercely. One of the main motives influencing those who settled in America was not to make possible any diversity in worship but to set up their own form of church as the official one. As Quakers were later to find, in most of the colonies there was no more toleration than in England. Hence the general agreement that there should be uniformity in the church led to an outbreak of bitter feuding, which was by no means ended by the defeat of Charles, or by the return of his son in 1660. In fact the extraordinary idea that the one state - one church linkage could safely be relaxed only began to take root just towards the end of Fox's life in 1691, and in some part only then through the forty years of Quaker struggle for complete independence in worship and church discipline.

Perhaps Charles could have survived religious opposition, but by 1640 he had stirred up other resentments. Yet all the disputes, whether about his extravagance, his unorthodox taxation, his indifference to Parliament, or even his encouraging Archbishop Laud to interfere with the accepted church, might have been contained or fudged but for Charles's one talent, to dishearten his friends whilst antagonising everyone who might be in doubt. Neither Charles nor the people he was willing to listen to had the skill to understand or conciliate the new Parliamentary spokesmen, so that, whilst George Fox was passing through his obscure adolescence, the men of power and influence in the country were drifting towards civil war.

Charles and Laud had brought their troubles to a head in 1637 and 1638 by trying to appoint English style bishops in Presbyterian Scotland, and by ordering the use there of a *Book of Common Prayer* very like the one they were trying to enforce in England. When Charles persisted the Scots turned to armed resistance, and he sent an army to cow them into a proper deference. Lacking efficient troops, officers, and the money to equip and pay them, it was defeated. By 1640 he was forced to summon an English Parliament. This only got him further into trouble because the members took the opportunity he had unwillingly given and made the granting of funds conditional on his first settling a long list of their own grievances. Charles both resisted and led them on by half promises so devious that they reluctantly started to call out the militia without his authority and to enrol troops as the only way of forcing him to negotiate and keep his word. To defy him, as king 'hedged about with divinity' rather than as exasperating Charles, cost much heart-searching, and perhaps accounts for some of their irrational fury. This was in any case a time when people's emotions were intense and their thinking more likely to be energetic than clear.

Despite a few large scale battles, the war was mainly fought

out in many smaller encounters, and in sieges of towns and for-
tified houses around the country. Garrisons sent out foraging
parties who collected horses, food and clothing, the loss of
which meant hardship for thirty miles around and for which
there was rarely payment. Until the end of the decade and the
final moppings up the risk of disruption to the business of survival remained. Since the country was for some years roughly
divided into royalist and parliamentary areas the worst damage
happened near the wavering boundaries. From the towns the
first troops of both sides were the 'trained bands', except that
they had little training or equipment and less desire to risk their
skins in fighting, especially if this involved going far from home.
In the counties landowners collected troops according to their
own friendships and inclinations, consisting mainly of their
own dependents from their own estates. Many soldiers had
been unemployed, and some were pressed men, given a choice
between army and prison, (as Fox was to be). Later came many
volunteers, most in the so-called 'New Model' army, associated
with innovations in fighting methods begun by Cromwell, who
joined up from conviction about the rightness of the cause. Yet
this removing of young men from their homes and keeping
them in large groups, with time enough to ask why they were
risking their lives, led to the troops joining in the reform process,
with demands far more socially disruptive than their superiors
had any intention of allowing. In addition, almost all the troops
shared one problem: their wages were unpaid. Long after the
fighting was over they stayed in the camps and garrisons, refusing to be disbanded without some back pay. In the end the problem of what to do with the army and its pay contributed to the
collapse of the Commonwealth. Many of the first Quakers had
gone through the experience of service and radical debate in the
army.

Charles's efforts to outwit his opponents by playing off one
section against another finally failed and he provoked some of
them into beheading him. This left the many obstinate conflicts
still as unsettled as ever. Even if his loyalists could be labelled
malignants and cowed by fines and confiscations of property
there was still the threat that his son would return and enable
them to rally successfully. When that threat seemed to be dis-

posed of by Charles II's defeat and flight after the battle at Worcester in 1651, the successful side, as usual in revolutionary situations, disintegrated into quarrelling factions. No agreed policies or stable government were possible. Only the strong personality of Cromwell, and the backing of men loyal to him from his days as army commander, kept the appearance of good order as long as he lived. Whilst Presbyterians contended with Independents for mastery, and the army watched them all, unorthodox thinkers could find the opportunity to put forward their ideas. The return of a 'merry monarch' as king, after the Commonwealth collapsed, meant that the people now in power had endless scores to settle and were going to take great care to get rid of any sort of dissent. The thirty years from 1660 were not a good time for people of independent minds.

Despite all that happened to him, George Fox was therefore born at an opportune moment. Earlier, he could never have had the opportunity to begin his long search without being picked up by the authorities or beaten by the material hazards of survival. Later, he would have been lost in the confusion or destroyed in the fierce reaction of the Restoration years.

Chapter Two

BEGINNINGS

Home

George Fox's origins were thoroughly undistinguished, and when he first came to public notice it was only as a passing nuisance to churchmen and magistrates. His life began in a small south Leicestershire village, about two miles from Atherstone, just off the main road once called Watling Street, and now known as the A5. Officially it was called Fenny Drayton, but Fox sometimes used a less complimentary local variant, Drayton-in-the-Clay. The flat low-lying area may well have lived up to those names. The nearest place was another small village called Mancetter, now almost lost in Atherstone.

In the religious conflicts of the Sixteenth Century many local people favoured the more radical Protestant reformers, possibly keeping attitudes first derived from the Lollards and from John Wycliffe, who came from Lutterworth, a few miles further down the road. Several Protestant martyrs came from the district, and the last man killed in England for heresy was burned at Lichfield in 1613. Fox refers to 'martyr stock' as an honour to a family. The main landowners, the Purefeys, (or Purefoys), through having the living in their gift, controlled the choice of parish priest at Fenny Drayton, and consistently appointed men of ability and strongly reformist outlook. One of these, in particular, had been Anthony Nutter, a notable preacher whom the church authorities had forced out of the living in 1605. (He probably served later in the Yorkshire parish where James Nayler, another Quaker leader, grew up). His successor, Robert Mason, may have been more adaptable, for he kept the living till his death over thirty years later. The records show that some parishioners wanted more changes and got into trouble with the church authorities. Religion, theology, and church organisation were very much live topics in the village in Fox's boyhood.

27

The squire's family motto 'Purefoi ma Joye' [Pure faith my joy], echoed their name. Although Fox never mentioned it he must have been well aware of this motto, for it was displayed on their monument in the church and on other buildings. Thoughtful jingles heard in early life can have longlasting effects, and it is very tempting to think that this was true of Fox, for certainly 'joy in pure faith' can be seen as summing up his lifelong outlook. The search for truth might have led him into some withdrawn and private byways, but in fact took him through half a century of danger and adventure. Faith for him, as he at length found it, became a way of life which had to be shared with all the world, whether that required defying the establishment at home or venturing into wild places abroad. Fox was never still: a complex, energetic, irrepressible, sometimes disconcerting man, his was a remarkably full and varied life.

Journals

The preoccupation of that extraordinary century with religion and politics led many unlikely people to turn author. In the days of the Catholics, people had been able to shed their troubles in the confessional, but now the Calvinists were putting the responsibility back on each individual. Some groups actually made church membership depend on an adequate experience of repentance and conversion. Were you one of the elect? Did the signs of righteousness show in your life? These questions led to introspective diaries, kept up like spiritual account books, or to narratives of conversion experiences, which were gathered into collections for the guidance of younger people. One comprehensive list of these writings has 223 entries, 123 of them by Quakers, (Watkins, Appendix). Fox expected the painful experience of religious awakening to expand into a new life of worship and service, so that Quaker journals usually say less about preconversion distress and struggle than we find in the works of others, Bunyan, for example. People of a decidedly less religious outlook like Evelyn and Pepys also went in for this new self-conscious kind of recording and stocktaking. Spiritual self examination was so much an accepted form that later on it was imitated in popular novels like Defoe's *Robinson Crusoe* and *Moll Flanders*.

Fox based his whole message on the devotional experience and unique worth of each person. Obviously therefore he could be expected to value the story of what he had gone through in his great adventure in the renewing of Christian discipleship. He seems to have been one of those fortunate people who enjoy a near perfect memory, although this could let him down over dates and places. Most of the leisure for getting his story on to paper came unwillingly from imprisonment. He began the first version during a long spell in Lancaster and Scarborough Castles in the mid 1660s, and the second some ten years later in Worcester Gaol. He then finished this whilst recuperating at home in Cumbria. One drawback for us is that the pages of the manuscript which deal with his early years have been lost, so that we have to depend on the version edited for publication after his death by his friend Thomas Ellwood. Although Ellwood did a very careful and scholarly job, he sometimes smoothed out what to him were everyday trivialities, or topics - especially from that long rejected Civil War and Interregnum - which he thought it might be embarrassing to revive.

Apart from his journal, Fox also kept, - even hoarded - letters and records of all kinds, and encouraged his friends to do the same. They thought that if their work was to renew the true original Christianity, their story would become a sort of further *Acts of the Apostles*. The result is that we have far more information about them than we could possibly expect about people of their time and standing. However, unluckily for us, they thought everyday affairs irrelevant to the spiritual life and left out many details we should have welcomed. Nevertheless, Fox's vivid memory and unquenchable enjoyment of life often led to his letting slip a great deal more about the incidentals of behaviour and appearance than he intended. Although he is now looked on as a pioneer in self-expression he had no such ambition. If he could ever have guessed that his story would one day be read only for 'human interest' he would have thought it a thoroughly perverse notion. Personality and motive, as understood today, meant little then. Moreover, his total preoccupation with the message and the action made him indifferent to how he himself appeared. Sometimes this means that he shows up rather unfavourably, so that he has been ridiculed for being humourless or arrogant. How therefore did his friends see him? There is no lack of comment from his enemies.

In the very first sentence of the *Journal* Fox set out his own reasons for writing: 'that all may know the dealings of the Lord with me, and the various exercises, trials and troubles through which he led me in order to prepare and fit me for the work unto which he had appointed me . . .' Most people today would be very hesitant to say even this much, and would be even less likely to continue: '. . . and may thereby be drawn to admire and glorify his infinite wisdom and goodness.' Nevertheless, with Fox, as with his contemporaries, we have to come to terms with this approach, for we are dealing with people whose world outlook was not our own, and to get to know them we have to take them on their terms. 'Pure faith' was then an overwhelming preoccupation, which led sometimes to heights of saintliness, but often to embittered arguments about distinctions now almost unrecognizable, and from them to spiteful persecutions. Perhaps we should ask ourselves how the complicated political and economic disputes of the present day will appear to our successors three centuries on. In fact, substitute 'political' for 'religious' and little seems to have changed.

Family

In his opening paragraph Fox added, 'I think fit (before I proceed to set forth on my public travels in the service of Truth) to mention how it was with me in my youth'. He then said very little.

> I was born in the month called July in the year 1624, at Drayton-in-the-Clay in Leicestershire. My father's name was Christopher Fox; he was by profession a weaver, an honest man, and there was a Seed of God in him. The neighbours called him 'Righteous Christer'. My mother was an upright woman; her maiden name was Mary Lago, of the family of the Lagos and of the stock of the martyrs. (N p.1)

Family historians have traced scores of Lagos, but none of them amongst the victims of the religious persecutions. We have to accept that there was a family tradition, and that the family took pride in it.

Only one 'Mary Lago' has been found in the likely parish

Fenny Drayton, supposed birthplace of George Fox

registers. Since her birth year was 1588, it seems unlikely that she can have been Fox's mother, who would more probably have been born around 1600, and her husband some years earlier, for men in those days were often several years older than their wives and married only in their late twenties when they had set themselves up in the world and obtained a house. It is just as well for us that Fox did give the date of his birth, because the church baptismal papers for that year were later destroyed. (The tradition is that a parish clerk's wife tore out the pages for kitchen use.) Occasionally he referred vaguely to his 'relations'. In fact he seems to been the eldest of four. A sister called Dorothy was baptised in 1626, on April 9th, and had apparently died before he wrote out his will in 1686. A brother, John, was baptised on December 20th 1629, and was quite generously treated in the will. A Katherine Fox also received a legacy, and she may have been another sister, born during the years of the missing register pages. These three, along with his parents, must be the core of the group of 'relations' that he returned to visit and who tried to help him during what they considered very regrettable scrapes. His father we last hear of in 1655, with an emphatic comment on his son's success in a debate with some priests in Fenny Drayton church.

> My father in the flesh thwacked his cane on the ground and said, 'Well', said he, 'I see he that will but stand to the truth it will carry him out', though he was hearer and follower of the priests. (N p.190)

Christopher sounded fit enough then, though he might well have been around sixty. When he actually died is not known, yet both parents reached ages which suggest that they were exceptionally fit or fortunate. Perhaps their son got his stamina from them.

'In the flesh' may today suggest some disparagement, but many uses of the phrase make clear that the sense of belonging to a divine father then carried an immediacy and importance almost as great as it had done for the first disciples in the Gospels, without a lessening of ordinary affection. Fox and his father had very different outlooks, but it is pleasant that he was able to have this moment of success in front of him. The thwacking cane suggests someone who knew his own mind and was sure of his standing, even if only as the village worthy that his neighbours called 'righteous Christer'. As a churchwarden in the 1630s he was involved in the making of some locally important decisions. His church accounts were exceptionally well kept and his signature strongly-formed.

We should have liked to know more of his business standing. Although 'weaver' could mean a man who worked his own cottage loom it was also used of someone who organised the work of many cottage weavers, arranging the supply of their wool, or possibly linen, the collecting of the finished cloth, possibly as blankets or sheets, and its sending off for sale. Some of these people came as near as their time allowed to being the owners of large and prosperous businesses. However the wool trade itself was rather in recession, even without the disruptive effect of Civil War, and Leicestershire was not one of the major weaving areas, so that Christopher Fox may have been operating only at a local level. His house was unpretentious, for when a new tax on hearths was introduced after the Restoration his widow was assessed on only one hearth. Yet he was certainly not without self-assurance, as shown in the incident above, or in resources, as some later incidents reveal. The family's financial status concerns us in connection with George and his means of livelihood, about which the *Journal* gives only a few hints and takes a great deal for granted.

Fox's mother may herself have had has some property, perhaps including the family house, for the known Lagos were prosperous yeomen farmers. She evidently remained in Fenny Drayton, for during some complex legal arguments at the time of his 1674 imprisonment in Worcester, Fox accounted for his movements about the country by sending the judges a statement, which

> . . . sheweth that whereas George Fox was travelling with his wife, son and daughter-in-law, [= son-in-law and stepdaughter] from London, intending to visit his mother, an ancient woman of above seventy years old, who greatly desired to see him before she died, being weak and aged; who when she heard he was stopped and sent to prison, it struck to her heart and killed her, as he received a letter from a doctor of that country to that effect. (CJ II p.294)

In another note he wrote,

> I did in verity love her as ever one could a mother, for she was a good, honest, virtuous, and a right-natured woman, and, when I read the letter of her death, it struck a great weight upon my spirit. (BQ p.32)

There is one other scrap about his mother. His friend William Penn wrote a Preface for the *Journal* in which he said that Fox's parents endeavoured to bring him up 'in the way and worship of the nation . . . especially his mother, who was a woman accomplished above most of her degree in the place where she lived'. It has often been assumed that Fox cut himself off from his natural family, but these statements show both loyalty and a continuing close communication, especially with his mother.

Upbringing and Education

Penn's remark about the 'accomplishments above her degree' of Fox's mother is faintly coloured by his own attitudes. As one of the people of property and standing with access to the king, he was inclined to be patronising about other Friends. Nevertheless it does appear that Fox's limited formal education came from his mother. This education is something of a mystery. It would have been natural for a promising son of a settled and apparently prosperous family to go to a village teacher and perhaps to a grammar school, such as that at Atherstone. Fox later was obviously enthusiastic about schools, yet about his own education we have only one ambiguous remark. 'Afterwards, as I grew up, my relations thought to have made me a priest, but others persuaded to the contrary; whereupon I was put to a man . . .' (N p.2). At around twelve, like most boys then, he became an apprentice.

The family argument does suggest that more schooling was considered for the boy. We can say only that Fox shows no sign even of the smattering of Latin that bright boys were given, sometimes by the local minister, in anticipation of a possible Cambridge matriculation at about fourteen, for he seems to have begun by thinking that the priesthood needed some study at University. When the time came, 'others persuaded', and we are left to wonder who they were, or why, and how disappointed the boy could have been. Nor can we do more than guess whether the actual parish priests had any part in the family decision, though it might be relevant that at about that time the old man, Mason, was replaced by his curate, Nathaniel Stephens, a dedicated Puritan, who for some years praised Fox, but later opposed him fiercely. Penn later wrote of Fox as a very quiet and serious child, precociously bright and thoughtful.

He appeared of another frame of mind from the rest of his

brethren; being more religious, inward, still, solid and observing beyond his years, as the answers he would give and the questions he would put . . . manifested, to the astonishment of those that heard him, especially in divine things.

Penn only came on the scene thirty years later, so that we may wonder how he learned this, if not from Fox's own talk. In his later life we can also detect both the attempts to show off scraps of erudition and the obsession with the setting up of schools which sometimes mark out the self-educated.

The boy probably educated himself by reading any tract or pamphlet that came his way, and by paying attention to the endless sermons and lectures which were beginning to be a feature of local life. Many children were expected to take notes of them, and then not only to repeat the arguments to their teachers and parents but to join in discussions during which the whole subject was chewed over. Education could be oral and informal to an extent incredible in our days. There is nevertheless one aspect of Fox's education which has come in for a good deal of comment, from his enemies in his own day, and from scholars later on. His handwriting was clumsy; his spelling, although mainly phonetic, could be strangely erratic. In this he was not alone, for, as we see from manuscripts, so was that of many people at the time, even of those considered well taught. By the end of his life standards were rising, but we have to judge him by the difficult years of the 1630s. Fox evidently disliked writing, because as soon as he was able he got copyists to take his dictation, even in prison. The main manuscript of the *Journal* has over twenty handwritings in it, mainly of his friends and family. He was also a great employer of shorthand writers. In his last years he probably had another very good reason for seeking help. We know that by then hardship and exposure had left him very much crippled by rheumatism.

There are of course other possible reasons for his educational problems, such as left-handedness, or even dyslexia. The story of William Stout, a Quaker of a generation later, shows that left-handed youngsters then got little sympathy. He began school at thirteen, as Fox might have hoped to do, and 'entered into' Latin and Greek, but in his own *Journal* he accounted for his failure in this way.

Nor did I make any progress in writing, though much taught ·
by reason I was naturally left-handed, and could not be steady
in my right hand, and then it was supposed that one could not
learn to write legibly with the left hand, which was a mistake.
(Raistrick p.62)

The Quaker historian William Sewel, a scholar who knew Fox in
his later years, gave a fair summing up.

. . . it cannot be denied that he was no elegant writer, nor good
speller, yet it is true that his characters [= letters] being toler-
able, his writing was legible, and the matter he treated of was
intelligible, though his style was not like that of a skilful
linguist. (Sewell I p.44)

When someone has spoken and written as much as Fox and
influenced so many people, we naturally like to look at his own
training, but in this matter of education he really does seem both
to have had some handicap and to have been obliged to fend for
himself.

When the family consultations and the 'persuading to the
contrary' were over he tells us, '. . . I was put to a man, a shoemaker by trade, and that dealt in wool, and used grazing, and
sold cattle; and a great deal went through my hands'. It is sometimes said that in his early manhood Fox earned his living by
shoemaking, apparently on the assumption that he had served
an apprenticeship to that trade, but he said nothing that could
support such a view. In one account of his work in Cumbria he is
called 'George Fox, shoemaker', but this was written up in 1709
by someone who had been a boy of only twelve when he met
Fox. (FPT p.241.) The assertion usually came from his opponents, a few of whom continued long after his death to ridicule
the idea that a 'shoemaker' could have been a preacher or
teacher. In those obsessively class conscious days it was a
favourite form of insult. A cartoon from as early as 1641, for
example, has the caption, 'When women preach, and cobblers
play, the Fiends in Hell make holiday' (Watts). Bunyan, on the
other hand, was endlessly ridiculed because he really had
worked as a tinker. Shoemaking was a craft for skilled leather
workers, far above cobbling, but whatever its standing Fox can
hardly have practised it, for he changed his whole course of life
at nineteen.

Penn complicated the matter in his *Journal* Preface. 'As to his employment, he was brought up in country business; and as he took most delight in sheep, so he was very skilful in them'. This would have been more reliable if Penn had not called it,

> an employment that very well suited his mind in several respects, both for its innocency and solitude, and was a just figure of his after ministry and service. (N p.xxxix)

This seems more pretty than likely. There was after all nothing withdrawn or quiet about much of his life. That Fox had herded sheep we can well believe, for in a grazing area any boy might be drawn into this job, at least when the flocks were driven to market. What seems to be clear is that the lad was trying his hand at a number of country skills, but that his main one is indicated in his own words, 'and a great deal went through my hands'. He seems to have been learning the very important accomplishment of dealer in livestock and country products. This was no reflective backwater but a tough job needing quick wits and a firm will. It provided its own education into human wiles and enmities. Fox's final words about his youth support this view.

> While I was with him, he was blessed; but after I left him, he broke and came to nothing. I never wronged man or woman in all that time, for the Lord's power was with me and over me, to preserve me. While I was in that service, I used in my dealings the word 'verily', and it was a common saying among people that knew me, 'If George says "Verily" there is no altering him.' When boys and rude people would laugh at me, I let them alone and went my way, but people had generally a love for me for my innocency and honesty. (N p.2)

That was how he remembered himself, - very straightforward and very firm. His opponents found him stubborn. We can also see here the blunt way of setting down his facts which sometimes makes him look smug. Yet to him it was enough if he believed he was acting honestly and speaking truth, whatever he might suffer from this disconcerting indifference to public opinion.

Leap into the Unknown

His next move can hardly have come as much out of the blue as
his telling of it suggested.

> When I was towards nineteen years of age, I being upon busi-
> ness at a fair, one of my cousins, whose name was Bradford,
> being a professor, and having another professor with him,
> came to me and asked me to drink a jug of beer with him, and
> I, being thirsty, went in with them, for I loved any that had a
> sense of good . . .

'Professor' was the usual term for people who claimed to take
their religion with more than usual thoroughness. Fox later
often played on the distinction between those whose 'profession' went no further than words, and those whose way of life
showed that they really 'possessed' the spirit of Christ. Unfortunately, on that day his hopes for a pleasant talk after the morning's bargaining were frustrated.

> They began to drink healths and called for more drink, agree-
> ing that he that would not drink should pay all. I was grieved
> that any that made profession of religion should offer to do so.

The next remark seems odd, for this was an age of heavy alcohol
use, and leading people on to repeated toasts or rounds was as
common then as now, not least in the fairs and markets it was
evidently part of his work to visit. Yet he went on: 'They grieved
me very much, having never had such a thing put to me before
by any sort of people'. His reaction was decisive.

> . . . wherefore I rose up to be gone, and putting my hand in my
> pocket I took out a groat and laid it on the table before them
> and said, 'If it be so, I'll leave you.' So I went away; and when I
> had done what business I had to do, I returned home. (N p.3)

The brief ride, or walk, from Atherstone to Drayton did not
calm his mind. During the night his distress increased, for he
continued,

> But [I] did not go to bed that night, nor could not sleep, but
> sometimes walked up and down, and sometimes prayed to
> the Lord, who said to me, 'Thou seest how young people go
> together into vanity and old people into the earth, and thou

must forsake all, both young an old, and keep out of all, and be as a stranger unto all'.

He was then just nineteen. Some six weeks later, he acted on this urge to distance himself from being tempted or provoked.

> . . . at the command of God, on the 9th day of [September], 1643, I left my relations and brake off all familiarity or fellowship with young and old .

If he had really begun a seven year apprenticeship at twelve he could only just have completed it before this disruption.

So far in his resumé of his early years he had given no hint of stress or disagreement, and to his family this decision must have appeared perverse and impractical. Yet in reality such changes usually have their origins in emotions and thoughts which have been growing for years until some single, perhaps trivial incident, like the one at the fair, brings them into the open. Rejections of family standards still happen, though the reasons are unlikely to be religious. With Fox the trigger was evidently the contradiction between *saying* and *doing*, shown in the especially culpable hypocrisy of the conspicuous 'professors'. The same preoccupation with consistency had shown itself earlier, in the remark that his 'Verily' meant he could not be deflected once he had arrived at a line which he thought right. Nevertheless, this explosive response seems surprising, and perhaps was fuelled by other such incidents, or by arguments within the family, or perhaps even a recent sermon. Yet whatever its hidden roots, this decision cut Fox off from the life for which he had seemed destined, as a morally strict, and moderately successful local tradesman and, worthy like his father.

The immediate result was three or four years of restless, unhappy wandering and searching, out of which grew the convictions on which all the rest of his life was founded. His whole purpose and his great happiness then became to share his insights with everyone he could reach. Thirty years later he had occasion to look back, and wrote to some Quakers, who knew that he was neither exaggerating nor boasting.

> And you have known the manner of my life . . . since I went forth and forsook all things. . . . And my travels hath been great, in hungers and colds, when there were few [sup-

porters], for the first six or seven years; that I often lay in woods and commons for the night; that many times it was a by-word that I would not come into any of their houses, and lie in their beds; and prisons have been made my home the great part of my time, and in danger of my life, and in jeopardy daily. (Ep. No 308)

Relationships

Some people, even today, interact all their days with the people and places they had known in childhood. But not Fox, for whilst he was learning market skills in Leicestershire, others whose lives were to be most closely interwoven with his were also growing up, sometimes in very different ways. Many were in farming in Cumbria and the Yorkshire Dales, whilst slowly evolving the approach to religion that would make them respond so eagerly to Fox's early ministry. A few had left their homes because of the Civil War and were trying to work out their convictions, religious and political, in the Parliamentary armies. One of these was James Nayler, son of a prosperous farmer in West Ardsley, near Wakefield, who suddenly set off from home and wife in 1642, to enlist. He worked as a quartermaster, then took to preaching amongst the troops. In 1650 he went back home on the sick list, with high praise from his commander, and returned to farming, until he encountered Fox a couple of years later, and began his short sad final career.

In the south, one of the more radical London Aldermen, Isaac Penington, was having trouble with his son's religious anxieties, and a naval officer, William Penn, busy with furthering his own promotion and building up a fortune, was hoping that his son William would do credit to the family, as he did, but not in the way that Admiral Penn wanted.

Much further north, in what was then the Furness district of Lancashire, was another family, headed by Thomas Fell, of Swarthmoor Hall near Ulverston. He was heir to a wealthy estate, and had prepared himself for an independent career by studying law and being called to the Bar. This was in 1631, when he was aged thirty three. The next year, perhaps as the result of having made this promising start in life, he married the daughter of a neighbouring landowner. She was Margaret Askew and was, at seventeen, almost exactly half his age. Nevertheless, the relationship was co-operative and affectionate, for Margaret grew into a very active and capable woman, able to take responsibility both for her husband's affairs during his long absences on his legal work and for their increasing family, three daughters in the first five years, then a son, who by coincidence was named George. Later, in the years up to 1653, there were four more daughters. Whatever Judge Fell desired he found himself with a houseful of lively girls, but with only one son as a prospective heir. When the Judge first heard of Fox from a fellow Justice in 1651, the last thought in his mind was of the way he and his family were to be closely linked with this troublesome young preacher.

Chapter Three

FINDING HIS WAY

Student or Seeker?

For all its later importance to him, Cumbria was very far from Fox's thoughts in that summer of 1643, when he 'came towards nineteen years of age' and was shaken by the pub incident. Then, after some weeks of uncertainty, and no doubt uneasy conferences with the family, and even, one hopes, his employer, he left home. In this early part of his story, where dates are few, he unexpectedly gives an exact day for this event: the 9th of the Seventh Month [= September] 1643. Does this indicate that the family reminded him of it? Or did he come to recall it as an unforgettable experience, the day on which his own life was 'turned upside down'? In those days, moreover, Biblical parallels, and overtones of exodus and trial would easily come to mind. Over the next four years a rather solemn youth transformed himself into an evangelist with a revolutionary interpretation of both religion and society. Whether our interest is in Quakerism or human behaviour in general, this is change of a kind worth examining.

For the story of this change we have only Fox's brief account, still in that part of the *Journal* for which only the text as edited by Ellwood survives. This summarises the four years, up to 1647, in this way.

> Now during all this time I was never joined in profession of religion with any, but gave myself up to the Lord, having forsaken all evil company, and taken leave of father and mother, and travelled up and down as a stranger in the earth, which way the Lord inclined my heart, taking a chamber to myself in the town where I came, and tarrying sometimes a month, sometimes more, sometimes less in a place. For I durst not stay long ... being afraid both of professor and profane, lest, being a tender young man I should be hurt by conversing much with either. (N p.10)

42

The Experience of Guilt

He was by no means exceptional in this agonizing. People lived with an all-pervading assumption that human beings are fallible creatures, always at risk of suffering or destruction in a vast and mysterious universe. This insecurity surfaced also in the extraordinary preoccupation with death and the after-life found in writings and paintings, and especially in church monuments, where skulls and skeletons flourish for all to take in their grim lesson. The diary-keepers were endlessly busy with their spiritual balance sheets, and their totting up of favourable events as providences or misfortunes as signs of divine disfavour. John Crook, who became one of Fox's friends, wrote of his pre-Quaker feelings, '. . . I was so possessed with fear, that I could have looked behind me lest the devil stood there to take me.' (Journal p.9) A rather later journal keeper, a Lancashire apprentice in 1663, wrote with an engaging diffidence, 'I was pensive and sad and went into the town field and prayed to the Lord, and I hope the Lord heard'. (Q in Ashley p.38) Fox probably seemed rather like that to the people near him.

Spiritual awakening led to the recognizing of one's moral weaknesses, failures, and faults: one's sinfulness. Often people who had thought their lives quite acceptable came to feel that they had been too easily satisfied and were as much at fault as more obvious sinners. A time of self-doubt and questioning, with a feeling of unworthiness, was a necessary stage in the spiritual journey. Through the admission of guilt, need and helplessness came the hope of receiving the forgiveness of Christ, and the salvation he had won through the crucifixion for those who believed in him, in spite of their unworthiness.

One of the most prominent and seemingly unlikely sufferers from such introspective religious doubts was Cromwell, despite his public life as the resolute General and politician. In 1628, when he went to London as a new M.P. he was in so much trouble that he consulted a notable doctor who specialised in mental distress and the associated physical symptoms. The case notes survive in which he is called 'extremely melancholy, has stomach pains and very dry and withered flesh.' (Fraser p.36) Fox said much the same about himself, when in 1645 the priest physician, Machen, at Lichfield found that no blood could be got from him, 'my body, being as it were, dried up with sorrows, grief and troubles, which were so great that I could have wished I had never been born to see vanity and wickedness.. ' (N. p.6)

Usually these miseries were resolved in an experience of conversion, and Cromwell was typical also in this, as was shown ten years later in his letter to a cousin about his newly found happiness. He was very willing to

> ... honour my God by declaring what He hath done for my soul . . . Truly no poor creature hath more cause to put himself forth in the cause of his God than I . . . The Lord accept me as his son, and give me to walk in the light, and give us to walk in the light, as he is the light . . . You know what my manner of life hath been. Oh, I have lived in and loved darkness and hated the light . . . O the riches of his mercy . . . Praise Him, that He hath begun a good work and should perfect it to the day of Christ. (Fraser p.37-8)

'Walk in the Light' is a phrase Fox used so much that to find it here is a useful reminder that, whilst his meanings may have been his own, his words were often drawn from the Bible and shared with others.

The Journey South

Since Fox seems never to have been inconvenienced by lack of money, but was rarely in one place long enough to have had regular work, he must have had some parental allowance or income of his own. An obviously penniless youth risked being whipped as a vagrant and passed from parish to parish back to his birthplace, but Fox never mentions such a possibility. Yet as a stranger and wanderer he would have found well paid work hard to get. Probably he managed like many a wandering student, even of our time. He had money enough in his pocket to pay for simple lodgings, but when he had free time or opportunity he used one of his skills in a casual job - seasonal farm work or even leathercraft.

Another sign that he was not hard up came in his remark that at Christmas he would look out 'poor widows from house to house,' and give them some money, and that, when he was invited to a marriage, he refused to attend, but 'the next day . . . I would go and visit them, and if they were poor, I gave them some money.' He accounted for all this by adding,

I had wherewithal both to keep myself from being chargeable to others, and to administer something to the necessities of others. (N p.7)

It is hard to see why he should have avoided a wedding. His reaction could have come from some youthful misogyny, but he may have been objecting to any marriage by a priest, or even merely to weddings still using the old episcopal form. His alms-giving looks like the efforts of an earnest young man to follow strictly the practical directions of the Gospels, and his Christmas activity, 'while others were feasting and sporting themselves', was in line with a recent controversial ordinance against the cel-ebration of that pagan and papist festival, which had provoked riots amongst some 'apprentices and common people'. (Morton p.35)

The route of his initial wandering, even if he had not worked it out in advance, drew him southwards towards London, then beginning to be the centre of unorthodox ideas of all sorts, and consequently a great magnet. Even so, his journey took nine months, until June 1644, with stopping points mostly about a day's walk apart. He wanted to hear what notable preachers had to say and was probably influenced by oppor-tunities for convenient lodgings and promising contacts with people or congregations already questioning for themselves the accepted ideas: encounters concealed in his phrase 'professors took notice of me and sought to be acquainted with me'. His reason for moving on was the usual one - the inconsistency to which he was so sensitive: 'I was afraid of them for I was sensible they did not *possess* what they *professed*.' (N p.4)

In his journal he almost ignored the Civil War, which had been disturbing the country since 1642. It had little to do with his theme, and when he was writing had become an old story that most people were ready to forget or suppress. Yet it could hardly be chance that all his stopping places were within the zone generally controlled by Parliament. One, Newport Pagnell, was so close to the edge that it had been briefly occupied by a Royalist garrison in October 1643, and the resulting losses must have been fresh in people's thoughts and talk when Fox turned up not many weeks later. The town had a reputation as a base for radicals, including the extremists called Ranters, with whom he was later to have many difficult dealings. It was in that town, incidentally, that some time later the sixteen year old John Bunyan was 'pressed' into the army. Could that young tearaway and the sober nineteen year old Fox have shared the excitement of listening to any of the activists in the town?   When Fox reached Barnet he lingered there for some weeks before going the final twelve miles to London, and went through a very unhappy time.

> A strong temptation to despair came upon me . . . sometimes I kept myself retired in my chamber, and often walked solitary in the Chase there, to wait upon the Lord. (N p.4)

In his hunt for the cause of his feelings of guilt and misery he blamed himself: had he, for example, done wrong to leave home? Then he reviewed his boyhood: 'I was brought to call to mind all my time that I had spent and to consider whether I had wronged any.' (N p.4). But this threw up no explanation. He began to feel 'snares ... and baits to draw me to commit some sin', as if he ought to do something extravagant to account for his misery. Still hopeful that he would find help from the professionals, he 'went to many a priest to look for comfort but found no comfort from them.' The feelings which affected him during these years have led to his being labelled depressive. If depression means a sense that there is nothing of value anywhere, and that all are 'miserable sinners' with 'no health' in them, as the *Book of Common Prayer* said, the word hardly fits him. His distress soon had more to do with a sense that humankind is not what it could be. It was a helpless frustration, as much anger as despair, at the aggression and selfishness he found about him. He persisted in his struggle, not to live with this sense of guilt or futility, but to find a basis for action, a way of stirring people to change their behaviour.

depression

London

Whatever hopes he had built up about it, London, when he got there, did him no good. He turned away from both the 'great professors', presumably the leading preachers, and the associates of his Baptist uncle, Pickering, even though he admits to some sympathy of outlook with the Baptists ('they were tender then'). Many of his early supporters came from them, disillusioned by their increasing divisions and formalism. Later on, Fox had trouble disentangling his movement from theirs, at least in the official mind. Even at this time, however, he does not seem to have been a completely passive listener. Something in his behaviour or talk was making an impression on those he met, for 'some tender people would have had me stay, but I was fearful' (N p.4). Fearful of what? That the multitude of ideas whirling around London would overwhelm him? Or that he might find himself preaching whilst he was still unsure?

He may have been disappointed in the city, but so much was happening that even in two or three months he could not have gone unaffected by the multitude of sermons and pamphlets and slogans which would have come crowding in on him. The details may be hidden, but the formative influences were real enough and we should be wrong to dismiss this period, as he does, in a few lines. Many of the matters on which Fox was later to take a stand were being fought over that winter as the preachers stormed away at each other with no pretence of impartiality or distancing from political or military topics. Fox was not a scholar who carefully collected other people's views to reassemble them, still recognizable, in a system of his own. His way was that of the artist who absorbs ideas and perceptions which are then dissolved in the hidden levels of his mind, to reappear transformed when he has need of them. Quaker historians, especially at the beginning of this century, tried to find direct connections between Fox's ideas and those of the religious mystics of the sixteenth and seventeenth centuries, mainly Dutch or German groups, such as the followers of Jacob Boehme, or those called the Family of Love. We can never be sure what Fox picked up in these years, but the arguments and feuds of the Presbyterians and the Independents were all around, even if he still had to encounter some of the more radical critics, such as the Levellers. With all this, the Bible, and his own reflections, it hardly seems necessary to look further afield for the origins of his teachings.

London: Cheapside & Cheapside Cross c1650

A few scraps may illustrate this ferment, in one of the critical years of a momentous decade. In July 1644, just after Fox reached Barnet, appeared *The Bloody Tenant of Persecution for Cause of Conscience*. The undeclared author was Roger Williams, a Baptist, driven out of Presbyterian Boston in America for his views on the right to freedom of worship, who had succeeded in founding a settlement of his own on Rhode Island. This remained a haven for open-minded people - including some Quakers - all through the century. The main topic of his book was that 'the doctrine of persecution for cause of conscience is most evidently and lamentably contrary to the doctrine of Jesus Christ the Prince of Peace'. It was a proposition on which Fox was to put much emphasis. Even amidst all else that was going on, the book caused a stir that no one could have missed, and made the author fortunate to be already out on the Atlantic, with the Charter for his settlement that he had come to London to get.

In September, Parliament appointed a committee 'to endeavour the finding out some way how far tender consciences, who cannot in all things submit to the common rule which shall be established, may be borne with according to the Word'. The attempt failed, for the people with most influence were fearful about its consequences, as much for civil as for religious order. The Presbyterians, and especially the Scottish Covenanter representatives in London, pushing for a presbyterian church organisation in England as the price of Scottish support against Charles, hated the thought that people should be left free to choose their faith or their pastors. By other decisions of the autumn Parliament ordered the use of a new service book *The Directory of Public Worship,* and tried to re-enforce a rigid parochial system. Naturally therefore the authorities rejected any relief from the unpopular tithes by which parish priests were supported, even for those who were also trying to find contributions for their own Separatist ministers. Perhaps Fox left London too soon to see another work, which might have appealed to him, the outspoken defence of free speech and unlicensed printing, with the strange title *Areopagitica*, by a young scholar-poet, John Milton, already notorious for daring to write in favour of divorce. As events turned out, for forty years it was Fox, his fellow Quaker writers, and their printers, who most persistently defied all censorship.

Fox mentions that the 'great professors' were 'dark and under the chain of darkness'. One of the darkest was Thomas Edwardes, already collecting material for the first edition (in 1646) of his *Gangraena*, a malicious catalogue of all the people and opinions he disagreed with, but notable for its racy gutter-tabloid style. He hated toleration, asserting that if ever it were granted 'men should never have peace in their families more, or ever after have command of wives, children, servants.' (Coward p.75). With such views dominating the establishment, Fox and any real dissenter could expect a rough time. Another of the sort was William Prynne, who had lost his ears in the pillory years earlier through his venomous attacks on Charles and his queen. He was now busily hounding Charles's favourite Archbishop Laud to execution and defending every possible gloomy and strict prohibition. Laud was not the only victim, for during that winter several others, political enemies or Catholic priests, were taken from prison to be messily hanged or beheaded. There was plenty of inhumanity to horrify a sensitive young man.

Prynne's bitter fanaticism led a rival from the 'left' of the Independents - who had once been a fellow victim of Charles's repression - to take the risk of putting out an open letter to him asserting that 'it is the incommunicable prerogative of Jesus Christ alone to be the King of his Saints, and law-giver to his Church and people and to reign in the souls and consciences of his chosen ones'. This was John Lilburne, out of the army for refusing to take a new oath, and soon to issue one of the chief books leading to the Leveller movement, whose astonishing programme of social justice, and even political equality, was to horrify the authorities, and cause difficulties for Fox. With such views it is hardly surprising that Lilburne later on declared himself a Quaker.

Back Home Again

Messages from home suggested to Fox that his parents were worrying about him, and he set off back to Leicestershire, 'lest I should grieve them who, I understood, were troubled at my absence'. Once he was back home, after days of walking along the wet tracks of winter, the family tried to find some way of getting him to settle. After all, they knew that many young men went through a phase of religious doubt and fervour, or wasted time 'gadding after preachers', and the family could reasonably hope that with a little help this awkward son of theirs would get over his unrest.

'My relations would have had me married.' That is a most surprising move, for fathers of respectable girls wanted evidence of security and status in a possible husband. Was this just a vague idea, or had they some girl in mind who might consider taking on a life with George Fox as her career? It does at least suggest that his family had acceptable worldly standing, even in the hard days of civil war and slump. Fox parried: 'I told them I was but a lad, and I must get wisdom.' (N p.4). He usually could find the last word! By contrast, at a different social level, the not yet redeemed Bunyan married young and without thought about how he was to manage.

> This woman and I came together as poor as poor might be, not having so much household stuff as a dish or spoon betwixt us both. (Bunyan p.10)

Or so he said later, when making the point that her one possession, an old devotional book, had been enough to start his spiritual search.

The family's next scheme was quite different: 'Others would have had me into the auxiliary band among the soldiery.' Enlistment in the new armies of the Parliament might well have seemed to them a very handy outlet for an active young man who couldn't settle, especially at a moment when the prospects for the war were not looking at all hopeful and fresh men were very much needed. Fox refused, 'grieved that they profferred such things to me, being a tender youth.' He was not likely so early to be consciously a pacifist. Probably, whilst his own thoughts were so unclear, he simply shrank from killing, and wanted to avoid being mixed up in some violent and distracting goings on.

One of Fox's most useful gifts was his exceptional memory. In those endless walks and broodings he could clearly recall past arguments, heard or read, to compare them with his own reflections or check them against what he found in the Bible. This was not a conventional scholarly training , but there is no reason to

consider it ineffective or shallow. In fact his development may
have been helped by the chances that kept him from a university, for much that went on there was so formal and outdated
that the original minds of the time had to find their real education somewhere else. Fox was certainly not alone in his contempt for them. In 1652, for example, William Dell, a prominent
preacher associated with the Levellers, wrote that the university
divines preached a 'dead doctrine which other men have spoken, but they themselves have no experience of'. (Q in Hill, *Intellectual Origins* p.113) As the Master of a Cambridge college Dell
was in a position to know.

The universities were places where youths, some as young
as thirteen, went to collect the smattering of classics that would
satisfy the requirements for ordination, or else to pass time pick-
ing up a little polish and more bad habits before taking up their
inherited properties. University studies were valued by those
who did work, not for the degree but as evidence of intellectual
ability and stamina. If Fox had a handicap at all it was his lack of
Latin, still the language used for many learned studies. Yet Fox's
three years of self-education probably meant that he was
exposed to more ideas from the variety of preachers he encountered and the writings that came his way than he might have met
in a university environment. Sermons amongst the Presbyterians were serious intellectual exercises and were often accompanied by daylong debates between the preachers assembled
from a whole county. Many laymen not only listened but joined
in vigorously. The Restoration grandees Fox was later to meet
may well have felt that he lacked cultural polish, but it would be
unwise to write him off as uneducated.

For about a year he remained at home, with short forays to
hear preachers in Coventry and other places around. Still 'in
great sorrows and troubles', he 'walked many nights by myself',
agonising over the problems of sin and redemption, 'being at
that time in a measure sensible of Christ's sufferings and what
he went through'. (N p.5). Yet two of his comments are revealing, because they suggest that he was already able to put forward ideas of his own. His answers pleased one priest, and
another, Stephens, the local man, used in his Sunday sermons
points got from Fox during the week, for which, he noted, rather
acidly, 'I did not like him' (N p.5).

At nearby Mancetter he clashed with another priest, for when Fox went to reason with him about the trouble which oppressed him, 'the ground of despair and temptations', (N p.5) the man told him to take tobacco and sing psalms. It sounds more like flippant dismissal than serious counsel. Moreover, the priest gossiped about the incident to his servants, 'so that it got among the milk-lasses' (N p.6). In his gloomy self-absorbed state we may wonder which most hurt Fox, the breach of confidence or the giggling and teasing of the girls. Since it stuck in his mind for thirty years it must have thoroughly needled him. Another priest, at Lichfield, recommended medicine and bloodletting as a cure. At Coventry his accidental stepping on to a priest's flower border led to a storm of rage, 'as if his house had been on fire' (N p.6), an outburst which provided Fox with yet another instance of the detestable contradiction, even in someone of great reputation, between words and conduct. There was no comfort in such encounters.

Criticism and Insight

Over these four years Fox grew from fairly conventional dissent to his own distinctive understanding of religion. One of his first steps was to reject the idea that a university training could make a priest, a name that he used for anyone doing the work as a profession or receiving payment. It is strange that this seems to have surprised him, for not all priests were graduates and by this time he had met the Baptists, and must have heard the fierce complaints from the Presbyterians about unqualified men, some of them 'mean tradesmen', daring to preach. As soon as he reached this insight, or 'opening', according to one of his favourite words, he acted on it with his usual forthrightness by refusing to join his family in the church, preferring, like many a seeker since (and a few daring ones in his own time), 'to get into the orchard or the fields, with my Bible by myself'. He defended himself with the question, 'Did not the apostle say to believers that they needed no man teach them?' (N p.7)

Nathaniel Stephens turned up at the house asking questions about this non-attendance, and telling his parents that 'he was afraid of me for going after new lights'. This led to a rather engaging glimpse of youthful arrogance. 'I smiled in myself ...

but I told not my relations who, though they saw beyond the priests, yet they went to hear them, and were grieved because I would not go also', (N p.8). In mundane terms it was a risky line, for loners could be suspected of dark and dangerous ideas. Possibly this disposing of priests pleased him the more because it 'struck at Priest Stephens's ministry', and freed him from deference to the man. Yet for over twenty years they went on sparring, with an uncomfortable mixture of hostility and respect. But the incident shows Fox already reaching towards his conviction that 'the true church, having the invisible Christ as its head, as its "bishop, priest and counsellor"', had no place for human priests, for "the Lord would teach his people himself". This view meant that he felt equally unable to join with any of the 'Dissenting people', 'but was a stranger to all, relying wholly upon the Lord Jesus Christ', (N p.8)

Along with the priests, Fox rejected their consecrated buildings. 'God, who made the world, did not dwell in temples made with hands . . . but in people's hearts . . . His people were his temple, and he dwelt in them'. Though some still venerated the churches, during this time they were often treated very casually. Very mundane matters were discussed in them. Civil War soldiers used them as garrisons and even as stables. (Lichfield and Hereford Cathedrals, for instance, were so knocked about that they needed almost complete rebuilding.) Mock ceremonies went on in them, such as the baptising by soldiers of their horses, or even of pigs and sheep. And of course they suffered from the high-minded destruction of sculptures and wall paintings. Rebuilding and refurbishing churches became a project for the bishops after the Restoration. Fox called churches by a derogatory secular name, 'steeple-house', although he did not invent it. His interest, and that of other Quaker speakers, was focussed on the activities of people. When he reacted emotionally to a church as a building he was affected by some association with inhuman action or hostile preaching. In the early years of the movement he went often to churches simply because in them and around them could be found people already assembled and priests with whom to debate.

The Bible came next under Fox's scrutiny. He carried the book with him, and knew it thoroughly, so that he could often catch out opponents, but he rarely accepted it blindly, although in argument he could quote texts as readily and as wearisomely as any of them. Where they treated the text of the Bible as the sacred authority, Fox looked on it as secondary, the written out record of past teaching and experience. It was not itself the teaching, or Word, even though it deserved the most serious attention. The true Word, the real teacher, was the eternal Christ. Guidance was to be found not only in what had been written long ago, but in his leadings, recognized through the attentive worshipper's waiting in quiet expectation. Fox expected the Bible, especially the new teachings of the Gospels, and the genuine leadings of the Spirit in worship, to be consistent, so that each could each test the other.

Nevertheless the Bible remained central to the thought and language both of Fox and all who heard him. The characters in its stories provided examples of behaviour that everyone recognized. Its imagery and descriptions, and the well known phrases of the English translations, especially the King James version, contributed to a vivid landscape of the mind, where people sometimes seemed more at home than in the real one. Our own century's abandonment of all this wealth of symbol and association often makes their writings seem hardly comprehensible. At a more intellectual level they could treat the Bible as a reliable authority, not only for moral topics but for the historical record, because no research was available to challenge it. Their own time was to see the beginnings of such studies. In fact, a few years later, in 1660, Fox's companion, Samuel Fisher, wrote one of the first scholarly works to examine the linguistic and historical discrepancies in the Bible. Their span of history was also minutely intimate, for the genealogies in the Old Testament had just been used to show that Adam and Eve began their lives in 4004 B.C. The enigmatic timescales of the apocalyptic books, with their strange forecasts about the imminent return of Christ and the end of the world, led many to Millenarian hopes, and some, especially the Fifth Monarchists, to dangerous conclusions, which seemed to the authorities to implicate Fox and his troublesome Quakers.

But Fox at this time still had his own way to find, 'for I saw that there was none among them all that could speak to my con-

dition . . . I had nothing outwardly to help me, nor could tell
what to do . . .' When he searched for the essence of religion he
discovered that it was not to be found in the careful, legalistic
arguments of the preachers, but in personal experience. In this
moment of stress, coming after the long months of brooding, he
'heard a voice which said, '"There is one, even Christ Jesus,
which can speak to thy condition."' This word, 'condition', was
to become one of his favourite words. Although it shaded out-
wards to include other psychological or social aspects, he meant
by it one's moral state, usually that reached at a particular
moment in one's life or development. Fox accepted that he and
all others were imperfect, ('concluded under sin, and shut up in
unbelief as I had been'). Yet he believed that his passionate long-
ing to learn the way to perfection could be satisfied, but only
from a perfect teacher, who for him was God in Christ, met
within his own being.

His conclusions matter more than the route through an
obsolete cosmology by which he reached them. Basing himself
on the Bible, Fox thought of history as divided into three ages.
Paradise had been the first, where 'God was the first teacher of
men and women, . . . and as long as they kept to, and under
God's teaching, they kept . . . in righteousness and holiness . . .'
The second was that of the 'serpent', when God was disobeyed.
The third was introduced by Christ Jesus, 'the third teacher, the
way to God, the Truth, the Life and the true Light.' (Ell. p.384 -
5). Fox concentrated on this age of Christ, insisting that his life
and sacrificial death had ended completely the penalties and
limitations of the age of sin, as it was perceived according to the
Old Testament. Humanity was once more no longer bound to
act wrongly, but, as in the first brief age of innocence, was able to
make spiritual and moral progress towards the perfection spoken of by Christ in the Gospels. Fox sometimes seemed to give
less attention to the crucifixion than might have been expected.
He was not interested in talk about it; he looked on it as a self-
sacrifice which provided a model for a discipline by which to
live. What he called the experience of the Cross meant first to
recognize in oneself the faults with which people begin, then to
realise that a new way was possible, and thereafter to persevere
patiently in trying to live according to it.

This understanding, and the boundless hope it offered, was so different from that of the Calvinists that he decided that he had been led, for his own good, away from all other teachers and books, 'that Jesus Christ might have all the pre-eminence, who enlightens, and gives grace, and faith, and power... And this I knew *experimentally.'* (N p.11). That for him was the key word: experimentally. It hardly matters whether it is given its modern meaning of 'by experiment', or its earlier one of 'through experience', its force is the same. Fox was asserting that his knowledge was no longer external, like clothing which could be taken off, or merely based on argument, but had become a quality of his own being. This led to a time of great contentment: a sense of increasing understanding of the nature of the world and of himself amongst other people.

> And then the Lord did gently lead me on, and did let me see his love, which was endless and eternal, and surpasseth all the knowledge that men have in the natural state, or can get by history or books; and that love let me see myself as I was without him. (N p.12)

Yet this was not without its downturns. For him, grounded in the Bible and still under the influence of the mediaeval dualism, his uncertainties appeared as a contest between actual forces, the Devil against Christ. But in the biblical record Christ defeated the devil, (according to the strange metaphor Fox often used, he had 'bruised the head of the serpent',) and this gave him confidence that with the help of Christ he and others too could find the courage to stand up to the stresses and temptations facing them. This spiritual progress appeared to him so important and so attractive that he was surprised how people could carry on, apparently content with what were to him just pointless outward things.

> If I had a king's diet, palace, and attendance, all would have been as nothing, . . . And I saw professors, priests and people were whole and at ease in that condition which was my misery.

and so came again to his conclusion,

> Therefore, all wait patiently upon the Lord, whatsoever con-

dition you be in; wait in the grace and truth that comes from Jesus; for if you do, there is a promise to you, and the Lord God will fulfil it in you . . . I have found it so, praised be the Lord. (N p.13)

His favourite, endlessly used name, drawn from John's Gospel, for his perception of the eternal Christ was 'Light'.

. . . it was opened to me by the eternal Light and Power, and I saw that all was done and to be done in and by Christ . . . (N p.14)

John . . . did bear witness to the Light, [with] which Christ . . . hath enlightened every man and woman that cometh into the world, that they might believe in it, and become the Children of Light, and so have the light of life, and not come into con- demnation . . . (N p.16)

And so on, almost every time he spoke; so often, indeed, that 'Children of Light' became the first name for his followers. This Light in the soul was not, as many preachers said, merely a 'natural light', the activity of the conscience, it was genuinely divine. He insisted endlessly that everyone, good or bad, Chris- tian or non-Christian, had some share, some 'measure' of this Light, and wanted people to 'be faithful to the measure of Light' in them, and to live so that they increased it.

In moral terms, however, this Light was never for Fox a mere cosy glow, or even a convenient beacon. It could show up not only what was sensible or good, but also, as rubbish in dark corners may be detected by a probing torch, it could lead to the painful exposing of one's inner failings and convenient complacencies. 'The divine Light of Christ manifesteth all things; and the spiri- tual fire trieth all things . . .' (N p.15). Indeed, the first effect on those who came up against Quaker teaching was often great dis- tress, as they saw that they had been too easily satisfied with their ideas about how they should live. From this understanding of the divine Light in its moral aspect Fox reached his own interpreta- tion of 'Law' in religious thought. He thought the Bible had much to say about the external law of the Hebrews, which he saw as a collection of regulations put forward by servants doing the best they could to meet the wishes of an absent master, and contrasted with it the new inner law of Jesus, distinguished by having the simplicity and first hand authority of a master who was present to interpret and advise. As he put it,

> . . . I saw many talked of the law, who had never known the law to be their schoolmaster, and many talked of the Gospel of Christ, who had never known life and immortality brought to light in them by it . . . (N p.15)

Fox's hearers shared with him a vocabulary, an experience of life, and a sense of urgency. He was confident that when he 'proclaimed Truth', people would recognize it in their own experience.

> And they that walk in the light come to the mountain of the house of God established above all mountains, and to God's teaching, who will teach them his ways. These things were opened to me in the Light . . . These things are to be found in man's heart.

Many who heard him reacted like the John Crook who had so feared the devil. 'This kind of preaching appeared . . . like as if the old apostles were risen from the dead, and began to preach again in the same life and power . . .' (Crook p.xv) The establishment did not agree: '. . . to speak of these things being within seemed strange to the rough and crooked and mountainous ones'. (N p.16.)

When his opponents 'argued for sin', and said 'they believed no such thing that any could be free from sin while upon the earth', (N p.56). Fox asked them what they made of such sayings of Jesus as 'You, therefore, must be perfect, as your heavenly Father is perfect.' (*Mat*. VI 48). His insistence that no one was doomed to sin and failure, and that everyone had in them some 'measure of the Light', some capacity for good, or 'that of God', fuelled the hostility of Calvinists. But as if this rejecting of their doctrine was not exasperating enough, he soon came to to make an even more sweeping claim. He dismissed the whole church establishment as a 'fifteen hundred years' apostacy', which had lost its way amongst imposed hierarchies and rules. He argued that, by demanding conformity and persecuting those who refused it, the churches had betrayed the message of Jesus, who 'persecuted none'. By assertions like this, and by making the inward individual experience the basis for faith and life, Fox was condemning all contemporary claims to authority, rank, and status, including those of magistrates and priests. This could lead not only to charges of heresy, but of subversion, and so to collision with the powers of both church and state.

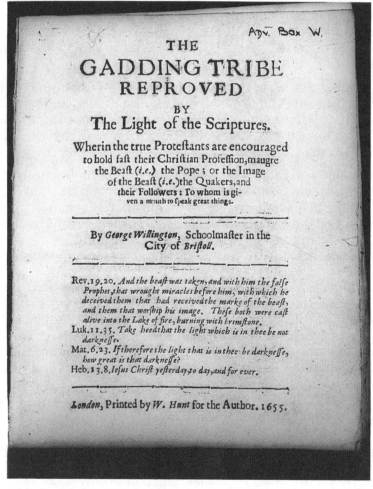

An anti-Quaker pamphlet dated 1655

Chapter Four

HIS WORKING LIFE BEGINS

Getting a Hearing

By 1647, Fox, now twenty three years old, was gathering the confidence to share his exhilarating new experience with everybody who would listen, and during the first phase of his working life, up to 1653, only prison checked his strenuous pace. In that crowded time almost all the problems and experiences of his career can be found.

At first he had no guaranteed group or welcome, but was just another young man trying to get a hearing at any gathering where he could ask questions or join in a debate. He travelled on foot, for no horse is mentioned until 1651, and was often alone. On muddy, isolated roads it was a strange life. When he could, he stayed with a sympathizer, but more often he used inns, and where he could not reach one, or was refused accommodation, he slept out, under a hedge or a haystack. Very sensibly, therefore he took to wearing the leather breeches which attracted a remarkable amount of comment. 'It was a dreadful thing [to priests and professors] when it was told them, "The man in leather breeches is come."' (N p.83). Since these were often worn, at least out of doors, it is difficult to see why Fox's leather clothes should have caused the stir they did. They would seem to be very practical garments for anybody leading his sort of life, even better than the industrial jeans or PVC jacket that a successor of his might choose today. Leather garments were not cheap, and his were apparently not strange in style or colour. Apart from being weather and thorn proof, they could deflect knifethrusts, as apparently in 1653, when after a beating up he 'saw a great hole in [his] coat, which was cut with a knife, but it was not cut through [his] doublet.' (N p.150). How long he went on wearing leather is not very clear. A reply by Margaret Fell to a satirist in 1665 implied that by then they were not his everyday wear.

In the early days he admitted that he had great difficulty even in nerving himself to face a preacher in church: 'I was in sore travail, and it came to me that I was moved to go to the steeple-house and tell the people and the priest . . .' (N p.20). During this time he felt the mixture of hope and inadequacy which have been experienced by many an evangelist. 'And I saw the harvest white, and the Seed of God lying thick in the ground, as ever did wheat that was sown outwardly, and none to gather it, and this I mourned with tears'. (N p.21). Yet even during the first year or so he got some encouragement. 'A report went abroad of me that I was a young man with a discerning spirit; whereupon many came to me from far and near, and I spake unto them the things of God, and they heard with attention, and silence, and went away, and spread the fame [= report or news] thereof.' Before long, people were not only listening to him, but responding, even to the extent of following his provocative example. 'Many were moved by the Lord to go to steeple-houses, to the priests and to the people, to declare the everlasting Truth'.

As he moved further afield from his home area, perhaps assisted by the ending of the war, he got news of a sympathetic group in Nottinghamshire, around Mansfield. They had belonged to a Baptist fellowship which had lost faith and cohesion, so that they were open to a fresh leading, (although one section had opted out and taken to spending Sunday mornings playing shovel board). Before long those who responded to Fox began to use the name 'Children of Light', from his directing his listeners to respond to 'the Light of Christ within them', and perhaps from its use in the Unjust Steward parable (*Luke* XVI 8). Though Nottinghamshire was not in the end a leading Quaker centre and not much is known of these people, their early support should not be underrated, for without something of the kind Fox might never have got started at all.

Amongst them was 'a very tender woman whose name was Elizabeth Hooton', ('tender', in religious matters, meant receptive and free from self-righteousness). She has the distinction of being Fox's first named follower and one of his most loyal fellow workers, whose house became for several years his base and refuge. No material trace of Fox's earlier life has survived, for his supposed family home in Fenny Drayton has disappeared, but in Skegby, near Mansfield, stands a stone built yeoman's house, thought to be that of the Hootons, and still called the 'Quaker house'. It is about equal to a present day three bedroom detached house but with an attic storey, perhaps once used as a dormitory for servants, children, or travelling Quakers. Elizabeth was then in her forties, the wife of a well-off farmer, as his house suggests. Oliver Hooton too became a Quaker. In many ways the couple were typical of Fox's supporters. Their home was used for meetings; the plot of land beside it became a burial ground, and both Elizabeth and their son, also Oliver, travelled as ministers, with the consequent beatings and imprisonments.

Public buildings were very scarce, and the endless debates had to be held where space could be found, even if that was an open field in winter. Inns were used for many purposes, and congregations often adjourned to them after church, some people to drink and some to go on with the arguments. Small groups met in private houses, often the halls of the gentry, as shown in Fox's reference to a 'meeting of priests and professors at a Justice's house and I went among them'. (N p.22). The only large halls were the churches, used not only for the Sunday services, but for the weekday lectures and 'disputes' [=debates].

At one of these Fox got into trouble for his extraordinary idea that women might have some rights equal with men.

> As I was passing through the fields, I was moved to go to Leicester . . . I heard of a great meeting for a dispute and there were many to preach, Presbyterians, Independents, Baptists and Common-prayer men [= Anglican, though that word was not yet in use] . . . in a steeple-house, . . . some being in pews and the priest in the pulpit.

A woman ventured a question and was snubbed by the priest. Fox objected, first against the sexual discrimination, ('for the woman asking a question, he ought to have answered it, having given liberty for any to speak'), and then against the idea that the building could be the 'church'. He insisted that 'the church was . . . a spiritual household which Christ was the head of, [not] . . . an old house made up of lime, stones and wood'. (N p.24). His ideas proved too disturbing. 'They all turned against me . . . The priest came down out of his pulpit, and others out of their pews and the dispute was marred'. Afterwards Fox 'went to a great inn, and there disputed the thing with the priests and professors of all sorts, and they were all on fire'. One man 'appeared for a while to join with me, but he soon turned against me'. In the end, however, 'there were several convinced that day; and the woman that asked the question aforesaid, and her family'. (N p.25.) She of course had most reason to be impressed. For Fox it had been quite a profitable day: some response and no pelting with stones.

He was eager to share with everybody his delighted assurance that the new era of Christ really had begun.

> Now was I come up in spirit through the flaming sword into the paradise of God. All things were new, and all the creation gave another smell unto me than before, beyond what words can utter. I knew nothing but pureness, and innocency, and righteousness, being renewed up into the image of God by Christ Jesus . . . I felt [the Lord's] power went forth over all, by which all might be reformed, if they would receive and bow to it. (N p.27 - 8)

He could not understand why the priests 'argued for sin', leaving the people weighed down not only by their own failings but by ancestral guilt, like the burden carried by Bunyan's Pilgrim.

Ranters and Others

Fox's opponents saw the matter differently. To them his supporters seemed to run into two heresies. Their trust in private inner leadings not only displaced the authority of priest or Bible, but looked like an unwelcome by-product of the election doctrine, the inference that if you were among the saved anything you pleased could be right or wrong for you. You could safely indulge in any speculation. This idea had got the name 'antinomian', and this word became a favourite term of abuse. One label for those supposed to hold such irresponsible and extravagant views was 'ranter'. It seems possible that there were hardly any self-styled Ranters and that the word was an abusive nickname coined by opponents, rather as the word Quaker was, and applied loosely to anybody whose radical views annoyed the establishment. Associated with ranters were a few notorious people who held that any sexual activity was commendable, even polygamy or group sex, practices which at least gave the makers of satirical cartoons some sensational material. Others took pride in their capacity to swear, apparently enjoying the emotional release of seeing for how long they could keep up the flow of fantastical oaths. Perhaps more had shrugged off theological complexities and were, as the phrase of our time has it, 'just enjoying themselves'. The very strictness of Presbyterian teaching could sometimes lead to reactions of an exaggerated and certainly an imprudent sort. It was always possible to find someone who could be accused of a heresy such as pantheism or materialism. Newcomers to Quakerism, happy in its liberating hope, could overlook its increasing emphasis on the need to test personal leadings by reflection, by relating them to the Gospel, and by conference with other Friends.

Quakers regularly had the name Ranter thrown at them by those who did not trouble to distinguish one kind of unorthodox behaviour from another. Fox spent much energy asserting the moral uprightness and self-discipline expected of his supporters. This was made harder because at first the excitement of Quaker rallies drew a fringe whose behaviour really was eccentric, and since there was very little Quaker organisation the Presbyterians could use them as evidence that the movement was a brand of ranterism. Unluckily, some of the people actually accepted as Quakers went in for actions that looked just as objectionable. They not only contradicted preachers in full flow, but tried to demonstrate their message with provocative and memorable tricks that might now pass as 'street theatre,' although they were really modelled on the example of prophets in the Old Testament. A few people paraded in sackcloth and ashes, or with a lighted candle at noon, as a comment on worldly values or the futility of the preachers. Others 'went naked' through the streets to demonstrate what little would be left if people's pretences were taken away. ('Naked' seems to have meant wearing at least loincloth or vest, and sometimes having the company of another Friend formally carrying the discarded garments.) In the early years, if it seemed likely to stir consciences, Fox did not reject this unconventional behaviour, but he practised it only once, in a very restrained way, at Lichfield.

In those brief heady years of almost free speech Fox was not the only one with an unorthodox message, to delight some hearers and scare the establishment. The Levellers, for instance, apart from their ideas on social justice, sometimes favoured pantheism. Others, including those associated with Ludovic Muggleton, later a persistent opponent of Quakers 'did say . . . that there is no God but nature only'. (Muggleton's *The Acts of the Witnesses*, 1650, Q in Hill, *The World Turned Upside Down*, p.173) Another, from amongst the shovel-board players of Mansfield, was a rather unstable man called Rice Davies. He responded to Fox and for several years lived as a Quaker, but by 1651, he had returned to his atheism and enlisted in the Parliamentary army. When he encountered Fox, then in Derby gaol, he ridiculed him for believing 'in a man that died at Jerusalem', when 'there was never any such thing' (N p.63). Rice Davies himself for some years led a group of his own, known as 'Proud Quakers', and attacked Fox for his moral strictness.

Fox's Way of Learning

Two incidents illustrate Fox's characteristic way of learning how to deal with the arguments and emotions confronting him. Whilst he was resting by the fire in someone's house, he was shaken by a fundamental doubt: What if there is no God? What if 'all things come by Nature?' He refrained from fretting, or trying to argue his way out of it, but waited, so quietly that 'the people in the house perceived nothing', as he 'sat still under it and let it alone' until he felt the answer. 'A living hope arose in me, and a true voice, which said, "There is a living God who made all things"' (N p.25). The implicit assumption was that the intolerable alternative would be moral and material chaos. At another time, as he sat alone thinking, 'the Lord showed me that . . . those things that were hurtful were within . . . the natures of dogs, swine, vipers, of Sodom and Egypt, Pharaoh, Cain . . .' He was terrified to feel in himself the emotions belonging to the various moral plights in this list, (symbolised in images drawn, of course, from the Bible), for he 'was never addicted to commit those evils'. But in this mental dialogue, 'the Lord answered it was needful I should have a sense of all conditions; how else should I speak to all conditions?' (N p.19). He realised that if he were to speak effectively to people in differing spiritual states, or in the grip of various hates and cravings, impersonal analysis would be useless. He needed to endure an imaginative re-creation of such drives and obsessions as if he were their victim. Both stories show him learning as much by a sort of emotional empathy as by logic. It was the way of the artist.

When emotions surfaced quickly and were expressed freely this capacity to identify intensely with mood or need may have underlain the visible trembling of the 'Children of the Light' when they spoke in public, and of those affected by their words, from which soon came the nickname 'Quaker', although this incident of 1648 appeared free of the later scorn.

> . . . to Mansfield, where there was a great meeting of profes-
> sors and people, and I was moved to pray, and the Lord's
> power was so great that the house seemed to be shaken.
> When I had done, some of the professors said it was now as in
> the days of the apostles, where the house was shaken where
> they were. (N p.22)

Social and Economic Challenge

Those who detested Fox's religious views soon found him open-ing up even more objectionable topics. The 'Light of Christ' for him meant much more than talk, for the real Christian had to 'live in the Light'. This meant that you needed to look critically , not just at your own behaviour but at public and social conduct. How did you treat your servants? Were you offering fair wages? If you were a craftsman, did you turn out work of first-rate qual-ity? If you were a trader, were your prices fair? If you had the chance to pass off poor goods, or overcharge an unwary cus-tomer did you take it? (Fox's early years in Fenny Drayton had no doubt left him well aware of the tricks used by traders.) If you were a magistrate, did you deal justly with the poor and the unpopular? When Fox asked such questions, with all their repercussions on profit and privilege, he could expect to stir up hatred even from those able to overlook a little priest-baiting.

One early incident illustrates the stress that Fox experienced as he became drawn into his campaign for a society fit for the eternal Christ. Amongst their many other functions the Justices regulated employment conditions, and were naturally inclined to do so to the advantage of the employers. Fox walked to an inn where some Justices were setting wage levels for servants, but found 'a company of fiddlers there', and turned tail. When he returned the next morning, the Justices had already gone, and he was so overcome with guilt at his failure that he felt he was losing his sight. Finding that the Justices had transferred their sitting to a town eight miles away he ran all the way there, his sight returning as he acted on his resolve. Catching them still at work, surrounded by a crowd of servants, he

> . . . exhorted the justices not to oppress the servants in their wages, but to do that which was right and just to them; and I exhorted the servants to do their duties, and serve honestly . . . [etc.] (N p.26)

To his relief, 'they received my exhortations kindly', perhaps because the servants had also come in for some advice.

He was heading for more trouble when he took on powerful professional groups: lawyers who were 'out of the wisdom of God', because they failed to act fairly by not doing 'to others as they would others should do to them', and doctors, because they failed to study 'the creatures and . . . their virtues' [= the properties of everything in nature]. Before long Fox had further aims.

> I was to bring people . . . that they might visit the fatherless, the widows and strangers . . . And then there would not be so many beggars, the sight of whom often grieved my heart, to see so much hardheartedness amongst them that professed the name of Christ. (N p.35)

Nobody was left out: teachers were to take care about the behaviour of pupils, employers should train servants carefully and bring them up 'in the fear of the Lord' by being 'patterns of sobriety and virtue' to them. Parents were to be especially responsible about their rearing of children. Innkeepers were warned 'that they should not let people have more drink than would do them good' (N p.37). Astrologers, the 'star-gazers' with their popular predictions, were misleading people and making them feel less responsible for their own lives. Entertainers should not stir up foolish emotions with their tricks and bawdy jokes. Even clothing, he thought, should reflect a quietly sensible outlook, free of extravagance and attention catching show. He expected those who had 'come to the new and living way of Christ' (N p.35), both to practise and to find pleasure in whatever was helpful and well done. He wanted indeed nothing less than a total transformation of customary political and social attitudes.

Hats and Pronouns

These ideas were radical enough to be reckoned thoroughly dangerous, if not downright seditious, but soon Fox's passion for equality set him off on a lifelong campaign against two other practices. Although he chose to think of them as 'small things', his stand generated some of the most embittered antagonism against Quakers and caused them almost more suffering than the more economically significant testimony against tithes, when that later gathered momentum. To Fox all men and women were equal in the sight of God; everybody should therefore be treated equally. Unfortunately, he was dealing with people who were obsessed with ideas of status. Everyone expected the incessant acknowledgement of social rank through elaborate language and gestures. Perhaps the very intimacy with which they lived amongst their families and servants, and the insecurity of life and fortune, reinforced their desire to show where they stood in the world. Since another feature of the period was the high level of aggressiveness, those who thought themselves belittled went on the attack, not only with words but with fists, sticks and swords.

In Fox's time the old singular words ('thou', 'thy' etc) were still used, but only to inferiors: servants and juniors, (and also, with some lack of logic, to lovers and the deity). It struck him that this was improper. Speakers should keep strictly to the logical distinction between singular and plural, so that no one would be humbled as a servant, nor flattered as a superior. The same passion for logic and truth led to another quirky verbal irritant. The names of the months and the days of the week were pagan. He therefore rejected them and used numbers, so that, for example, Sunday became 'First Day'. Most of the people he addressed thought he was insulting them. In addition, social interaction in those days involved more than words: every encounter required not only bowings and curtsies but elaborate raising and sweeping around of hats. This was the more frequent because hats were on people's heads everywhere, not only out of doors, but in court, in church, and at their own dinner tables. Children kept their hats off when with their parents and everybody else; servants when with their masters and all gentlemen; gentlemen when received by the aristocracy; nobles before the king, and the king before God. There was even a feeling of guilt around that the actual king had been compelled to lose his head as well as his hat.

Into this intricate and elaborate social dance entered Fox, hat firmly on head, daring to claim that before Christ, all, - servants, priests, and Justices, - stood on a level, so that the gestures by which everyone asserted or acknowledged his position in the national pecking order were a ridiculous masquerade. 'Small thing' Fox might call it but, on top of all his other outrageous ideas about a Christian society, it gave a pretext for

> . . . the rage and scorn that arose! Oh, the blows, punchings, beatings and imprisonments that we underwent for not putting off our hats to men! For that soon tried all men's patience and sobriety. Some had their hats violently plucked off and thrown away so that they quite lost them . . . beside the danger we were sometimes in of losing our lives. (N p.37)

The battle over 'hat honour' went on until attitudes changed and the whole elaborate ritual was moderated. It became the quick means of identifying a Quaker. Along with the use of 'thee' it was a sort of ordeal for newly convinced Quakers to survive. It was a good excuse for taking offence and beating someone up, or for refusing him justice. Perhaps the oddest aspect was that even though they condemned the social pride that demanded hat honour, Quakers were as obstinate about keeping their hats on as others were in knocking them off. No one was willing to be seen hatless.

Prisons and First Imprisonment

Stuart prisons were inhuman places, not intended for custodial sentences, but for holding offenders until the Quarter Sessions or the half-yearly Assizes. Sentences ranged from fines and binding-over orders, through whipping and stocking, to branding and ear mutilation, and finally hanging. Prisoners were usually held only till they found sureties for their good behaviour, paid their fines, or had the other penalties carried out. Apart from a few 'Houses of Correction', set up originally to house and employ - in a punitive way - the unemployed poor, the prisons were all old and makeshift: castles, town gatehouses, old monastic buildings, inns and private houses. Nobody, whether king, County Justices, or borough corporation, wanted to pay for their upkeep. When Margaret Fell during one of her trials, complained of the conditions at Lancaster, the Justice told her 'they were to commit them to prison, but not to provide prisons for them.' (HJC Natt. Pap. p.113). Gaolers depended mainly on allowances related to the numbers in their charge, and on the fees paid by prisoners themselves. Many gaolers seem to have been recruited from the rougher sort of ex-offender. Prisoners with money to spend could live fairly comfortably. Those who refused were deliberately illtreated to induce them to pay up. Often the prisoners' relatives brought in their meals, their clothes, and even the materials of their trades so that they could earn their keep. Within a few years thousands of Quakers, mostly from social groups above the usual run of wrongdoers, overloaded the system and congested the prisons. Their non-cooperation about oaths, fines, promises of good behaviour and fees to gaolers led to their being worse treated and kept in custody for much longer than the expected few months. Prison buildings were not meant for such people.

It was inevitable that before long Fox would be arrested, although he was usually careful to give no pretext. In church, for example, he waited to speak after the sermon in the time allocated to people from the congregation. However, in 1649, something provoked him to rasher protest.

As I passed to Nottingham on a First Day in the morning with Friends to a meeting, when I came on top of a hill, as I looked upon the town the great steeplehouse struck at my life when I

spied it, a great and idolatrous temple. And the Lord said unto
me,'Thou must go cry against yonder great idol, and against
the worshippers therein.' (N p.39)

He interrupted the preacher, and was taken off to prison, 'a piti-
ful, stinking place, where the wind brought all the stench of the
house of office in the place, where the stench . . . was in my
throat and head many days after' (N p.40). He was always
acutely sensitive to smells. Sanitary arrangements were
generally sketchy, but in prisons, - since offenders didn't count,
- they could be left out altogether.

The treatment of prisoners was unpredictable, depending
on the prejudices of the officers involved. Here the sheriff in
charge of him was so impressed by Fox that he transferred him
to his own house. The man's next move reminds us again how
people then felt intensely and turned quickly to action. He not
only confessed to some unjust dealings, but 'the next market
day, as he was walking with me in the chamber, he said, "I must
go into the market and preach repentance to the people"; and
accordingly he went, in his slippers . . .' (N p.41). The Justices
naturally had Fox returned to the prison. When the Assize came
on a man 'was moved to offer himself up for me, body for body,
yea, life also'. It was the first of many such gestures, but it is
remarkable that at this early point the personality of the young
Fox should have made so great an impression that someone was
willing to accept the risks of prison for him. Nothing came of it,
because after about six weeks one of the many administrative
mix-ups in his career led to his being released without charges,
and he was able to return to his Skegby base.

Witchcraft and Healing

There he had brought to him a demented woman, 'possessed'
for thirty two years. Quakers were often accused of witchcraft,
and this patient's plight was turned into a kind of test. Careful
arrangements were made for many Friends to assemble, and
after several days of prayer the patient stopped 'roaring and
tumbling on the ground', sat quietly beside Fox and spoke
lucidly. Cautiously Friends

. . . kept her a fortnight in the sight of the world . . . and then sent her away to her friends . . . And then the world's professors, priests and teachers never could call us any more false prophets . . . or witches . . . it did a great deal of good in the country. (N p.43)

This was only one of many healing episodes, sometimes of mental trouble, but mostly of illness and injury. The rough handling by mobs meant that Fox himself was often injured, for with the obvious approval of priest or magistrate this disturbing young man was fair game, a licensed target for some of their own frustrations. Though he admitted frequently to being 'mazed and dazzled with the blows', or 'so bruised that I could not turn in my bed, and bruised inwardly at my heart', his ability to recover quickly always surprised those with him and helped him to keep going when they thought it impossible. One notable quality indeed of these first few Quakers was their persistence in trying to put forward their message and their indifference to brutal knocks and beatings. Fox and his friends firmly accepted the reality of spiritual healing, and it remained a continuing strand in their lives.

Soon afterwards, whilst in Derbyshire, Fox had another brush with Nathaniel Stephens, who raised a suspicion of witchcraft by his claim that Fox had been 'carried up with a whirlwind into heaven, and after was found full of gold and silver'. Fox's family wrote asking him to come and show himself, but were inclined to credit the story, for 'said they, when he went from us he had a great deal of gold and silver with him.' (N p.50). Later on, Fox had capital of his own, but if this money had been provided by his family it indicates that they were quite well off. Another sign of prosperity came a few months later, when his relations, 'much troubled that [he] should be in prison, for they looked upon it to be a great shame', offered sureties 'in one hundred pounds, and others in Derby, fifty pounds apiece.' (N p.61). The 'others in Derby' might have been supporters rather than relatives, but if so it suggests that people of substance were already amongst those attracted to him. Most people thought themselves fortunate if the value of their whole estate came to a hundred pounds, and few would have £50 of disposable money to risk.

Derby Prison

In the autumn of 1650, in Derby, Fox heard the church bell ring-
ing for a lecture. He joined in the debate, but when he told them
that their formal activities, 'all their preaching, baptism and sacrifices, would never sanctify them', he was arrested. The justices
soon convinced themselves that by saying Christ 'abided' in him
Fox was claiming to be equal to Christ. Under a new law that
counted as blasphemy, and they committed him to the House of
Correction for six months, unless he gave surety for good behaviour. Of course he would not, nor would he allow his family to
do so for him. In prison, crowds, hoping to see some sort of
freak, came to stare at this man 'that had no sin'. Fox was not to
be silenced by prison. He kept up his campaign by a stream of
letters, many to the magistrates, and others to encourage his
own supporters not to lose heart. According to him, it was
during this trial that the name 'Quaker' was first used, by the
Derby Justice, Gervase Bennet, 'when we bid them tremble at
the word of God.' (N p.58). The sarcastic name may not have
been quite new, but it was soon linked only with Fox and his followers, who were beginning to call themselves, no longer 'Children of the Light', but 'Friends', although the Mansfield group
had already used the word before Fox met them. Perhaps the
remark of Jesus, 'Ye are my friends if you do whatever I command you', had suggested it. For many years the name continued to vary. Fox later used 'people of God', and Sewel, the
first Quaker historian, resorted to 'the people called Quakers'.
Fox began his letters with a range of phrases, from 'Friends in
the Lord', 'Friends in the eternal Truth of God', 'Friends in the
Immortal Seed of God', to 'Dear Brethren in the Covenant of
Life'.

As the six months imprisonment ended, a recruiting drive
was going on, linked with the alarm about Charles II's Worcester
campaign. Fox was offered a place as an officer, because of his
admitted ability to influence people. He refused, and his reply
gave for the first time his considered rejection of fighting. He
would not take up arms, because he 'lived in the virtue of that
life and power which took away the occasion of all wars, and
knew from whence all wars did arise . . .' Official exasperation
led to his getting another six months' sentence, not in the com-

paratively humane conditions of the House of Correction but in 'the dungeon amongst thirty felons in a lousy stinking low place in the ground without any bed.' (N p.65). His only relief was an occasional walk in the garden. This prison gave him first hand experience of another social evil. It fell to him to play the pastor to two men sentenced to hang for 'small things'. Although he had to 'admonish' them for their theft he assured them that their heavy penalty was against the law of God. After the execution he noted, 'their spirits appeared to me as I was walking, and I saw the men were well'. (N p.66). This apparent clairvoyance he took as a matter of course, a fact of life to be expected when there was occasion for it. In the end the authorities could not agree on how to dispose of him, and after a year he was turned out, in October 1651.

Lichfield

As soon as he was free, Fox was on the move again, looking forward with fresh hope to the spreading of the 'light and truth and glory of the Lord'. Soon afterwards happened one of the strangest incidents of his life. This has become something of a legend, though only from his telling of it, for there seems to be no other record. Except that it did not result in a confrontation with priests or Justices it seems a more intense form of the compulsion which had led to his protest in Nottingham church.

Whilst walking near Lichfield with other Friends, he saw 'three spires' which also 'struck at his life'. A mile from the town he pulled off his shoes and gave them for safe-keeping to some shepherds. He then walked around the streets shouting, 'Woe unto the bloody city of Lichfield!', seeming to see 'a channel of blood down the streets, and the market place like a pool of blood.' (N p.71). Fortunately he was left unmolested and some friendly people brought him back to the commonplace with: 'Alack, George! Where are thy shoes?' As a burning sensation died out of his feet and body, he returned to the shepherds, paid them soberly for minding his shoes, washed his feet in a ditch and put his shoes on again. Then, recognising that the townspeople could not be blamed for the bloodshed during the recent siege, he began to wonder why he had been overcome by such an unexpected urge. When he later heard of a massacre there in

Roman times he decided he might have picked up some impression of this. Unfortunately, despite the tradition, there may never have been such a massacre.

During the war Lichfield had gone through a bitter and destructive siege, in which the cathedral had been wrecked and its great central tower shot away, so that in reality on that day he could hardly have seen *three* spires. This very visible destruction may have suggested to Fox a parallel which excited him into re-enacting an Old Testament prophecy, for the phrase 'Woe to the bloody city' echoes the censure of Ninevah by the prophet Nahum (*Nahum* Ch. 3). Exhaustion after the hardship in the Derby prisons could have contributed to an hallucinatory reaction. The episode was a one-off, out of character and difficult to account for. By the time he came to write his account in the *Journal* Fox himself seemed to be puzzled by it. It was even too much for his longsuffering family, for he noted, 'my relations were offended at me.'

Towards Yorkshire

Fox soon began to edge northwards, through the Nottinghamshire and Derbyshire territory where his support had so far been strongest and where Friends were keeping up meetings without his presence, and then into Yorkshire. By this time news of him must have gone ahead, circulating amongst the gatherings of separatists and other thoughtful people unhappy at the ways of the Presbyterians. Nevertheless to people such as innkeepers he was merely a suspicious character who should present himself to the village constable to prove that he was an lawful traveller. This was in order, though rather officious, but Fox, as might be expected, took what would now be called a 'civil liberties' stand, saying that he would rather lie out all night than prove his innocence. Sometimes this did lead to his sleeping by a hedge, (even in a snowy December), although this discomfort could also result from an innkeeper's taking offence at his 'thee and thou'. Once this leads to a glimpse of his taste in food. Refused milk, he 'asked her if she had any cream, though I did not greatly like such meat, [i.e. kind of food] but only to try her' (N p.77).

During this sweep he met and convinced several in Yorkshire who became notable co-workers, especially two farmers,

James Nayler and William Dewsbury, leading members of an Independent or Congregational church near Wakefield. Another encounter near Beverley may have had an effect of a different kind. Fox was taken by another Friend to the house of a Justice Hotham, who received him very warmly. Durant Hotham and his brother Charles, rector of Wigan, were enthusiasts for Jacob Boehme, the one writing his biography and the other translating his works. Despite the theory that Fox had drawn some of his ideas from Boehme, this may have been the first time he met someone who really knew these mystical teachings. After some conversation about Fox's ideas, Hotham 'took him into his closet', and said,' he had known that principle this ten year, and he was glad that the Lord did now publish it abroad to people' (N p.75).

In York Minster, Fox was told 'to say on quickly', because of the cold, the frost and the snow, - a remark which shows that people then were not always indifferent to the discomfort of their great unheated buildings. At his charge that they 'lived in words but that the Lord looked for fruits' they threw him down the steps. Disappointed at the lack of response he continued towards Cleveland, on foot again, though back at Beverley he had for the first time spoken of having a horse. Unfortunately, the people he had looked forward to meeting had 'spoken themselves dry'. Some responded to him, but others kept to meetings in which they 'took tobacco and drank ale'. He thought that there were a lot of Ranterish groups in the area.

An incident at Robin Hood's Bay showed the practical caution which was one of Fox's qualities. A hostile priest invited him for a walk along the cliff, but he made sure that a sympathizer came too, as a precaution against the priest misrepresenting his words after he had gone, or, as the locals expected, pushing him over the edge. Yet the priest and his wife afterwards became Quakers and were Fox's hosts during a further tour twelve years later. It is clear that during all this time people were affected not only by Fox's arguments but by his manner. Though the news of his arrival could fill a church and lead to a riot, it sometimes seemed that by his personality and attitude he could win over all but the most prejudiced.

He continued his way round the county, endlessly active

with his preaching. In Pickering he had to use the schoolhouse for a long discussion because the Justices were holding their Sessions in the church itself. The senior Justice, named Robinson, impressed at being told that Fox had won an argument with the local priest, whom he admired, later received Fox 'at his chamber door', and the incident shows they could overcome the difficulties brought about by Fox's 'hat on head' principle. 'I told him I could not honour him with man's honour, and he said he did not look for it.' A little explanation - hardly an apology - smoothed away any awkwardness that might have given offence. As they parted, Robinson told him that 'it was very well that I did exercise that gift which God had given to me'. (N p.86). The encounter later had a critical effect on Fox's life.

On his way south again Fox had a further talk with Justice Hotham, from which comes a hint why the establishment for once was less hostile,

> If God had not raised up this principle of light and life, the nation had been overspread with Ranterism and all the justices in the nation could not stop it with all their laws . . . (N p.90)

The comment shows the social groups Fox was thought to be addressing: only those below the level of the all powerful landowning gentry. It also suggests that the authorities feared Ranterism as another widespread or worrying threat to social order, and were willing to tolerate Fox to counteract it. Ranters, however, unlike Quakers, were ready to recant or keep quiet under pressure, and after a clampdown on unauthorised groups around 1652, most of those thought of as ranters disappeared. Fox went on referring to them, and some historians have said that he emphasised the contrast with them to help him clarify Quaker essentials, and to provide warnings of the follies that could arise if obedience to the Light of Christ gave way to self will.

Pendle Hill

As Fox kept at work he won more interest and got increasingly sympathetic hearings, although in this period of 1651 and early 1652 his headlong recollections of places and incidents cannot be put into a firm sequence. Often he spoke at length, but some-times puzzled the crowd, as once at an open-air debate when he put himself on a haystack and stayed silent for several hours, provoking anxious questions about when he would begin. He called it 'famishing them from words'. It was a striking evidence of the level of interest in religious matters that the crowd were willing to wait so long, and perhaps a way by which he could show them that learning could go on through silent expectation. The tense anticipation guaranteed such concentration that 'there was a great convincement amongst them'. This was at once demonstrated in practice, for the proof of convincement was to behave in a more honest way, even over an unpopular tax: a number of people called to the priest to report tithes they had been withholding. The priest on this occasion was so taken aback that he excused the arrears. (N p.88). In view of Quakers' later stand over tithes it is worth noting that Fox here seemed to be taking the view that people who had already accepted a liab-ility should not default on it.

In Holderness he had a rough time, despite some response, and some cries that he was mad. Refused shelter at several houses or inns, he said he 'discovered a ditch and got a little water and refreshed myself and got over the ditch and sat among the furze bushes, being weary with travelling, till it was day.' (N p.91). Back on the road, he was arrested as a vagrant, and marched some twelve miles to a Justice, whom the constable expected to be already drunk. He then came up against another risk for strangers, for, after the usual difficulty over the hat, they wanted to search his pockets to see whether he might be a Royal-ist spy carrying letters. When Fox pulled his shirt open, the Justice was surprised into the remark, 'He is not a vagrant by his linen'. How Fox did look after his clothing is never said, though there are hints that he was unusually fastidious about it.

One incident illustrates both his method, and also what could sometimes go wrong. At Tickhill, near Doncaster, he left Friends at a Meeting whilst he went to confront the priest, but when he began to speak, the 'clerk up with his Bible and hit [him] in the face'. This must have provoked a nose-bleed, for his 'face gushed out with blood, and it ran off in the steeplehouse.' He was then punched, beaten with books, fists and sticks, and thrown over a hedge, and lost his hat, before he could reach the house where Friends were waiting. Yet he soon spoke to the crowd from over a yard wall and so shook the priest's assurance that the people started mocking, 'Look how the priest trembles and shakes, he is turned a Quaker also.' He noted that when the Justices 'sat to hear and examine the business, he that had shed my blood was afraid of having his hand cut off for striking me in the church, but I forgave him and did not appear against him. So I came without my hat to Balby, about seven or eight miles.' (N p.99). Fox seems to have been most troubled, not by the savage penalty, nor by his own beating, but by losing the hat with which he made his social protest.

Despite attempts to imprison them, and more threats of violence, Fox, with Nayler, Farnsworth, Dewsbury and others were preaching and causing so much of a stir that people were saying Friends 'made more noise in the country than the coming up of the Scotch army', [probably the soldiers who came south in August 1651 to support the unsuccessful campaign of Charles II]. Then, with Farnsworth as company, he headed further north, busily and confidently speaking,

> . . . for the Lord had said to me that if I did but set up one in the same spirit that . . . the apostles were in . . . he or she should shake all the country . . . ten miles about them. (N p.103)

Perhaps because he had grown up in a flat country, mountains seem to have had an exhilarating effect on Fox. When he came to the great shoulder of Pendle Hill, near Clitheroe, he felt impelled, like an Old Testament prophet, to scramble up and survey the view. There he was 'moved to sound the day of the Lord', 'and the Lord let me see in what places he had a great people to be gathered' (N p.104). The news of enquiring and perhaps receptive groups had evidently reached him. For several days, in his excited anticipation he had 'eaten and drunk little', but on the way down he 'found a spring of water and refreshed' himself. That night he and Farnsworth wrote a leaflet giving a summary of their message,

> . . . concerning the day of the Lord, and how Christ was come to teach people himself, and to bring them off from the world's ways and teachers to his own free teaching, who had bought them and was the Saviour. (N p.104)

Draw Well, near Sedbergh, home of Thomas Blaykling

The keeper of the alehouse where they lodged was so impressed that he 'spread the paper up and down'. The copies of this must have been made by hand, but as the years went on printed leaflets were used during the speaking tours.

Fox's continuing expectations led to another Biblical echo. When he came to a river he had some impression of 'a great people in white raiment by a river's side', like the 'worthy' ones of *Revelation*. More prosaically, he and Farnsworth 'passed on among the fell countries, and at night got a little fern or bracken and lay upon a common'. After parting from Farnsworth he continued to Askrigg in Wensleydale, where he narrowly escaped the embarrassment of being locked up as a young madman until his family could be sent for. After clearing himself as sane, he continued alone up the dales, until he came to Dent, 'where many were convinced'. By now he was evidently able to move on with introductions from one host to another, though not always without a problem. He recalled, for example, that he 'came to Major Bousfield's in Garsdale' and from him, after some asking of the way, to 'Richard Robinson's.' Robinson, a younger man who was soon working hard for the spread of Quakerism, received him hospitably, but not without some qualms, for 'a dark jealousy riz [= rose] up in him, after I was gone to bed, that I might be somebody come to rob his house, and he locked all his doors fast.' (N p.106)

The next day Fox reached Sedbergh, at the time of its great hiring fair in June. Refusing to enter the church, he spoke for several hours from a tree in the church yard, with his usual message that they should give up the 'world's ways and teachers and turn to the 'one true teacher, Christ Jesus' (N p.107). A Separatist preacher defended him from the complaints of an army captain, with the comment, 'This man speaks with authority and not as the scribes'. It was a remarkable tribute to the kind of impression Fox often made on people, though it could then have brought danger. The preacher turned out to be Francis Howgill, and it was hardly a surprise that he should soon become one of Fox's leading fellow workers.

The following Sunday Fox went to a chapel on the side of the nearby Firbank Fell, to one of the periodic regional rallies of the Separatists. Many had already come close to his outlook, but were hesitant about where it would lead them. Fox's assured explanation, their response to the force of his personality, and all the conversations which followed, drew so many people to him that this weekend of June 1652 came to be recalled as the moment of lift-off for the Quaker movement.

Chapter Five

SWARTHMOOR AND BEYOND

The Cumbrian Scene

Fox's movements so far have one rather strange feature. It was natural that he should begin his work by circulating round his home area of the east Midlands. It made good sense that he should move some way north when he heard of the Nottinghamshire sympathizers, but after that we might have expected him to gravitate south again, towards London, the region of the greatest ferment. Instead, in several circuits he had worked his way northwards, gathering groups of supporters at various places, and had then headed over the Pennines towards Cumbria. This was the region those in authority were inclined to call apprehensively the 'dark region of the north'. Few people then would have expected much good to come out of it.

For nearly a century this area had been troubling the government and the church authorities. Its people were poor and scattered, as can still be recognised from the absence of rich churches and impressive houses. In 1649, after plague had spread north from Lancashire, there were thought to be, in only what was known as Cumberland, thirty thousand impoverished, starving families. If we remember how many people then saw misfortune as a punishment for their own shortcomings, the level of distress and anxiety must have been very high (Horle p.2). For other reasons the authorities thought North Lancashire 'the very sink of Papacy', with 'more seditious spirits . . . than in any other part, drawing the people from their due obedience to her Majesty and her laws' (Richardson p.5). That had been written before 1600, but little changed in the following years. The Bishops of the two dioceses, Carlisle, and remote Chester, almost ignored the area. All governments had difficulty in coercing clergy into the poor livings and complained about the low standards and unorthodox views of many who were there. In 1644 one Presbyterian divine, seconded to the Furness area,

83

found the inhabitants 'exceedingly ignorant and blind as to religion' (Richardson p.4), often keeping remnants of Catholic practice.

The clergy agreed that the parishes were too large and that the priests of the chapelries into which they had been divided were inclined to Independency and too financially dependent on their congregations (Richardson p.16). The need to use houses for meetings led to family-centred worship and this could let Independency slide into Separatism. The authorities grumbled about every kind of irregularity, from drunkenness, [some of it the result of passing the times between morning and afternoon services in the alehouse (N p.112)], to keeping hats on in church in what was thought to be a spirit of dumb insolence (Richardson p.80). On the other hand some refused to attend if there was no sermon, or came with their Bibles to look up the scripture quotations they expected (Richardson p.101). The area clearly had its problems and possibilities. The Separatists and Seekers who worried the authorities had already reached an outlook very close to that of Fox, and were the very people most likely to welcome him.

Rally at Firbank

Fox reached Sedbergh at the beginning of the Whitsun Fair week, and stayed close by. Amongst those he convinced was his host, a Captain Ward, one of the many impressed by his bright eyes and direct look, according to the comment, 'He said, my very eyes pierced through him' (N p.108). When the First Day, or Sunday, came, Fox was taken to Firbank Chapel. This was a small building on the fellside above Firbank hamlet and intended for the people of that part of the dale, a few miles from Sedbergh. The congregation here was one of several who had already set up an informal grouping, in the area stretching southwards to Preston Patrick, where a notable preacher, Thomas Taylor, had been based. Taylor had recently moved away to Richmond, and his congregations were having to rely on their own lay preachers, mostly local farmers, two of whom, Francis Howgill and John Audland, 'preached in the forenoon to a seeking and religious people separated from the common way of national worship' (FPT p.243). The arrival of Fox, this much talked about visitor with his air of authority, his hopeful message, and his sharp handling of the priests, caused a stir, and some edginess about what he would do. Some people came, or perhaps were sent, to ask him not to be too hard on the morning's preachers, and not 'to reprove them publicly, for they were not parish teachers but pretty sober [= serious, responsible] men', (N p.108).

Fox stayed amongst the overflow outside. Howgill was nevertheless very apprehensive, for later on, when they got to know each other, he told Fox that he thought he had noticed him looking into the chapel and that Fox' might have killed him with a crab-apple'. After their preaching, they and the locals went to their dinners, whilst others stayed to wait for their return. Fox was evidently feeling the tension himself. At the afternoon session everyone would expect to hear from him. This was the first

Firbank Fell, near Sedbergh, with Fox's Pulpit

time he had ever had so large an audience, (tradition says up to a thousand), amongst whom many might well be receptive, and even hopeful that he would help them to see a way through their uncertainties over belief and practice. As often, Fox ate nothing, but got a drink from a stream, and reflected on the challenge facing him. In a rather conscious copying of Christ's using similar vantage points he took up a place on a ledge of rock. Older people, who thought that preaching should be done decently in a church, made their point by going inside and peering out through the windows.

In three hours of that June afternoon he gave one of the most effective sermons of his life, in which he covered the whole of his message. The gruelling struggles, the endless meeting of challenges from priests had led to the defining and focussing of his teaching. Although he could look back to meetings already settled, where his friends were carrying on his work, and finding, like him, that it led them to prison, this was his most demanding opportunity. In an area where so many had come close to his vision, failure might well be the end of his hopes, but a favourable response would be almost enough in itself to guarantee a future for his campaign to 'publish the Truth'. The after-effects show that the sermon was a triumph. Fox made only one comment, that 'several Separate teachers' were in the crowd and 'all . . . were convinced of God's everlasting Truth that day' (N p.108). That was his significant gain: he had won over the leaders, and these proved to be an outstanding group of campaigners. The rock ledge later came to be thought of as a kind of monument, now marked by a plaque and identified on the Ordnance map by the label 'Fox's Pulpit'. The chapel was later abandoned and has disappeared, though its burial ground remains.

After the sermon came anti-climax. At his host's house a young man confronted him, lit a pipe of tobacco and urged him to smoke it, saying, 'Come, all is ours'. Smoking could be another expression of the antinomian notion that people are free to do what ever they please, for tobacco had at that time something of the aura that now goes with cannabis. It was a sort of dare. Fox disposed of it by taking the pipe, lifting it to his mouth and then returning it. He hoped that John Story, a 'lad' with a 'flashy, empty notion of religion' would therefore neither be able to ridicule him for scrupulosity, nor claim that he had been shown up as inconsistent. This sort of incident was not uncommon, for only a few weeks later, in Kendal, another young man offered Fox a whole roll of tobacco. He commented 'I accepted of his love, but denied [= declined] it'! (N p.110). Fox's assessment of Story at this first encounter may have been sharpened by the difficulty he and his friend John Wilkinson were causing Quakers at the time the Journal was taking shape.

The Firbank congregation and the others with whom it was linked had 'a common practice . . . to raise a General Meeting at Preston Patrick Chapel once a month . . . to which resorted the most zealous and religious people in several places adjacent' (FPT p.244). It was a wide area over which to travel so regularly, riding along roads like packhorse trails, from Sedbergh, Kendal, Yealand, Underbarrow, and so on. The next of these meetings happened to be due the following Wednesday, and Fox was taken there by Audland and others, including John Camm, from a farm not far away. The meeting began hesitantly, for Fox was unwilling to use the bench with the other preachers at the front, whilst they stayed edgily quiet,

> . . . about half an hour, in which time of silence Francis Howgill seemed uneasy, and pulled out his Bible, and opened it, and stood up several times, sitting down and closing his book, a dread and fear being upon him that he durst not begin to preach.

Then came what they were all waiting for.

> G.F. stood up in the mighty power of God, and in the demonstration thereof was his mouth opened to preach Christ Jesus, the Light of life and the way to God, and Saviour of all that believe and obey him; which was delivered in that power and authority that most of the auditory, which was several hundreds, were effectively reached to the heart, and convinced of the Truth that very day, for it was the day of God's power.

The writer of this account added a comment which itself is a spontaneous tribute to the power of that sermon.

> A notable day indeed never to be forgotten by me, Thomas

Camm . . . I being then present at that meeting, a schoolboy
but about twelve years of age . . . that blessed and glorious day
in which my soul . . . was effectually opened, reached and
convinced, with many more, who are seals of that powerful
ministry that attended that faithful servant of the Lord Jesus
Christ'. (FPT p.244).

Present day Quakers, at least of the British variety, shrink from
this enthusiastic language. Yet there is much evidence that Fox
was an orator with the power to change the thinking and the
lives of great audiences as readily as he could sit in silent atten-
tiveness amongst a very few.

    Many of Fox's sermons are said to have lasted for 'several
hours', but we must not think him exceptionally long-winded.
An hour was standard measure. Few speakers then in religion or
politics would have sympathized with our present day demand
for terseness, although 'tub-thumping', or 'taking hold with
both hands at one time of the supporters [= posts] over the
pulpit, and roaring hideously to represent the torments of the
damned', (Richardson p. 42) had fallen out of favour. Fox's hearers had made a lot of effort to get to the meetings from their scattered farms and workshops. They wanted not only a
comprehensive account of the new teaching, but a recital of the
Biblical support for it, and a rebuttal of the opponents' case. As
yet no books contained it, so that all depended on the speaker's
clarity and their own attentive hearing.

    One of the Cumberland Separatists who responded to Fox
in the Wigton area later wrote,

So in the latter age of the world, 1653 . . . there were many in a
fervent [desire] after the Lord and the way of worship that
might be the most acceptable to him, which caused many to
leave the formal, dead way of worship . . . [and] caused us to
separate ourselves from among them, so that it pleased God to
look down upon us with an eye of pity, and he sent his servants amongst us to preach the glad tidings of the gospel of
peace, which directed our minds to the measure of Light or
grace manifested within our hearts and consciences . . .
(FPT p.57).

It has been traditional to call this group Seekers, the people
whose attitudes have been summed up in this way:

The characteristic Seeker conclusion was that all Christian ordinances had been lost by the apostacy of the churches, and could be restored only by those who, like John the Baptist and the Apostles, had a special commission to do so. Until such qualified administrators appeared there could be no true Christian ordinances and no true Christian church at all. (Tolmie, p.54).

These Cumbrians, however, mostly called themselves simply Separatists. They were certainly not Seekers in the modern sense of people holding that religious assurance is so totally beyond human reach that only a perpetually provisional frame of mind makes sense. They clearly looked forward to being able to settle in a church and into congregations which would embody the fresh vision of the Christian life they longed for. For instance, although many objected to practices such as Baptism and the Lord's Supper, they did not do so on principle. They felt that the church had collapsed so that no properly authorised administration of these ordinances remained and the people were left waiting for the gathering of a new Christian church. (Barclay p.178). They may be better described in the words of a pamphleteer of 1657 as 'sheep unfolded and soldiers unrallied, waiting for a time of gathering'. They were people who 'acknowledged no visible teacher but the word and works of God, on whom they wait, for the grace which is to be brought by the revelation of Jesus Christ' (Barclay p.177). When Fox offered these Separatists a way forward towards a new church and ministry, they listened to him with relief. Howgill's comment at Sedbergh could be thought of as an exclamation of delight that Fox might be one of the 'qualified administrators' with the authority to renew the 'gospel order' of the church. Yet, whatever they expected, as they grew in Quaker experience they found that their old practices were still unnecessary. Fox showed them that worship needed neither words, nor outwardly expressed sacraments and rituals.

Westwards to Swarthmoor

Still moving westwards, Fox passed through Kendal, where he spoke at a meeting in the town hall. At Underbarrow, three miles further on, he asked a priest and others who had been arguing with him to appoint a meeting in the 'steeplehouse'. The next morning the 'professors' were very much in two minds about it, and whilst they were still arguing amongst themselves some 'poor people . . . travellers, that I saw were in necessity', passed by. The professors thought them cheats, refused them charity, and went in to breakfast. Fox dashed after the travellers and gave them some money, but caused a sensation because some of the others who came out of doors at that moment insisted that Fox 'could not have gone so far in such an instant except I had wings (N p.111). Although the ugly suspicion of witchcraft evidently overhung their minds, the incident is more revealing for showing that Fox was exceptionally fit and fast on his feet. 'Sober and serious' in outlook he may have been but he was not physically staid. He was after all only twenty-eight, and, from some hints, youthful looking for his years. The meeting, when they got down to it, was profitable, though not for the priest, 'who fled away' (N p.111). Although Fox spoke for 'some hours', parish officials and professors remained to argue with him outside 'in the steeplehouse yard', so that he 'took a Bible,and showed them chapter and verse and dealt with them as one would deal with a child in swaddling clothes' (N p.112). Usually Fox drew freely on the Bible, but without staying to give all the references. There is a sort of humorous pity in his recalling how he had needed to treat them like a babies' class.

Fox kept moving on, through Newton-in-Cartmel, to Staveley, where he met the first serious hostility for weeks. A priest incited the crowd, who threw him over the churchyard wall in a way that might well have broken his back, and was perhaps intended to do so. Yet he was still able to notice the more receptive temper of the 'youth in the chapel who was writing after the priest' (N p.112), (another reminder of how sermons were preserved), and to bring about his convincement. Fox spent the midday break amongst the people round the alehouse, whilst they were waiting for the afternoon service. By way of some more talk at another chapel at Lindale, he came at the end of a busy day 'from thence to Ulverston and so to Swarthmoor to Judge Fell's' (N p.113). In view of what was to follow, this is a remarkable throwaway line. If the Firbank Fell sermon and the following weeks in south Cumbria settled the course of his mission, the arrival at Swarthmoor at the end of June just as effectually determined the rest of his personal life.

At Swarthmoor

Swarthmoor Hall, once a mile from Ulverston, but now swallowed by its new housing, is a grey, clifflike, stone hall, still impressive even though its stable and service blocks were demolished long ago and its estate has shrunk to a paddock. In the twenty years since his marriage to the teenaged Margaret Askew, Thomas Fell had become one of the senior judges and administrators in the northwest. He had been a member of the Parliament first elected in 1640, but had given up attending its sittings before the final conflicts over the fate of the King. The little we know of Fell suggests that he cared most for a stable administration, moderate and tolerant in outlook. His house had become known as a place 'open to entertain ministers and religious people at', and the family had heard of the Quakers, 'and did very much inquire after them.' (Ell. p.ii). Fox knew that Swarthmoor was a house where he could expect hospitality. When he arrived he was accepted, even though only the children of the family were at home.

Because the news of Fox's progress had gone ahead the curate of Ulverston, William Lampitt, turned up very soon afterwards. Whether he wanted to safeguard his own authority in the house, or to have a friendly exchange of views, he had an uncomfortable evening, according to Fox's tart recollection of the encounter. He apparently came to the conclusion that Lampitt, a Puritan, with Millenarian views, lacked both the Calvinist's deep sense of sin and his own profound commitment to discipleship. He told Fox 'that he had been under a cross in things but he could now sing psalms and do anything'. (N p.114). Fox said he 'was still a Ranter in his mind . . . and would talk of high notions and perfection and thereby deceived the people' (N p.113); ('Notions' became Fox's usual term for speculative thinking, especially of the sort unlikely to lead anywhere.)

In the evening, when Margaret Fell returned, her children told her of the disagreement. If all of them joined in, with the usual children's pleasure in reporting a falling out amongst adults, she must have found it a noisy time, for by now she and Judge Fell had a family of seven, from Margaret, then about eighteen, down to two year old Susannah. There were three daughters, then a son, George, of about fourteen, then three more daughters. To keep the son company two lads were living with the family, William Caton, employed as a secretary, and a young man, Leonard Fell, who worked as an estate steward, and was one of the many Fells who, despite the name, may not have been a relative. Fox spent the rest of the evening with them, discussing his views, or, as he says, 'declaring the Truth to her and her family', though it would be strange if in that group he got off without much questioning.

Much later, Margaret told Fox that she had 'had a vision of a man in a white hat that should come and confound the priests, before my coming into those parts' (N p.119). If other Journals of the time are to be relied on, people thought psychic experiences not unusual, attracting no very great attention. On the other hand people then often expressed themselves in very concrete or pictorial terms, and she may have been saying no more than that she had been given some description of Fox. The unexpected detail is the 'white hat', for the hats seen in portraits are sombre in colour. Fox tells the story without comment, but could the hat he so provocatively kept on his head have been of an unconventional, distinctive shade? From many hostile comments it is known that the hair underneath it was abundant and shoulder length, because to Fox this was an unimportant option and he rejected the crop or bob of some Puritans. In fact, he was not an exception in this. The shorter hair fashion apparently started as a sort of defiant gesture amongst the London apprentices in the 1640s, was taken up, perhaps for convenience, by others, especially some of the radically minded troops, and then died out.

No descriptions survive, and probably none were ever written, from which we could learn what Fox looked like at this pivotal time in his career. In later life he was called a 'burly man', but in these years he was very robust and quick in his movements. He may not have been above middle height, perhaps by today's standards rather short. Many who met him mentioned

his bright eyes and direct look, his 'penetrating gaze'. It is tempting to imagine him as having the build and vigour of a quick-
moving Rugby forward, for the many assaults and hardships he
survived certainly suggest that sort of toughness. Later on,
when ministering in worship, he seems to have spoken force-
fully but with slow deliberation. In these middle years he was
obviously well able to think on his feet, whether in discussion
with priests or when confronting a judge in court. His memory
was alert, so that he was rarely caught searching for a reference
or quotation. From the number of priests who are mentioned as
having run off rather than face him in debate he was a formid-
able opponent, though he usually seems to have exercised a
kind of placid authority, free from anger. It is perhaps no surprise that gossip went ahead of him, and that priests hated to see
this stranger, in his distinctive leather breeches and coat, standing in the congregation before them.

The anxious Lampitt turned up again the next morning, but
he lost ground, for 'Margaret Fell soon discerned the priest
clearly, and a convincement came upon her and her family of the
Lord's Truth' (N p.114). In those days children took young to
religious discussion. A day or two later they all went to a 'peni-
tence day' service at Ulverston Church, for the government was
fond of ordering these periods of public prayer and fasting when
the going was difficult. Fox, as often, waited outside until he
was clear about whether he should speak or what line he should
take. When he had 'walked in the fields' which surrounded the
building, then a tiny place, without the aisles and chancel it was
given a couple of centuries later, he at last took his turn, in a dis-
tinctly critical mood about Lampitt's views. But his own teaching so startled Margaret Fell that she 'stood up in [her] pew, and
wondered at his doctrine, because [she] had never heard such
before'. (Ell. p.ii). Very soon, another dignitary, Justice Sawrey,
shouted to the constables to remove Fox, but when Margaret Fell
protested, and Lampitt supported her, not knowing which of his
patrons to displease, Fox was allowed to go on. Sawrey soon
exploded again, and this time Fox was taken outside, where of
course he went on addressing the people in the churchyard.

In the following weeks Fox continued his tour of the area,
with mixed results, although in Rampside the Independent min-

ister, Thomas Lawson, welcomed him to his church. Lawson was soon convinced and gave up his church, along with his tithes, so that he had a period of poverty before he was able to open a school not far away. He was later to distinguish himself as a botanist. In Walney Island, where the priest 'went to hide in the haymow' to avoid a public discussion with Fox, James Lancaster 'was convinced', and later became a much travelled Quaker minister, both independently and as Fox's companion. Like most of those drawn to Fox, both these men were young, Lawson, despite his already having a church, was only twenty-two, and Lancaster lived to 1699, so that in 1652, he also must have been in his twenties.

Fox returned to Swarthmoor, and then set off east again, past Kendal towards Sedbergh. One who met him, perhaps during this return, was an even more youthful seeker, the sixteen year old George Whitehead, who said much later in his autobiography that he had been 'drawn to be inquisitive . . . towards the knowledge of the blessed Truth . . .', but who 'was at a loss in [his] spirit . . . as one bewildered, and wandered further . . . though the Lord had raised good desires in [him] towards Himself, that [he] might know true repentence unto life, yet those desires were often quenched.' He began attending meetings in the houses of Robinson and others of the group around Sedbergh, and was

> . . . already resolved to persevere among Friends before I heard our dear Friend G. Fox. I was then very low, serious, and intent in my mind, willing to see and taste for myself . . . and I saw and felt his testimony was weighty and deep, and that it proceeded from life and experience, and did bespeak divine revelation, and tended to bring to an inward feeling and sense of the power and life of Christ . . . His speech was not with affecting eloquence or oratory, or human wisdom, but in the simplicity of the Gospel . . . (Whitehead p.5)

Fox evidently remained in touch with Margaret Fell, for when Judge Fell returned home she sent a messenger all the way to Grisedale, beyond Sedbergh, to fetch him back to meet the Judge. He had been received as he neared home by an indignant bevy of priests and Justices, telling him that his household had

Swarthmoor Hall interior

been bewitched, and was therefore 'greatly offended'. The first
Quakers the Judge had to encounter were Nayler and Farnsworth, who had come looking for Fox and had stayed to counsel
the family. They spoke, in Margaret's words, 'very moderately
and wisely', so that the Judge, though hostile when they were
first brought to him, was soon won over. When Fox reached the
house Margaret shrewdly let the Judge finish dinner, whilst she
sat with him. 'And . . . the power of the Lord seized upon me,
and he was struck with amazement, and knew not what to
think; but was quiet and still. And the children were all quiet and
still, and could not play on their music that they were learning.'
(Ell. p.iv). This trembling, or even crying out, hardly seems surprising, even without any religious basis, for the tension may
well have been unbearable. She had felt the pull of the new mes-

sage so strongly that she knew her whole future way of life was at risk. 'And any may think what a condition I was like to be in, that I might either displease my husband, or offend God.' (Ell. p.iii). It was no wonder that the children were scared and subdued, even if they did not realise all that was at stake.

When Judge Fell allowed him to be brought in, along with Nayler, Farnsworth and the family, Fox 'spoke very excellently . . . that if all England had been there I thought they could not have denied the truth of those things. And so my husband came to see the truth of what he spoke . . .' (Ell. p.iii). Her recollection of all this was still vivid when she wrote her story half a century later. In the long talk that followed Fox says he 'answered all his objections and satisfied him by Scripture, so as he was thoroughly satisfied and convinced in his judgement' (N p.118).

These interviews with the Judge are worth noting. By all that is known about him Thomas Fell was a very well educated and level-headed man, a Presbyterian moderate who held a series of important judicial and administrative posts and had been used to the London scene for twenty years. If Fox had been unable to explain and defend his teaching calmly, rationally, and with the expected Biblical evidence, it is not credible that the Judge, despite his known tolerance, would have allowed him, not only to remain in the house, but to make it his base, and almost his home. Another fact which came out during the interview was that the Judge had already heard a favourable report from the Justice Robinson whom Fox had met in Yorkshire, for he went on to ask, 'Art thou that George Fox that Justice Luke Robinson spoke so much in commendation of amongst many of the Parliament men?' (N p.118). Robinson was a determined republican, and one of the leading M.P.s. If Fox had been noticed and praised in such circles it may be wrong to think of him even then as a minor unknown amongst the preachers.

The next day happened to be a Saturday, and the Friends in the house were wondering where they could hold a meeting. The Judge overheard, and volunteered his permission for them to meet in the Hall. To the continuing exasperation of the local Justices they went on doing so regularly till 1690, when a purpose-built Meeting House was put up nearby, at the expense of Fox himself. In fact, of the whole household, only the son

George rejected Quakerism, for even the Judge, although he never took the politically inexpedient step of identifying himself with Friends, gave them extremely helpful protection against their enemies and could be said to have shared sometimes in meetings for worship by sitting in his own adjoining private room near an open door. Even more astonishing for those days, he allowed his wife to work enthusiastically for Quakerism, writing and receiving innumerable letters about the travels and problems of the 'spreaders of Truth', and organising the funds, (later called the 'Kendal Fund'), for their maintenance and relief. His house was sometimes full of them. His servants were convinced, and he lost Caton, who wore himself out within a few years, chiefly spent in visits to Holland, and Henry Fell, who went as a missionary to the West Indies. Margaret and the older daughters shared in the travelling, the girls facing the filth and dangers of visiting Quakers in prison. Margaret also wrote a great deal, not only letters, but longer pieces, including five about the Jews, whose conversion was thought to be one of the necessary signs of the approaching millenium.

The Provocative Message

Fox has generally not had a good report from theologians or church historians, although more recent writers seem to take both him and the early Quaker movement much more seriously. The line has been that he was notable for some spiritual insights but that he had no coherent doctrine.

His ideas were usually conveyed through a cluster of symbols, derived from the Gospels, which interact and take on lives of their own. It is true that his writing was almost all the by-product of his campaigning, directed at immediate issues. Yet that is by no means to say that he was an incoherent thinker. From his own experience and from thoughts about religion already in circulation, he cleared away accretions, and arrived at what was for him simply the delighted rediscovery of the original Christian message, which provided a foundation for lives of great value. As can now be seen, it had a further merit. The insights and experience at its core proved to have the potential for growth able to cope with a changing society and, indeed, a world beyond any seventeenth century foreseeing, for all their millenial visions.

Underlying his faith was the conviction that God, who 'made the world and all things in it', was totally real and all-important, for 'God is dead' was an idea then accepted only by such people as the Ranters. As he wrote five years later to Quakers in the West Indies, some of whom, incidentally, were slave owners,

> God that made the world, and all things therein, and giveth life and breath to all, and they all have their life and moving, and their being in him . . . He is no respecter of persons . . . And he hath made all nations of one blood . . . (Ep. 153)

Fox rejected the distinctions he heard from the preachers.

> And ye professors, who have given new names to the Father, the Word, and the Holy Ghost, as *Trinity* and *three distinct Persons*, say Scripture is your rule . . . but there is no such rule. (GTD *A Testimony of What We Believe about Christ* p.446)

In his experience *God, Father, Christ, Holy Spirit,* and also *Light, Truth, Power,* stood for one reality, and he often used all these words in various permutations, according to the aspect uppermost in his mind. He accepted that in Jesus was to be found fully the eternal Christ.

He held that each human being had a capacity for spiritual and moral growth, which he often called the 'seed'. Equally within each one was some 'measure' of what he pictured as a Light, coming from God and Christ, and therefore not, as others of the time called it, a merely 'natural light' of the conscience. Everyone had an ability to respond to it, although many rejected or were unaware of it. A stimulus was needed, a spiritual awakening spoken of symbolically as a second birth. This came about through dissatisfaction with one's present state leading to a desire for change: 'as many as receive Christ, he gives them power to become the sons of God . . . and this is the birth that sees and enters God's kingdom'. Fox saw no limits to this: Christ is the 'Light of the world . . . who hath enlightened every one that's come into the world'. This universality of this conviction meant that Quakers were ready to meet people of other faiths with open minded sympathy. What mattered was whether they were truthful and humane, rejecting oppression and persecution.

Fox fully recognized the moral dilemma of sin, that all people fell into selfish and harmful conduct, even, as it seemed, forced into it against their wills. He accepted the Biblical explanation for this: that a flaw had got into humanity at its beginning, like a sort of primaeval virus of evil. He saw that the people of the Old Testament had found a way to contain this by the discipline of a code, the Hebraic law he called the 'first covenant'. He then turned to Jesus and said that through his life, death and teaching, all men and women had the opportunity to begin again, with no trace of that ancestral taint. Fox did not question the sacrificial and redemptive character of the death of Jesus, but he was far more interested in his life-changing power and truth and love.

The mercy of God, which the theologians called grace, and which the Calvinists had for long said was open only to a selection of people, he said was open to all. To those who felt trapped helplessly by guilt, he said that the Light was as much in them as in everyone else. It would show them what was wrong with their lives, and would stimulate in them the courage to change their ways. Fox did not dwell on the crucifixion as an event. The Cross stood for a ruling principle in one's life, by which one learned to grow from a self-centred existence to a life of service and worship under the teaching and in the presence of the eternal Christ. This change might begin with a single agonising struggle, but more often was achieved through small advances, each causing the 'evil to weaken and the good to be raised up'. To Fox and the Quakers this continuing discipline was the experience of living 'under the Cross'.

To his Biblically expert hearers Fox said that the 'first covenant' of the Hebraic law had been replaced by the 'second covenant' of Christ, which would never change. To those who talked of the sin and death brought into the world by the first Adam he replied that Christ was the 'second Adam', through whom came the symbolic new beginning. Fox accepted in their full emotional and moral force sayings like 'Be ye perfect even as your father in heaven is perfect', or 'to such as believed he gave power to be sons of God'. Perfection might be a long way off, but it was not a forbidden dream. He compared the priests with slave owners, who cheated their captives by promising to free them but who kept them as slaves till they died. On the other hand he had no use for the antinomian attitude that moral distinctions did not matter. For Quakers, conduct was not justified merely because it seemed enjoyable. Nor had they any use for a simple goal of 'self-fulfilment'.

From Fox's belief that the eternal Christ was the only priest, who superseded all human priesthoods, it followed that all gatherings for worship were spiritually in his presence and under his direction, so that human priests, or external tokens such as baptism or a Lord's Supper, were no longer relevant. Whatever was external could turn into a matter of form only, practised without sincerity or commitment, and was therefore to be avoided. For Fox the invisible Christ had taken over all the 'offices' of the church, and was the only *priest, bishop, prophet,* and above all, *shepherd* or *teacher*. ('Bishop' he used in its literal sense of 'overseer', and 'prophet' in its sense of 'preacher' or 'evangelist'.) This underlay his repeated assurance that Christ, (or 'God and Christ') 'was come to teach his people himself', and his insistence that this teaching and leading happened within them, even 'when they were in their labours and their beds' (N p.155). For Fox the Church was the faithful community meeting and living in the presence of one invisible and universal priest, the eternal Christ. As Christ stood for what was eternally true, it followed that, as people learned more and came closer to him in devotion and service, they would find themselves in closer unity with each other, and their conduct would be more reliable and consistent. The unity of Quakers in the Truth and the need for consistency of behaviour soon became leading features of Fox's teaching.

What led Margaret Fell to stand up in her pew with surprise when she first heard Fox was the unqualified universality of his message,

> . . . and so he went on and said that 'Christ was the light of the world, that lighteth every man that cometh into the world, and that by this Light they might be gathered to God . . .'

But what shook her more deeply, and caused her to 'sit down and cry bitterly', was the personal challenge,

You will say,' Christ saith this', and 'the apostles say this', but what canst thou say? Art thou a child of Light, and hast walked in the Light, and what thou speakest, is it inwardly from God? (Ell. p.ii)

As usual, Fox contrasted the profession of faith with its *possession*, its following out in everyday living. Perhaps this realisation led to her cries,

'We are all thieves . . . we have taken the scriptures in words, and we know nothing of them in ourselves.' So that served me, and I cannot tell well what he spake afterwards. (Ell. p.ii)

In this she described the experience in which a fresh life began, the conviction, or the 'being convinced', as Fox often said, that the old way of living would no longer satisfy, and that there was need for a new life in the divine presence and service. Explaining this could be, as Fox often said, 'declaring Truth', to hear it sympathetically could be 'affected by the Truth', but to accept it as the basis for one's future life was to 'receive Truth.' Perhaps the excitement and relief with which many thousands received Fox's simple and liberating message can best be appreciated by observing the enthusiasm shown by people who now see their way out of an authoritarian political regime. But as those who responded to Fox soon found, he was asking not for subscription to a creed but for a comprehensive overhaul of every aspect of life and conduct. This could lead to great distress through the surfacing of hidden emotions, contradictions and compulsions.

The Millenium and the Fifth Monarchy

Many people were then affected by the millenarian dream, the mysterious 'Second Coming' of Christ and the 'Last Days', apparently foretold in the strange visionary works *Daniel* and *Revelation*. Scholars struggled to interpret their timetables and looked over the changes of history, in the hope of fitting them into the various 'monarchies', at the end of which history would collapse in turmoil and give way to the rule of the Heavenly King, the returned Christ. The many remarkable events through which people were then living led them to expect that the crisis would arrive very soon, with dates like 1656 or 1666 being especially favoured. One group, when the great events seemed to be delayed, were willing to hasten them by an armed overthrow of the current regime (the 'Fourth Monarchy'), expecting that this would lead to the 'Fifth Monarchy' under the direct rule, in some miraculous way, of a returning 'King Jesus'. In our own time we still see these longings being expressed, sometimes even through the same apocalyptic visions of the Bible. And, like the old Fifth Monarchists, we are inclined to be impatient when change comes slowly.

Fox dealt with the millenial expectation not by talk of an outward event but by assuring people that Christ in spirit had always been present. His outlook has been called a 'spiritual millenarianism'. In this spiritual kingdom all who 'received' Christ would live safely, whatever the outward troubles to be suffered. Where Bunyan imagined life as a dangerous journey to a haven attainable only at death, Fox said that the real life of Christians was going on all the time in the divine presence, and that external or physical matters, even the beatings and imprisonments that came their way, were to be accepted as incidents having a function within that real life. But when the authorities heard Fox say that 'Christ is come to teach his people himself', and that his followers could already live in that Kingdom, they saw danger. His explanations sounded altogether too innocent to be true. To them they looked like a cover for insurrection, though they were never sure of what kind, Jesuit, political, or Fifth Monarchist. Their fears and suspicions gave them another reason for hating and suppressing Fox and his followers.

Chapter Six

THE CROMWELL YEARS

The Work Increases

After the first excitement of his encounter with the Fell household Fox spent several months in a vigorous campaign around the region, from Lancaster northwards, interspersed with returns to Swarthmoor. Although many people were 'convinced' or 'satisfied', Fox's presence sometimes led to terrifying violence. Twenty years later he told of these mishaps, and many others like them, with a detail and a racy vigour, and even a sense of an underlying comedy, which can stand comparison with episodes in the novels of Defoe or his successors. Occasionally he got so caught up in the tale that he seemed almost to forget that he or his friends were at the receiving end of the blows. Quite apart from the Quaker involvement, such stories suggest that people were then used to a high level of brawling and disorder.

In Ulverston Church, for example, after Justice Sawrey had forbidden him to speak, the 'rude people' said,

> . . . 'Give him us!' So all of a sudden the people . . . were in a rage and an uproar, and they fell upon me in the steeple-house before his face, with staves and fists and books, and knocked me down and kicked me and trampled upon me . . . Many people tumbled over their seats for fear and were knocked down, and the Justice and priests among them.

When Sawrey regained control he told four constables to whip Fox out of town. They preferred to drag him 'through mire and dirt and water', and to 'knock down and break the heads' of many friendly people, and of others who were there only for the market. When the fourteen year old George Fell ran up to see what was going on, they threw him into a ditch of water and cried, 'Knock the teeth out of his head!' (N p.127). Perhaps this adolescent humiliation helped to sour George and underlay his hatred of Quakers, or perhaps he had resented being the only boy in a houseful of sisters, all of whom became enthusiastic Quakers.

The trouble was not over. With the mob following, the constables led Fox to the 'common moss'. There, he said,

> . . . they gave me a wisk over the shoulders with their willow rods, and so thrust me amongst the rude multitude, which then fell upon me with their hedge stakes and clubs and staves . . . and mazed me, and at last I fell down . . . and when I . . . saw myself lying on the watery common, and all the people standing about me, I lay a little still . . . and I stood up again in the eternal power of God and stretched out my arms amongst them all, and said with a loud voice, 'Strike again, here is my arms and my head and my cheeks.' . . . And a mason . . . gave me a blow with all his might just a-top of my hand . . . with his walking rule-staff. And my hand and arm was so numbed and bruised that I could not draw it in again . . . And I looked at it in the love of God, and I was in the love of God to them all . . . The Lord's power sprang through me again . . . and I recovered . . . my strength in the sight of them all . . . and I never had another blow afterwards (N p.127-8).

As the years passed many Quakers were whipped, but this was one of the few times when Fox himself was at risk. As usual, he listed with a sort of connoisseur's enthusiastic precision all the weapons brought out against him. Back at Swarthmoor, he found the household 'dressing the heads and hands of Friends and friendly people.'

A fortnight later, whilst going with Nayler to visit Lancaster on Walney Island, Fox was threatened with a pistol, which misfired, and then met on shore by the locals with 'staves, clubs and fishing poles', apparently set on by Lancaster's wife with a tale that Fox had bewitched her husband. When he came to, after being knocked into the sea and half drowned, the wife was pelting him with stones whilst her husband lay stretched over his shoulders, trying to protect him. After Lancaster had got Fox away in a boat they all turned on Nayler. Back on the mainland, a crowd received Fox with 'pitch-forks, staffs and flails and muck-hooks', crying, 'Kill him, knock him in the head, and bring the cart and carry him away to the grave-yard'. Instead, they merely hustled him away from the town. He managed to get himself to Rampside, three miles away, and was put to bed, 'with a little drink of beer', so bruised he could 'turn no more than a sucking child'. When Margaret Fell sent a horse for him he admitted he could hardly ride 'for the torture of the bruises' (N p.131). Yet in the end, 'James Lancaster's wife came to be convinced, and many of those bitter persecutors . . .' (N p.132). Meanwhile, Justice Sawrey and a Justice from Lancaster issued a warrant charging Fox with blasphemy, although a sign of the unsettled times was that the return of Judge Fell, who had been away during the rioting, forced them to defer serving it.

The Lancaster Sessions to which Fox was summoned were due at the end of October. The Judge and he rode there together. Legality had a different meaning then, and nobody wondered that Judge and defendant should pass the time discussing how Fox should best present his defence. This time he was successful, for the witnesses could not swear they had actually heard the incriminating words, and Fox was able to show that they had misheard or misinterpreted him. Justice West, a sympathizer, even allowed him to explain his teachings to the crowded court room. When the Sessions were over, Nayler wrote a report to Friends, with the comment that even many 'bitter spirits' had 'cried the priests had lost the day' (N p.138). He added that he himself had later escaped detention at Appleby because Justice Benson had frustrated the issue of a warrant as 'not according to law'. Nevertheless, in November, he and Howgill were put into Appleby Gaol, and in the January of 1653 Nayler himself was charged with blasphemy. He too was able to clear himself on the ground that his words had been misrepresented, but both men were kept in custody till the Easter of 1653.

Fox meanwhile had been in a further difficulty. The Lancaster Assizes became due and the hostile party persuaded the Assize Judge to order the issue of a fresh warrant, whereupon Colonel West, who was acting as clerk, refused to make it out, saying 'he would offer up all his estate and his body' for Fox. The Judge gave in, so that the 'envy both in priests and Justices' was stopped for a time, as the news spread through the county. The whole affair demonstrated the vagaries of the legal administration. Fox and Richard Hubberthorne, another of his new fellow workers, returned to Swarthmoor, losing their way and nearly their lives in crossing Morecambe Sands.

Fox stayed around Swarthmoor during the winter, whilst travel was difficult, busy with writing. In these early dangerous days of his ministry Fox's tongue had its rough side, and some pamphlets, or letters like this to Justice Sawrey can hardly have lessened ill-feeling.

> Friend, Thou wast the first beginner of the persecution in the north . . . Instead of stirring up the pure mind in people, thou hast stirred up the wicked, malicious and envious. But God hath shortened thy days, and set thy bounds, broken thy jaws . . . and brought thy deeds to light . . . Let not John Sawrey take the words of God into his mouth until he be reformed . . . [and so on.] (Ellwood p.94)

Lampitt also came under the lash, and we may wonder whether he and Sawrey compared letters.

> The word of the Lord to thee, O Lampitt! who art a deceiver, surfeited and drunk with the earthly spirit, rambling up and down in the scriptures . . . To that of God in thy conscience I speak . . . (Ellwood p.96)

This is not the language of mature Quakerism, but the racy colloquial eloquence of the time joined with Biblical imagery to generate astonishing fountains of denunciation, or praise. Even the children joined in, for in 1655 the eight year old Mary Fell wrote, (and the family carefully kept the scrap of paper),

> Lampitt,
>   The plaiges of god shall fall upon thee and the seven viols shall bee powered upon thee and the milstone shall fall upon thee and crush thee as dust under the Lords feete how can thou escape the damnation of hell.
>   This did the lord give mee as
>   I lay in bed.
>   Mary Fell. (Ross p.27)

We might also willingly wish away another common idea, that the wicked could expect an unfortunate end. Life in those days was risky and unhealthy, even for those who were trying to live sensibly, so that many people did die through accident or painful premature disease. It was easy and tempting to link such misfortunes with earlier wrongdoings. Fox was wrong to see a link between Justice Sawrey's hostile treatment of Quakers and his later drowning, or others' 'miserable deaths' and their cruelty against Quakers, but such connections were then generally made, and perhaps are still secretly wished for. Fox noted a number of them, sometimes inaccurately, through lack of information. If he had drowned in Morecambe Sands no doubt his enemies would have been quick to see this as a divine judgement.

Amongst those drawn to Fox in that winter of 1652 were a few who could not disentangle themselves from the wilder ideas competing for attention, and who listened to a Furness man. After a fortnight's fast he had come up with a millenarian fantasy, that the Day of Judgement would be followed by a new creation marked by strange apparitions, all in that December. Fox's response to this difficulty also included a fast, but this led him, not to delusions, as often happened to others, but to pastoral messages demonstrating his essential calmness and rationality.

> Friends, when your minds go forth from the pure spirit of God . . . there the image of God comes to be lost . . . So, dwell in the Light, and wait upon God, to be restored by Christ Jesus, to be made like him . . . pure, holy, perfect and righteous. Dwell in that which is pure and eternal, which guides the mind to God . . . (Ep. 32)

The people whose excitable over-enthusiasm might have discredited Fox's mission soon 'came to see their folly and condemned it; and they came in again and died in the Truth.' (N p.147). Yet they were only the first of many whose judgements were thrown off balance in those heady days, and who would endanger the growing Quaker movement.

Fasting was not the unusual response to a crisis that it would have been in a later age. Popery might be condemned, but Government and Church were given to ordering fasts at moments of difficulty. Fox himself fasted occasionally when confronted with a difficult problem, but during at least the first dec-

ade other Friends did so more often. Nayler, for example, when
he arrived at Swarthmoor, 'was under a fast fourteen days'
(N p.119). Swarthmoor must have been a tolerant household to
accept strangers arriving to look for their leader, but holding
aloof from the general hospitality. Since the foods available for
anybody, especially in winter, provided a very unbalanced diet,
we may suspect that some of the strange behaviour reported in
these years was due simply to the weakness of
undernourishment.

Opposition and Carlisle Prison

Early in April 1653, after tours into Lancashire and Cumberland,
Fox was again at Swarthmoor. Whilst listening to Judge Fell and
Colonel Benson, who were 'talking of the news in the News
Book, of the Parliament, etc', he remarked that within a fortnight Parliament would be broken up and the Speaker pulled
out of his chair. By the time of Benson's next visit all this had
happened, for Cromwell had grown impatient and had disposed of the remaining Rump of the Long Parliament, first elected back in 1640, at the very beginning of the troubles. Benson
treated this as an example of second sight in Fox. However, it
does also show that news could then travel promptly, even from
London to Cumbria, and, much more to the point, shows that
Fox was alert to the national political situation. Such references
are scarce, for they were not part of his theme in the *Journal*, and
by the time he was writing he probably saw little point in men-
tioning topics belonging only to hopes frustrated by the Restoration.

   The incident again reminds us that Fox should not be written off as only a naive enthusiast. Although most Quakers at
that time were farmers and tradesmen, he and his companions
were very well aware that they needed the backing of propertied
and professional people. Even at this early stage we see him
happy to have the help of such men as Judge Fell himself, of Colonel Benson, landowner and magistrate, of Colonel West, member of Parliament, and of Anthony Pearson, 'a Justice of the
Peace in three counties' (N p.148). Fox quotes the Judge as
remarking during their very first conversation that he 'wished
that I was awhile with Judge Bradshaw to convince him'

(N p.118). Such a convincement might have led to interesting consequences, for Bradshaw, President of the Court which had tried and sentenced Charles I, was a man of high standing under Cromwell. They probably never did meet, but Judge Fell evidently knew his friend's mind, for, in 1654, the Quaker travelling speaker Thomas Holme wrote from Chester,

> Judge Bradshaw quit himself like a man at the assizes; the priests was mightily discouraged and weak Friends strengthened. Truly he did as much as a man in that nature could do. (CJ Vol. 1 p.409)

As 1653 went on the Quaker campaign spread through Cumbria, bringing in many people and causing a great stir. Fox learned that opponents in the Carlisle area were threatening to take his life if ever he came there and immediately set out to confront them. At Bootle, near the present Millom, the priest, hearing of his coming, had brought in another from London to help him. His preaching so upset Fox, that, 'for the Truth's sake', he was 'moved to speak in his time [i.e. the hour allowed for the sermon] . . . if I had been imprisoned for it' (N p.148). In the resulting uproar Fox was struck 'upon the wrist with a great hedge-stake', so that people thought his hand was shattered. He later found his coat had been slit by a knife. The constable made attempts to protect Fox and his companions, 'in the name of the Commonwealth'. In the afternoon Fox waited with some friends at the market cross, whilst several went into the church where they 'spoke to [the priest] in his time', because he was calling them 'false prophets and deceivers, and anti-Christs'. Fox joined them, and later managed to get a quiet hearing from most of the people, although the priests were in a 'fret and rage', at losing their congregation, especially to someone who condemned tithes (N p.149-50).

At an outlying church, when Lancaster gave notice of a meeting, the people 'came in as to a horse fair . . . above a thousand . . .' (N p.151). When Fox arrived, Lancaster was already speaking from a yew-tree to a crowd as thick as at a 'leaguer', or army camp, and he reluctantly agreed to use the pulpit indoors. Amongst those who had come to hear him were a dozen soldiers and their wives from Carlisle garrison, who then followed him

to Cockermouth, where they told the crowd to be quiet, 'for we
had broken no law'. This was to be expected, for in these few
years the army contained some of the most radical and adven-
turous minded people in the country. Another indication of how
seriously the clergy took Fox, unwillingly recognizing the
strength of his case and the force of his preaching, comes from
the remark of 'some of the great men of the town', 'Sir, we have
no learned men to dispute with you.' The admission may however merely support the national authorities' poor opinion of the
Cumbrian clergy.

From Cockermouth the party rode on to Caldbeck, where,
as often, Fox chose to leave his host's comfortable house, and
'lay out all night'. In July this was probably enjoyable, as well as
providing the quiet needed for prayer and resolution. Everyone
knew of his imprisonment two years ago in Derby for 'blasphemy'. For a second conviction the sentence was exile, or, if the
offender were afterwards found in the country, hanging. Courage was therefore certainly needed, for the next stop was Royalist Carlisle, so hostile that even the magistrates' wives had said
they would 'pluck the hair' off his head. His response was to
stand 'a-top of the cross in the middle of the market place', and
announce that

> the day of the Lord was coming upon all their deceitful ways
> and doings . . . and that they were to lay aside . . . all cheating
> . . . and speak the truth. . . So I set the Truth and the Power of
> God over them (N p.157).

Naturally uproar followed. Fox looked sharply at someone, a
very hostile Baptist deacon, and got the answer, 'Don't pierce
me so with thy eyes, keep thy eyes off me.' This bright and penetrating look constantly caught people's attention.

Later the crowd, including Baptists and soldiers, moved to
the cathedral. Here Fox took on the pastor over the key subjects
of 'election and reprobation', to such effect that the man later
'came to be convinced'. Next he went to the soldiers in the
Castle, where they beat a drum to summon up the troops to hear
him. Although Fox had himself refused to fight, many Quakers
did go on serving in the revolutionary army. He remarked that
he 'turned them to the Lord Jesus Christ their teacher, and

warned them of doing violence to any man'. When Sunday arrived, the 'steeple-house' was crowded and tense. Fox spoke when the priest had done, and soon a riot began. The military governor sent 'a file or two of musketeers' to restore order and to reclaim Fox's friendly troop, some of whom were put into the gaol to appease the authorities.

The next day the officers and Justices issued a warrant against Fox, whereupon he went to them at the town hall, where many people were gathered, 'and a great deal of discourse I had with them'. His answers were taken to be blasphemous and heretical, though he said they could not justly lay any such charge against him. Everything turned on the meaning they chose to give words, and by the end of several hours it would be quite easy for each side to give a different slant to what had been said. Fox insisted that his reply 'yes' to the question whether he 'were the son of God', meant that he was so simply in the same way as everyone who had received Christ. They took him to be claiming some exclusive sonship. Furthermore, as Presbyterians, they had little sympathy with his answer that the Scriptures were not in themselves the word of God but 'writings', and that 'God was the Word . . . before writings were.' (N p.159). In those days misery and death depended on such answers. The outcome was what the Justices had always intended, and Fox had expected: he was sent to gaol to wait for the Assizes.

The gaolers, 'like bear-herds', offered Fox the 'great chamber', the distinguished prisoner's room, but he refused to pay rent and board money, and sat up all night. The next day he was put into another room, where he 'got a thing to lie on'. Here he had a guard of three musketeers, one at each door between him and the street, as though he were a rebel. He was plagued with priests challenging his views, and with sightseers, including 'great ladies and countesses', - though it is hard to guess who these could have been, - who wanted to see the man 'who was to be hanged'. Hangings were hardly a novel entertainment, but who could tell what would happen at the death of a blasphemer? The Justices thought that they had Fox beaten, and by his death would dispose of his disruptive sect. They knew their man well enough to be sure that he would refuse the alternative penalty of exile, and that even if they went to the trouble of deporting him he would be back as fast as he could travel.

Unfortunately for them a legal snag developed, which meant that it would have been useless to have Fox put up before the Assize judges. However, these were in collusion with the Justices, 'giving them what encouragement they could to exercise their cruelty' (N p.161), and ignored a statement in defence of Fox by the sympathetic Justice Pearson. Friends were not allowed to see Fox, and the magistrates ordered that he should be kept

> . . . in the dungeon amongst the moss troopers; where men and women were put together and never a house of office [= latrine] . . . And the prisoners were exceeding lousy . . . But the prisoners were made all of them very loving to me . . .

Several Friends issued public statements, and so did Fox, although John Stubbs, one of his visitors, reported in a letter to Margaret Fell that Fox's pen and ink had been taken from him. A prosaic postscript adds, 'I have bought him a shirt' (CJ Vol. 1 p.121). After the dungeon he must certainly have needed a fresh one. Stubbs was a soldier, one of those who, as Quakers, had soon to leave the army, not directly on pacifist grounds, but because they could not swear the oath of allegiance which Cromwell required from the troops when he became Protector.

The jailer did his best to break Fox's spirit, with consequences like a black comedy. When Fox moved nearer the air grating the jailer went for him with a cudgel, 'as if he had been beating a pack of wool'. Fox sang whilst he did so, and the jailer brought along a fiddler, but Fox sang the louder, so that the fiddler 'sighed and gave over his fiddling'. Stubbs's letter mentioned that the beating had been to make Fox dance to the tune like a bear, but that he had refused. No one says what Fox sang; perhaps it was a psalm of rejoicing. At least it is evidence that he did sometimes find a fitting occasion for music! One other detail, in the light of what was later to happen to him, has a moving irony. Another visitor to the dungeon was 'a little boy, James Parnell, about fifteen years old, who had apparently been sent as a messenger from Nottinghamshire Friends. He was convinced, 'and came to be a very fine minister of the word of life and turned many to Christ' (N p.163). Unfortunately he is now remembered mainly for the cruelty with which he was treated in

Colchester gaol, and the pathos of his death there, when not yet twenty.

Meanwhile Margaret Fell had been working for Fox's release. She wrote to Colonel West, then in London as a member of the current Parliament. This was the body with almost as many names as months to its existence, the Little, or Nominated, or Parliament of Saints, made up of men chosen by local recommendation for their religious and moral soundness. They turned out to have many ideas on reform, but none on Cromwell's major problems: how to get some legitimate revenue, and especially how to find the money to pay off the army. One of their ambitions was to bring in religious toleration, so that when the news came of a young man in danger of death under the blasphemy law a letter was sent ordering his liberty. However, Justice Pearson had earlier gained the support of the army commander, the 'governor', and the two shamed the magistrates

Swarthmoor Hall at the present time

into improving the prison conditions, an action which led to the under-jailer joining Fox in the dungeon. The same pressure, along with the letter from Parliament, led to Fox himself being let out. This prison episode lasted seven weeks. After the usual mixture of brutality, squalor and legal confusion it had ended in no trial at all, and left the risks from a blasphemy conviction still hovering over Fox.

The Work Expands

Fox made his way south again, busy with meetings and interviews, until he again reached Swarthmoor. His next major move was to set out in the spring of 1654 across country to 'Bishoprick', as Durham was still known, from having been for so long ruled by its Bishop. His chief host in the county was the Justice Anthony Pearson, at whose house a 'very large meeting' was held 'where many were convinced' (N p.166). From there Fox moved north into Northumberland, with both convincements and yet more arguments with priests, but without being assaulted or arrested. He completed the circuit back to Cumbria by way of Hexham, and afterwards noted,

> So great a convincement there was and the plants of God grew and flourished so by heavenly rain, and God's glory shined upon them . . . In Bishoprik there were few steeplehouses but Friends were moved to go to them. Nay I may say few in England but Friends were moved to go to them and warn them of the mighty day of the Lord, to tell them where their true teacher was. And a great people was convinced. (N p.168)

This is rather an exaggeration for 1654, but at least in the north west the increasing number turning Quaker had upset the civil authorities and driven the clergy into frenzies.

One result of the many convincements was that by then a number of men and women were ready to follow Fox's example, and leave their homes for long and dangerous travels around the country. They should not be thought of as 'ministers' or 'pastors', and even less as 'priests', if those words are taken to refer to people in some way set apart, appointed or ordained. They were ordinary Friends moved by a strong desire to share their new awareness. As far as they could they paid their own way, leaving wives and servants to look after their farms or trades. In a stream of letters they reported back to Margaret Fell, and she passed on news, money, books and other practical comforts. One of their main strengths turned out to be the close links they were able to keep with each other, even under their great difficulties. Sometimes these Friends had to work alone, but the records show that whenever possible they moved at least in pairs, not only to further their work but to give each other companionship, and often first aid, after assaults or judicial whippings. They were sometimes impatient, often over-eager, and occasionally foolish in the means they took to catch public attention, yet they remained remarkably clear of the desire to dominate, and saw no arrogance in declaring their unfamiliar message. Whilst they were always ready to face a hostile church or to attract attention in some unusual way, their preferred method was to get an introduction to some one, or some small group, to whom they could explain their new vision of the Christian life. With encouragement and further visiting these could set up their own meetings, and begin their own travelling.

A generation later, when these people were elderly or dead, a systematic effort was made to collect the evidence of the 'publication of Truth' in the early years. Naturally the reports sent in were incomplete, but enough reached London to provide a record from which the extent of these campaigns can be gathered. The people who took part had a wonderful confidence that their message was a simple truth about the nature of faith and humanity. They were sure that if only people could be reached they would be 'convinced of the Truth' and their lives transformed. The usual count of the first generation of travelling speakers, or 'spreaders of Truth', who set out from the north gives a total of about seventy, of both men and women, but the real number was much greater if we include those who worked only locally, or for a short period, or as companions to others. Their number, and their travelling in couples, echoed the arrangements in the Gospels, for they thought they were bringing back the pure religion of those days. Some died within a year or so; others lasted for much of the century, alongside those who later, as 'public Friends', continued the work. Some left Journals or other writings, and in Cumbria a few houses survive with which they can be linked. Fox's own role began to change as he was slowly drawn into work of a more pastoral or even administrative kind. His letter-writing and his travelling together leave us wondering how he found time for so much activity.

Fox Moves South

Fox himself now set off south, after he had 'visited the churches [i.e. Quaker meetings] in the north and all were settled under God's teaching' (N p.177), moving down from Swarthmoor to Lancaster, then across to Yorkshire. Near Handsworth Woodhouse he took part in a regional rally of some two and a half thousand people; then he darted across to the people convinced in Holderness during his first journey north, and criss-crossed the other eastern areas till he came into Derbyshire, where he noted that two of Judge Fell's daughters met him, for they were now beginning to travel amongst Friends' meetings. Then, by way of his first centre at Skegby, he went on to Swannington in Leicestershire, to the home of a man convinced in one of his earliest tours, where, despite the season, the January of 1655, a conference had been arranged, attended by ministering Friends from as far afield as London and Bristol. The urgent reports, or rumours, from the local Justices to Cromwell betray their worries that all these strangers might mean a new rebellion. 'They say they had summons to rendezvous from one Foxe, who gave them information there should be between one and two thousand.' They were buying up horses at inflated prices. 'And though under pretext of peaceableness they have not so much as a cane or staff in their hands, yet some of them were accidentally seen to have pistols at their sides under their cloaks.' Even their going caused more alarm, for 'they dispersed themselves very early the next morning', after a report of arms being seized some miles away. (JFHS VIII. Oct 1911, p.148)

Fox's own account suggests that he too was disturbed, for others of a different outlook had turned up to argue with the Quakers, 'professors and Baptists, and Ranters 'who made a disturbance and were 'very rude' (N p.182). Amongst them was Jacob Bauthumley, whom Fox calls 'a great Ranter', and who is one of the few Ranters to whom a name can be given. Bauthumley provided an example of what could happen to anyone accused of a heresy. In 1650 he had been cashiered from the army, had his book *The Light and the Dark Side of God* burned in front of him whilst his tongue was bored through with a red hot iron. Bauthumley's ideas, including his saying that sin was only the 'dark side of God', looked like the antinomian trap, with its belittling of the difference between right and wrong. Fox had no sympathy for such notions, but in those early days it was easy to miss the growing Quaker emphasis on testing personal leadings by further quiet reflection, by seeing whether they were consistent with the Gospel, by conference with other Friends, and by considering their effects.

London Again

After this conference Fox made several other visits, and then at last, three years after his last stay there, he reached his parents' home at Fenny Drayton. His old opponent, Nathaniel Stephens, had made preparations by collecting several priests to debate with him. After Fox had out-argued him, he exclaimed rather despondently, 'Neighbours, this is the business: George Fox is come to the light of the sun, and now he thinks to put out my starlight.' To which Fox replied: 'Nathaniel, give me thy hand'; and told him that he would not quench the least measure of God in any, much less put out his starlight if it were a true starlight - light from the Morning Star' (N p.184).

Fox soon had other matters to think about, for in these early weeks of 1655 some muddled revolts by Royalists erupted. Although they were easily put down, the authorities were on edge about any unauthorised activities, such as Fox's wideranging travels, and his meetings with people from distant parts of the country, including the one at Swannington. Consequently, just before a small meeting at Whetstone, near Leicester, seventeen troopers came to arrest him and take him to their commander, Colonel Hacker. Fox was told he could be released if he would agree to go home (to Fenny Drayton). He refused, on the ground that this would imply guilt and make his home a prison. The result was that he finished his journey to London under military guard, and was detained at an inn, the Mermaid near Charing Cross. Hacker then rather illogically allowed him to travel to Northampton to see two Friends in prison there. Fox had always intended to join the Quaker ministers already active in London, but he must have been disappointed to reach the city, in custody, and with the handicap of being labelled a politically dangerous prisoner.

Southern Invasion

Quakers had reached London at least a year before Fox arrived. Early in 1654 two women handed out the pamphlet he had written for the purpose, *To all that Would Know the Way to the Kingdom,* and in the 'same spring Howgill and Camm also came south. They were evidently eager to get the ear of Cromwell himself, with his half royal position of Protector, but found him more interested in the sort of toleration that would enable him to keep everybody's support. The two men found little encouragement, and wrote that 'all is puffed up in knowledge and stumbles at the cross'. Their encounter with London sophistication led them, in their report to Margaret Fell, to remark happily, or perhaps a little primly, on their own good fortune, through the 'rich and boundless love of God unto us people of the North, who hath separated us from the world . . . and hath gathered us together in the unity of the Spirit' (BQ p.156). Nevertheless, before they set off north again they had met a few who responded to them, people who began to ask for the help of other experienced Quakers. Howgill returned with Burrough, and they soon caused a stir by their debates in churches and by their own meetings. One reason for this was that Puritan preaching had proved too difficult and unappealing. Two years later a group of ministers, led by Richard Baxter, despondently admitted this.

> We find by sad experience that the people understand not our public preaching . . . and that after many years preaching, even of these same fundamentals, too many can scarce tell anything that we have said. (Q in Hirst p.325)

The Quaker invitation to leave behind the 'notions' of intellectual theology, and to listen to the guidance of the Light of Christ in the spirit, along with people who became one's 'Friends in the Truth', evidently offered a welcome renewal of hope and vigour.

In the July of 1654, in a further interview Justice Pearson, from County Durham, told Cromwell 'what great things the Lord had done in the North, which was going over England, and should pass over the whole earth . . .' His letter reporting this to Fox shows the wide ranging hopes Quakers then held that their new-old message would lead to a complete transformation of the social order.

> And now was the Lord coming to establish his own law, and to set up righteousness in the earth, and to throw down all oppressors. And I showed him that now the controversy should be no more between man and man in wars and fighting. (BQ p.161)

Cromwell wanted no such change. The reports from the Quakers' clerical enemies and from John Thurloe, his own efficient Secret Service Secretary, meant that he was concerned about the political consequences of the spread of Quakerism, and was interested in Fox chiefly as a possible rebel. Consequently, as soon as Fox had been brought to London he sent to ask him for an assurance 'that he would not take up a sword against the Lord Protector or the Government as it is now' (N p.197).

Fox drew up a very careful reply, the rather strained style of which suggests how strongly he saw the need to make clear his position.

> I did in the presence of the Lord God declare, that I did deny the wearing or drawing of a carnal sword, or any other outward weapon, against him or any other man. And that I was sent of the Lord to stand a witness against all violence . . . and to bring [people] from the occasion of wars and fighting, to the peaceable Gospel; and from being evil doers, which the magistrate's sword should be a terror to (Ellwood p.137).

It is important to realise that in this, as in other early statements Fox was simply rejecting armed rebellion. The stand against international war had still to develop. The reference to the magistrates is a reminder that whatever his differences with them he always accepted the need for civil administration, and for some authority to deal with breaches of the ordinary criminal laws.

Cromwell's response was to call Fox to a private interview, during which he was again told about Quaker principles and the grounds for them. Fox recalled his rather emotional reaction, with tears and a handclasp, but in the long run Cromwell's conduct arose from political compulsions, and Quakers did not always find him sympathetic. They in turn failed to recognize either his political and military tightrope or that their own outspokenness could endanger the future for everybody. However, when Fox had withdrawn, declining an invitation to dinner in the hall, Cromwell told an officer to let Fox go free. He brought the message with the enigmatic comment, 'And my lord says you are not a fool' (N p.200). Fox at once set about the task for which he had come south, by joining in the London work of Friends, with 'great and mighty meetings' in the City, where his own presence helped to draw the crowds.

Chapter Seven

FROM PROTECTOR TO KING

London

By this time, March 1655, the numbers of Quakers in London had increased so much that Friends had hired part of a large old building, containing a hall said to hold a thousand standing. From the adjacent inn sign this meeting house in Aldersgate was always known as the 'Bull and Mouth'. The general plan was to use it for public addresses and debates and to gather the people who were becoming 'convinced' into smaller meetings, mostly in houses, for worship and discussion. Fox's own travelling companion, Alexander Parker, admitted to Margaret Fell, in one of the innumerable letters north, that the Londoners took a little time to recognize Fox's capacity. Howgill, in another, mentions that Fox, no doubt like most of them, had talked himself hoarse and speechless in the public meetings. It all seemed very unlike most modern Quakerism.

Meanwhile, other teams were travelling in the provinces. Unfortunately, what Friends might call a 'mission to the south' was to the Justices and priests the spreading of a plague, for the newcomers often won a sympathetic hearing, and, when they moved on, were able to leave a convinced group behind them. Worse still for the authorities was the discovery that many of the new Friends were liable to spread the infection. The London preachers, according to Fox, 'were in a great rage' through losing those of their congregations, who 'received the power of [Christ] and felt it in their hearts; and then were moved of the Lord to declare against the rest of them' (N p.202).

In these early days, with their high hopes, Fox himself was as busy as ever sending out pamphlets and open letters, including one to *The Pope and all the Kings in Europe*. At a very different level, he reacted to the fashionable society around him with a letter about the 'fooleries and vanities' of fashion, the men's plaited and powdered hair, the women's face patches, and the coloured

ribbons attached to all their garments, which he thought made
them look like 'fiddlers' boys and stage players'. In fact, he said,
the more fantastic the better, to be 'accepted and show he is no
Quaker' (GTD. *The Fashions of the World*, p.109). Evidently not all
in Protectorate London was as plain or drab as tradition suggests. Amongst these people were the gentry of the country and
the court, looking for any chance to re-establish their dominance
over radicals and dissenters.

Tithes and Social Opposition

When Cromwell appointed a committee to test the fitness of
ministers Fox made his usual comment on their claim to tithes.

> Christ, when he sent forth his ministers he bade them give
> freely . . . They did not go to a town, and call the people to
> know how much they might have by the year . . . The apostle
> . . . did not say take tithes, Easter reckonings, Midsummer
> dues, Augmentations . . . (N p.207)

Whilst Quakers had been few and the theological fervour of the
authorities greater, it had been enough to punish them for inter-
rupting preachers or for blasphemy, but by now property
mattered more. All through the century tithes, which were then
a major tax, had annoyed the people who had to pay them. They
were condemned by radical troops and Parliamentarians, and of
course by people of Leveller opinion. Two years earlier the anti-
tithes proposals of the Nominated Parliament had led to its dis-
solution. Where others had often grumbled and paid up, Fox
always expected Friends to keep up a more determined opposition against support for the 'hireling priests', Milton's 'blind
mouths' (*Lycidas* line 119). To turn Quaker was therefore no light
decision, for it led to the regular loss by distraints of goods worth
far more than the value of the tithes themselves, and often to
much damage by the collectors. A draft Parliamentary constitution in 1654 shows why the authorities thought tithes were
necessary, but gave up trying to reform the system.

> . . . until some better provision be made by the Parliament for
> the encouragement and maintenance of able, godly, and pain-
> ful [= painstaking] ministers and public preachers of the Gos-

THE GREAT
MISTERY
OF THE
GREAT WHORE
UNFOLDED:
AND
ANTICHRISTS KINGDOM
Revealed unto DESTRVCTION.

In Anſwer to many Falſe Doctrines and Principles which *Babylons* Merchants have traded with, being held forth by the profeſſed Miniſters, and Teachers, and Profeſſors in *England*, *Ireland*, and *Scotland*, taken under their owne Hands, and from their owne Mouths, ſent forth by Them from time to time, againſt the deſpiſed People of the LORD called *QVAKERS*, who are of the Seed of that Woman, who hath been long fled into the WILDERNES.

ALSO

An Invaſion upon the great City *BABYLON*, with the ſpoling of Her golden Cup, and delicate Merchandize, whereby She hath deceived the World and Nations: And herein is declared the ſpoyling of her prey, in this Anſwer to the multitude of Doctrines held forth by the many falſe SECTS, which have loſt the key of Knowledge, and been on foot ſince the Apoſtles dayes, called *Anabaptiſts*, *Independents*, *Presbyters*, *Ranters*, and many others; who out of their own Mouths have manifeſted themſelves not to be of a true deſcent from the true Chriſtian Churches: But it's diſcovered that they have been all made drunk with the Wine of Fornication received from the Whore which hath ſitten upon the Beaſt, after whom the World hath wondred.

By *GEORGE FOX.*

And the Merchants of the Earth ſhall weep and mourn over her, for no man buyeth their merchandize any more, Rev. 18. 18. *And they cryed when they ſaw the ſmoak of her burning, ſaying, what City is like unto this great City: And they caſt duſt on their heads, and cryed weeping and wailing, ſaying, Alas, alas, that great City, wherein were made rich all that had Ships in the Sea, by reaſon of her coſtlineſs, for in one hour is ſhe made deſolate*, Rev. 18, 18, 19.

LONDON, Printed for Tho: Simmons, at the Bull and Mouth near *Alderſgate*, 1659.

Title page of Fox's defense of Quakerism against many attackers

pel for instructing the people, and for discovery and confutation of errors, heresy, and whatsoever is contrary to sound doctrine, the present public maintenance shall not be taken away. (Gardiner p.443)

The authoritarian outlook of the people in power shows up even more clearly in the calm legal language of this document than in the heated pamphlets.

Quakers held that tithes belonged to the Old Testament covenant of the Jews, and that this had been ended by Christ's new covenant and his new command to share his message freely. Other objections were more material. As a tax, tithes were unequal and unfair, with towns avoiding them, many areas being exempt and so on. Corn and cattle might not be too hard to assess, but this account, from a Shropshire village, shows that adjusting smaller dues could be fiddly and open to abuse.

As for wool, lambs, pigs and geese, if there be seven, the Rector has one for tithe, and then he must pay to the parishioner three halfpence for those three that are wanting to make ten . . . But if there be above ten and under seventeen, then the Rector has one for the ten, and a halfpenny for every one that is above ten . . . The manner of tithing is for the owner to choose two out of every titheable number, and the tithesman to choose the third . . . [and so on, for several pages] (Gough p.46).

For the receiver, however, payment in kind at least had the merit of carrying its own inflation-proofing.

A major grievance was that in many places the rights to tithes had come into the possession of laymen, originally through crown grants of church property after the Reformation, and later through inheritance or purchase. The proportion of tithes diverted, or 'impropriated', varied from place to place, but in some areas over two thirds had become a sort of 'gilt-edged' investment, relied on as part of a normal income. Some of those who became Quakers drew income from tithes and had to find ways of giving it up. Cathedrals and the universities owned tithes, as did the crown and many of the gentry. Fox, perhaps unfairly, attacked the clergy rather than the laymen, but tithe owners were often unwilling to allow enough for church maintenance and clergy pay. Many parish priests or curates were therefore victims of the system, dependent on whatever allowances the lay tithe owners chose to give them, or left with poor and sometimes uncollectable tithes, so that they shivered at every fresh threat to what was left of their incomes.

Their refusing tithes was only one of the reasons for hating Quakers. When society was still seen as a single pyramid rising in obedient grades from children and servants through the gentry and nobles to the monarch or Protector, the Quakers' persistent refusal of customary dues and tokens of deference made them look like fanatics or outlaws, trying to overthrow all decent social order and set up a rival state. They not only used separate meeting places, but were insisting on other seemingly antisocial practices such as marriages and funerals without priests. They made separate arrangements for the welfare of their sick and needy, and they thwarted the legal system by rejecting the frequent oaths its processes required. Fox alone using the northern familiar 'thou' and keeping his hat on in the presence of his social betters was merely a passing irritant, but when the country seemed overrun with his supporters all doing the same it began to look as though another revolution was threatened. Cromwell and his friends might be inclined to religious toleration, but many country gentry and Justices saw these Quakers as social pests. Their rapid rate of increase and incessant activity made them seem more numerous than they were. Although no accurate count is possible, in the eight years after Fox left Swarthmoor the total grew from a few hundred to perhaps forty thousand. At that rate the establishment might well feel under siege. Yet one remark suggests caution. In 1658, young Ellwood mentioned his surprise during a visit to some friends, the Peningtons of Chalfont in Bucks, at finding they had 'become Quakers, a people we had no knowledge of, and a name we had, till then, scarce heard of' (Ell. History p.14). Within a year or so he too was an active Friend, being assaulted by his father and taking his turn in prison.

Work and Challenge

As soon as Fox felt free to leave the London work to his friends he set off again on his travels, teaching and encouraging the new groups reached by his fellow ministers. Often he headed for where the opposition was most bitter, as he did when he went across Kent, despite soldiers operating checkpoints. Friends there were still few and the priests had 'stirred up the magistrates to whip John Stubbs and William Caton', his own friends, and the first Quakers to preach in the county. From Dover Fox headed back to Reading, to a meeting at which once more he noted that 'two of Judge Fell's daughters' came to him. Next he was off to Essex, where in a fierce anti-Quaker campaign James Parnell, George Whitehead and many others were being ill-treated in prison. Yet even here the authorities were inconsistent, for when Fox had, 'walked out into the fields as [he] used to do', after one large meeting, some Justices passing on horseback recognized him, but ignored him and rode on to the house, where Friends sold them 'some books of our principles'. Perhaps they intended to base some future prosecution on them.

During that journey Fox happens to mention the pace at which he moved. After a day which included a forty five mile ride, he was ready to be off at three a.m. However, he and Hubberthorne were held up for a day on a phony charge of being 'two horsemen on grey horses and in grey clothes' wanted for burglary (N p.238). When they did get clear the day's programme included a long meeting near Ely, and ended in a late arrival at Cambridge, to complete another forty mile ride. It has been calculated that the places Fox mentions are often a day's vigorous riding apart. Since he can hardly have remembered such details for twenty years, even to delays caused by a companion's horse casting a shoe, he may well have already begun keeping itinerary notes, like those made for him in later years by his escorts. The rowdiness of the Cambridge students provoked Fox into a grim joke. When asked at the inn what he would like for supper he answered,

> Supper! Were it not that the Lord's power was over these rude scholars it looked as if they would make a supper of us and pluck us to pieces. (N p.219)

The first Quakers to venture to the University towns were women. The students, whether prospective priests or squires, had no sympathy for these critical strangers. At Cambridge Elizabeth Williams and Mary Fisher had been treated as vagrants, that is, 'stripped to the waist and whipped till their backs were bloody', to the entertainment of the students. Two other girls, who tackled Oxford, showed more courage than common sense, for Elizabeth Fletcher, aged only seventeen, as a dramatic demonstration against the 'hypocritical profession of the Presbyterians and Independents which the Lord would strip them of' (FPT p.259) went 'naked through the streets', though presumably only partially unclothed. The outcome was a whipping. The hostile reaction was against the symbolic criticism rather than the Quaker action itself, for poverty and the customary whipping of offenders must have made mere lack of clothing commonplace enough. Her companion Elizabeth Leavens was later thrown over a gravestone and spent the rest of her short life crippled and in pain.

The courage and dedication of Quakers at this time seemed to have no limit. Their usual response to some local outrage was for others to go to the place, as Hubberthorne and Parnell had already done at Cambridge, and as Fox was now doing. The later life of Mary Fisher herself is one of the most surprising, and illustrates the complicated interlinking of lives which characterized these early Quakers. In 1655 she and another woman made their way to Barbados, then a prosperous British sugar colony. Amongst those who responded to them were one of the wealthiest sugar planters, Lieutenant-Colonel Rous, and his son John. Before long John Rous and others had tried to infiltrate the rigidly bigoted Presbyterian centre of Boston, Massachusetts. The news of what happened reached Fox from Henry Fell, no longer a Swarthmoor clerk but a minister travelling in the West Indies, and sending long journal letters back to Margaret Fell and to Fox. In Boston, the group, including Rous, already punished by having part of his right ear cut off, 'were kept still in prison at the date of their last letters. They would not pay fees and be at the charge to pay the Marshall to convey them out of that jurisdiction'. (Sw. Ms. 4/265.) Other letters praised John Rous warmly, and we may wonder whether this good report interested not only Margaret Fell but her daughter Margaret, for when he later settled in England as his father's representative she married him.

Meanwhile a whole group of Quakers set out for the Mediteranean, to the centres of the Catholics and the Moslems. Mary Fisher's own sense of mission led to something even more outlandish. She and a companion managed to get past the Inquisition in the Mediterranean, and the hostility of British agents, to enter Turkey and interview the Sultan in his own army headquarters about Quaker Christianity and Islam. She returned safely, but in 1657 two men, John Perrot and John Love, went to Italy, where they preached against the Catholic church and tried to convert the Pope. Love died under the tortures of the Inquisition. Perrot, apparently because of his extravagant and incoherent language, was treated as mad. Quakers succeeded in getting him released in 1661, and he came back to England. Unfortunately they then had further trouble from his views and conduct. Such stories seem to take us far from Fox, but they illustrate the almost worldwide adventure that he and his colleagues had made of Quakerism in only five or six years from the expansion of 1652.

In London there was a fresh problem. In response to the fears of insurrection the Government had taken the power to demand from suspects an oath 'abjuring' Papal authority and the Catholic doctrine of transubstantiation. Nominally intended to expose or remove Catholics, this oath and its Royalist successor were eagerly used against Quakers, as secret Papists. A later incident, in 1659, illustrates the level of argument. When Whitehead was visiting Meetings in Cambridgeshire he was drawn into a debate with members of the University. Their representative alleged: 'He that is a Papist is a heretic; you are Papists: ergo, you are heretics' (Whitehead p.165). Whitehead objected and was told, 'You refuse the Oath: ergo, you are Papists.' Even the Justices who did not go along with these ideas could make the Quaker refusal to take any oath a ground for getting them into prison.

Fox sent Cromwell a protest, *Concerning his making people suffer for not taking the Oath of Abjuration.* He also wrote letters of sympathy and encouragement to Friends, and travelled around the Midlands, trying to keep up the courage of Friends trapped between prosecutions on other grounds and this new political scare. Nevertheless he and the others continued to attract lively attention, as when after a debate with some priests the hearers went off shouting, 'A Nayler, a Nayler, hath confuted them all!' We may wonder what topic nowadays would draw such a vocal and enthusiastic response. Fox was pleased, although admitting that he was beginning to be anxious about signs of stress in Nayler himself.

And so the Lord's day was proclaimed, and people began to see the apostasy and slavery they had been in, under their hireling teachers . . . And Friends came out of Yorkshire to see us and were glad of the prosperity of Truth (N p.223)

The Dark Country of the West: Launceston Imprisonment

Back in London again after a roundabout return journey, Fox reviewed progress. Then, although still uneasy about Nayler, he left him to continue the work in the City and set out himself for the west. After Portsmouth, where Fox and his companions were detained for questioning by the governor, they came towards an increasingly hostile West Country. Here Friends were so few that Fox's party could not find hosts and once at least actually had to ask at an inn 'for the sober people of the town'. At Plymouth they had 'a very precious meeting'. A few months earlier the first travelling Quakers had been imprisoned in Exeter as vagrants and rioters, but Fox's party reached Marazion in west Cornwall before some town officials tried to arrest them. They had no warrant, and when challenged merely showed a mace, which one of them 'plucked from under his cloak'. Fox got ready yet another outline of his message, in rather messianic terms, which he and his companions Pyott and Salt all signed, 'to be sent to the seven parishes at the Land's End'. The next morning Salt handed a copy to a man they met along the road. Fox was uneasy about this action, for the man turned out to be clerk to a Justice, Major Ceely of St Ives. He foresaw trouble, but decided that if it came he would 'crush it and make the good come forth'.

He had good reason for his presentiment. When they reached St Ives it 'was in an uproar . . . The Indians were more like Christians than they' (N p.238). Major Ceely, the Justice who was behind the riot, having asked Fox whether he had written the leaflet, with its millenarian tone, ordered him to take the Oath of Abjuration, and rejected a copy of the statement he had drawn up for 'Oliver Protector'. The only distraction came from a 'young, silly priest' who wanted to cut Fox's hair 'for it was pretty long.' The party were arrested and led to Redruth, where they rather cheekily took turns to draw off the soldiers whilst each addressed the people. At Bodmin, Major General Desborough, Cromwell's officer in charge of the western area, refused to help them, although he knew them. Still under guard, they reached Launceston Castle on 2nd January 1656, despite a couple of clumsy attempts to assassinate Fox. At the Assizes nine weeks later the crowd expected they would be hanged. As usual, Fox made a dramatic story of his debate with the Judge, whose rage and frustration at these strangely defiant prisoners is emphatically shown. When no other charge could be made to stick, the Judge fined them twenty marks a-piece [mark = 67 pence] for not putting off their hats, treating this as contempt of court, with an order that they should be kept in prison until they paid the fine. Since this would imply both guilt and submission to people they regarded as equals in the sight of God, they faced the prospect of being released only by death.

At first the conditions were not intolerable, and sympathetic people were able to visit them. Within a few days, however, knowing that the detention could last a long time, Fox refused to pay the gaoler's high fees, (fourteen shillings each a week, seven for the horse and seven for the owner), [shilling = 5 pence]. In revenge the man put them into the dungeon called Doomsdale, used only for witches and people waiting to be hanged. It was a 'nasty stinking place', under the other prisoners' rooms, so that it acted as a cesspit, where the sewage came up to the tops of their shoes. Lying down was impossible and the stench sickened them. Yet they found someone to take a report of all this to the Sessions, and were soon allowed out to clean out the place and buy food. They also wrote to Cromwell, and somehow Fox got to hear of the comment by his chaplain, the distinguished preacher Hugh Peters, that they 'could not do George Fox a greater service for the spreading of his principles in Cornwall than to imprison him' (N p.254). None of these efforts got them released, but did result in their removal from Doomsdale, where the worst period had lasted a fortnight.

Some time later, when Friends outside were being harassed, Fox saw how a little subterfuge could help them. One of his visitors had not entered by way of the town gate. Fox therefore drew up a report of the Mayor's excesses, and told his visitor to take it and return to the town through the gate. The trick worked. The guard took the young man to the Mayor, who had his pockets searched. When the letter was found and read, 'he saw all his actions characterized, and from that time meddled no more with the servants of the Lord'. Fox said this was from shame, but in the uncertain times the Mayor could have been afraid of getting into trouble with London (N p.259).

By this time they not only had an increasing number of visitors but the help of a young woman called Anne Downer, daughter of a parish priest, who had walked from London to help them. She lodged in the town, cooked for them, and served as a shorthand writer for Fox. After this she was not lost to the records, for she married George Whitehead. Amongst the visitors was a 'grave, sober, ancient man, a Justice of the Peace' named Humphrey Lower, who accepted the force of Fox's arguments. Another was his son Thomas, who was so pleased with what he learned from Fox that his own convincement began. So did that of Elizabeth Trelawney, 'a baronet's daughter', a young deaf woman, who had caught Fox's attention by her efforts to stand close to him. Soon afterwards she and Thomas were married, although parted by her death in 1662. A personal irony about Fox's story is that the very manuscript telling it is in the handwriting of Thomas Lower himself, by then one of Fox's closest friends and later married to Mary Fell.

One problem was that the year was 1656, one of the key dates for the Fifth Monarchists. The authorities did not know quite what to expect, and some of the Fifth Monarchists were alleged to be planning to hurry up the new era by an armed rising. Because Quakers also had so much to say about Christ's presence it was easy to misunderstand Fox's distinction, that, whereas the Fifth Monarchists 'looked on this reign to be outward', Quakers said that Christ 'was come inwardly into the hearts of his people to reign and rule there' (N p.267). Moreover, since the troubles began in the early 1640's, some preachers had been applying the fiery language of *Revelation* to their cause in the Civil War, calling it the 'Lamb's War against the Beast' (Capp p.36). Some Quakers took to this rather threatening image, and looked forward to the 'Lamb's victory', to be won through the 'Lamb's War'. Their hearers detected, not spiritual renewal, but everyday violence and rebellion. Fox himself occasionally used it, as in his leaflet of 1658, *The Wrath of the Lamb*.

> I will break into pieces, saith the Lord, I'll make nations like dirt . . . I'll make religions, professions, teachings, time-servers . . . I'll make mire of them. The wrath of the Lamb is risen upon all apostates . . .Trumpets sounded, The Just will rule, the Lamb will have the victory . . . [and so on] (GTD p.143 - 4)

When the year passed with no miraculous return the Fifth Monarchists were shaken, although for at least another decade they worried the government. One man much affected by the plot hysteria, or perhaps just over-zealous, was the Launceston gaoler. When the wife of Fox's companion sent him a cheese, the gaoler carried it to the Mayor 'to search it for treasonable letters, as they said, and though they found no treason in the cheese they kept it.' In fact they didn't, for when Fox's party passed through the town after their release a constable had an attack of bad conscience and came running after them with it. He was allowed to keep what must have by then been a battered and overripe object (N p.264 & 268).

At a more serious level a Friend in London went to Cromwell to offer to take Fox's place in prison. Although he was refused his action led the Protector to tell Desborough to release the prisoners. He however set a condition, that they should go home and preach no more. When they refused he kept them where they were and shelved the problem by handing it over to the officer in charge of the gaol. He tried another tack: they could go if they would pay the gaoler's fees. They still refused, but soon afterwards the officer gave in and let them out unconditionally, on the 9th of September. It had been an eventful and hazardous nine months.

Whilst Fox himself was out of circulation in Launceston other leading Friends had continued at work. Whilst they rejected any kind of professional pastorate as inconsistent with the spiritual priesthood of Christ himself and his freely given message, they saw that the new groups of Quakers could need support, and accepted the benefits of some organisation to hold together what might otherwise have remained rather random independent groups. Friends whose service had come to be valued took to conferring together 'about the affairs of Truth'. They were soon known informally as elders, or sometimes by the more curious term 'seasoned Friends'. Their conclusions were offered simply as advice. Anything more would have been out of place, for all the Friends who received it were considered to be equally open to the leading of the Light of Christ. This was clearly shown in 1656 in the postscript to some proposals about the organising of meetings put forward by the 'elders and brethren', including Farnsworth and Dewsbury, who had been meeting at Balby in Yorkshire.

> Dearly beloved Friends, these things we do not lay upon you as a rule or form to walk by, but that all with the measure of Light which is pure and holy may be guided, and . . . these may be fulfilled in the Spirit - not from the letter, for the letter killeth, but the Spirit giveth life.

The Balby postscript was later looked on as a classic statement of the Quaker attitude, and often reprinted; (e.g. CFP 'To the Reader').

The Nayler Crisis

The party got horses and were on the move at once. First they went to Humphrey Lower's, then to a 'General Meeting' for all Cornwall, and then back east, through Okehampton. Here, rather provocatively, they stayed at an inn belonging to the Mayor, who had himself been detaining Friends travelling to visit Fox in gaol. Amongst those arrested for this reason and imprisoned in Exeter was James Nayler, by now in a dangerously unbalanced emotional state, perhaps due to the weakness resulting from overwork. He had been reacting extravagantly to the excitement and praise of successful preaching and to the flatteries of a group of women who clung to him as if he represented a sort of messiah. On his way west, and especially at Bristol, these women had surrounded him with chanting and bowing, on the model of a Hebrew woman who fell at the feet of the prophet Elisha. Fox's visit to him in Exeter gaol was made in an effort to help him to recover his judgement and get back into unity with other Friends. During a meeting for worship in the prison, however, Fox noted that Nayler was one of those who 'could not stay the meeting but kept their hats on when I prayed' (N p.268).

Quakers had come to follow the usual practice of wearing hats in meeting, but of removing them when someone present began to pray. The deference refused to human beings was evidently felt due to the deity. Some were coming to think that even this action was an external formality which should be rejected unless the individual were moved to make it at that moment. Some held that the divine leading on any action could never be foreseen, and even that any planning or organisation was an interference with the spontaneous response of the soul to the divine. Nayler was very reluctant to question any action, even the women's provocative conduct. For Fox, on the other hand, 'the Truth, that is our Guide, is unchangeable' (Ell. p.237). He therefore held that conduct and beliefs should be dependable and consistent.

Nayler's own sense of the overwhelming presence of the divine spirit gave great richness and power to his ministry. His ability and his strenuous work made him one of the major Quaker ministers. To some of those in authority he was more the 'chief Quaker' than Fox himself, for he led the work in London whilst Fox had been out of sight in the North. Whilst in Exeter prison he fasted for a month, and although this began as an effort to overcome his own conflict of mind, it must in fact have weakened his judgement as well as his body. Friends generally were troubled; some were inclined to think Nayler's behaviour might be a right expression of genuine experience; others took Fox's view that Quakers should be as trustworthy as the principles they claimed to follow, and that they should recognize practical human needs or undertakings. In Exeter, Fox felt that he and Nayler could not reach any understanding, and this led him to reject an offered kiss from Nayler, convinced that he was still 'dark and much out'. This estrangement brought great grief to both of them. Yet Fox believed that his firmness was needed to safeguard the future of the movement.

The problem came to a head after Cromwell's Council in October ordered a general release of Quaker prisoners. Nayler, still with his circle of women, set off back for Bristol. There he allowed the women to re-enact with him the entry of Christ's entry on the ass into Jerusalem. He may have been clear that he was only symbolically drawing attention to the spirit of Christ within all men, but the authorities saw it as a blasphemous claim to be the returning Christ. It was after all still 1656, the year of millenarian hopes. Nayler himself later said: 'The Lord hath made me a sign of his coming.' (BQ p.254). Bristol Quakers, all the thousand or so of them, avoided the proceedings.

The Justices hesitated about how to deal with Nayler, and wrote for the advice of their town clerk, who happened to be in London as an M.P. When he reported the incident to the House, a Committee of fifty-five was set up 'to examine the truth . . . and to report'. Brought in custody to London Nayler and the four key members of his group attracted attention by their constant singing on the way. At the enquiry Nayler declared,

> I do abhor that any of that honour which is due to God should be given to me as I am a creature. But it pleased the Lord to set me up as a sign of the coming of the righteous one, and what hath been done in my passing through the towns, I was commanded to suffer . . . as a sign. (BQ. p.256)

One of those present was Anthony Pearson, who said that only some few 'violent men of the committee' were not satisfied. This Parliament, which had been convened in September, was another of the selective assemblies that Cromwell called in his desperate attempt to get taxes voted, both to keep the country going and to deal with the continuing problem of a large standing army still with its pay in arrears. But the attitude of the Justices and gentry who came to it was increasingly traditional and conservative, and in Nayler they were sure they had the leader of the dangerous and disorderly Quakers. Some of the most determined M.P.s saw their chance to destroy him and terrify his sect into subservience. Unfortunately for them, the legal punishment for a first offence of blasphemy was only six months imprisonment. Nayler had been charged earlier, in Appleby, but never convicted, and was therefore liable only for this short sentence.

This did not suit Parliament, which then decided on very shaky constitutional grounds that it had an inherent judicial power to impose any penalty it chose. The 'merciful ones' managed to avoid a death sentence, and Nayler was ordered to be pilloried at several spots, whipped through the City, with a total of 210 lashes, have his tongue bored through and be branded on the forehead. If he survived, most of these barbarities were to be repeated in Bristol, and he was then to be put into solitary confinement, at hard labour, 'until released by Parliament'. There were other grotesque details in this extraordinary attempt to torture him publicly to death. Despite various petitions asking for the remission of the Bristol beating and a cautionary letter from Cromwell, ten days later, on December 27th, the second half of the punishment was inflicted. Back in London, in January, Nayler was put into the usual damp, dark cell, where he stayed until an appeal from his wife was granted at the end of February, and she was able to bring him fire, candles and food. It would be wrong to think the treatment of Nayler unprecedented, for over the years a number of unfortunates had been burned and mutilated. The punishment attracted attention not because it was brutal but because it was held to be illegal and a dangerous precedent.

Whilst Nayler was suffering and convalescing in Bridewell prison, Quakers generally were faced with the shock and confusion resulting from this episode. Fortunately Fox and most Friends had made clear all along their disapproval of Nayler's extravagance and were therefore spared immediate prosecution. Nevertheless some supporters were left hesitant, and some were inclined to commend him. Fox has been blamed as being too hard on Nayler, and at the personal level this might be so. Yet he seems to have felt compelled to take into account the damage to the whole movement which could result from this loss of judgement in one of its major spokesmen. Official opin-

James Nayler, possibly based on sight of the man himself

IAMES NAYLOR

Of all the Sects that Night, and Errors own
And with false Lights posse\se the world, ther's none
More strongly blind, or who more madly place
The light of Nature for the light of Grace.

The Shaker *or* Quaker.

THe Quaker is an upstart branch of the Anabap-

ion turned even more hostile. As one petition said, 'They meet in thousands, and certainly will overrun all, both ministers and magistrates' (BQ p.268). Parliament passed a new vagrancy law which allowed Justices to arrest, whip and send back to their parishes, not just obvious vagrants as before, but anyone whose reason for travelling did not satisfy the magistrate. Since travelling in the ministry or attending a Quaker General Meeting would never be accepted as good reasons, a hostile Justice had a free hand. In the years that followed many prosperous and respectable men and women were illtreated and humiliated under this law.

Nayler had to wait for his release till September 1659, under yet another Parliament, and for a further three months before a full reconciliation with Fox. During his imprisonment he wrote his pamphlet, *The Lamb's War*, which has been described as a 'compact summary of Friends's understanding of the basic conflict of good and evil.' (EQW p.104). It is astonishing that anyone in his plight could write so clearly and calmly. Despite his injuries he found the courage and strength to take up his work with renewed spiritual awe and devotion, and with a moving personal humility. His life ended in the autumn of 1660. Whilst he was walking north to his Wakefield home, he was apparently mugged near Huntingdon, and died in the house of a Friend nearby. (BQ p.275)

Travels and Trouble

Fox spent the rest of the Protectorate in further tours. After leaving Nayler in Exeter, he went up to Bristol at the end of September, for his first visit there. He spoke for many hours in the Friend's orchard used for meetings to a large crowd, of two, or, according to an alteration in the manuscript, of ten thousand. This would be about half the city's population, and, though no doubt a sincere estimate, sounds very much over the top, although Bristol had admittedly become a major Quaker centre. Crowd numbers are still notoriously hard to estimate. Back in London, Fox again met Cromwell, some of whose servants had become Quakers, and drew his attention to the increasing harassment of Friends by the Justices, a consequence of the Nayler affair rather beyond Cromwell's power, or perhaps inclination, to soften. As soon as he had reviewed the London situation, and had himself put up with rough treatment from the crowds, Fox set off towards the end of 1656 on a further circuit of the country, to clear Friends from a fresh attack.

In the course of the millenary excitement of the year the priests had taken to accusing Quakers of being 'Antichrist', an expression of the riot and disorder which were thought to precede the millenium, according to the current interpretation of *Revelation*. This 'Antichrist' was the great bogey of the time and had been identified with almost everything people feared, from the Pope to Charles I. Other names, such as *fascist* or *red*, have since been used in the same emotive way. Fox called his journey 'the service for which he had been moved to travel over the nation, to answer the priests' objections, and enable people to have their minds settled.' (N p.280). Back in London again, he spent much time in writing, both arguments against opponents, and pastoral counsel to Friends. Like his fellow workers he retained a remarkable trust in the power of truth and reason and expected that anyone had only to be shown where his arguments fell apart to give them up. From about this time he set London Friends to collect everything hostile, and to get out a reply to clear Friends from each misrepresentation or slander. Truth had to be strenuously upheld. He himself began to prepare one of his few long works, *The Great Mistery*, published in 1659, in which he painstakingly quoted and refuted hundreds of assertions in anti-Quaker works.

At this time the increasing numbers of Friends led him to realise the need for some organisation rather more coherent than the spontaneous meetings and the informal area rallies which had served so far, inherited from Midlands Baptists and Cumbrian Separatist congregations. He therefore wrote around to urge the setting up of 'men's Quarterly Meetings', that is, meetings of representative, responsible men, to look after the welfare of Friends. Meetings of this sort had already developed in the northern counties, as the Balby conference showed, and Fox now thought they should be set up 'throughout the nation' (N p.285). Nevertheless, he was soon on the move again, this time taking Wales into his circuit. The Welsh tour had its mixture of success and violence, and some complications, including the language, which Fox could not speak, though some with him could. Arguments turned frequently on an old objection, whether the Light Fox spoke of was divine or merely natural. Thomas Holme, one of his companions, had an unusual story for a publisher of Truth. In Chester Castle he had committed the indiscretion of falling in love with another young Quaker prisoner, the Elizabeth Leavens injured earlier at Oxford. The two married, although neither had any income. Their maintenance therefore fell rather heavily on the 'Kendal Fund' for the help of travelling ministers. After Chester, the couple had settled in south Wales, where their work for Friends was going well, and people were said to enjoy their unusual accomplishment of singing in meetings.

The mountains excited Fox, although he did not consciously think of them as scenery. When he 'came a-top of a hill', which may have been Cader Idris near Machynlleth, he did as he 'had been moved to do in many other . . . rude places'. He treated it as a sort of grand prophet's platform, as he had done Pendle Hill five years before, from which he could 'see a great way, and sound the day of the Lord'. Further on, at Beaumaris, his Welsh companion John ap John was taken into custody and Fox was urged to keep indoors to avoid his own arrest. He replied by walking up and down the streets telling 'the people what an uncivil and unchristian thing they had done in casting John into prison, for they were high professors . . . So after a while they set John at liberty again.' (N p.305). As often, the bold stand paid off, and they got out of Wales with nothing worse than some distress at its poverty, and especially one sign of it, the stablemen's trick of filching oats intended for the horses, which distressed him for the animals' sake. After more activity in Cheshire and Merseyside, Fox headed north and for a couple of weeks 'got a little respite from travel' at Swarthmoor, though he spent even this time writing letters of counsel to Friends and others.

Yet the urge to get moving again soon took him and he admitted: 'I had for some time felt some drawings in my spirit to go into Scotland', and did so on Sept 10th 1657. The priests' strict Calvinism meant that Scotland was not a happy place for him. Where he did get a hearing, and 'a spring of life riz [= rose] up' in his hearers, the priests set up a great cry 'that all was undone and that I had spoiled all the honest men and women in England'. His route took him past Dumfries and Glasgow, north towards the Highlands, then east to Edinburgh, north as far as Perth, and then back towards Edinburgh in October, to find a warrant was out ordering him to appear before the Scottish Council, under General Monck. His report to Cromwell's Secretary Thurloe showed his opinion: 'You see by enclosed letters and books what pains these Qrs take to get proselytes'. The Council gave Fox a week to get out of Scotland. He spent this in further visits , sometimes being escorted out of towns under guard, once, with his companion, Lancaster, attracting attention by 'singing and sounding in the power of the Lord', and so embarrassing the soldiers that 'they would rather have gone to Jamaica than guard us.' When told about all the warrants out for him he made the infuriating comment: '. . . If there were a cartload of them I do not heed them, for the Lord's power is over them all . . .' It is hardly surprising that the authorities detested him.

Back in Durham, by way of Berwick, Fox found Anthony Pearson was eager for him to meet Sir Henry Vane, one of the more radical politicians, who wanted the republic to go on. In the difficult time to be expected after Cromwell, Pearson apparently hoped for some alliance between Vane and the Quakers, through which, along with other radicals, they might hope to gain control of the government and prevent a further shift of power, or even the return of a King. Fox found the interview unproductive and tense, for when Vane was asked about primary and all-important spiritual and moral issues he merely became irritable. Fox soon began to feel strongly that despite the attractions of political influence, Friends should keep out of all the intrigues and factions into which the Republic was disintegrating.

After this, Fox made his way back to Swarthmoor, and then south to London, by way of Beckerings Park near Ridgmont in Bedfordshire, the home of his friend John Crook, which had become such a Quaker centre that it could be called the 'Swarthmoor of the Midlands', (Hill, *Bunyan* p.80). Here a 'General Yearly Meeting for the whole nation' was appointed to be held. According to Fox three thousand or more attended, with the usual consequence of such a large gathering, 'the inns and towns around were filled.' (N p.339). Since some Civil War armies had hardly contained more troops it was easy for anxious Justices to see a threat of rebellion in such a coming together of people from all over the country. Fox gave one of his most important addresses, about Quaker belief, about helping the newly convinced, about meetings for worship, and how they should go about their preaching.

The Restoration Dilemma

In late July 1658 Fox tried to comfort Cromwell's daughter Elizabeth Claypole, whom he knew, by sending a letter of pastoral encouragement and consolation, to be read to her when she was ill. Its opening words have often been quoted: 'Be still and cool in thy own mind and spirit . . . and then thou wilt feel the principle of God to turn thy mind to the Lord God.' (N p.347) The tone of this message, in which Fox is speaking from the centre of his spiritual experience, is a very welcome contrast with the sharpness sometimes found in his controversial writing. Lady Claypole is said to have found the letter helpful before her death, probably from cancer, about a week later. Cromwell himself, already mortally ill before the heartbreak of losing his favourite daughter, died the next month. It was a difficult time for Friends, and many were in prison, or suffering other penalties because of the conservatives in this last Cromwell Parliament. Yet his death brought more threatening uncertainties, as authority collapsed. No group was competent to take power, yet each was able to prevent any other from forming a stable government. Fox had good reason for anxiety about the dangers ahead if Friends ignored his advice not to 'meddle with the powers of the earth' (N p.341).

In this situation, his distress at what was happening to his Friends, and what worse miseries could come about in the country, led to his own physical collapse, made more likely by the years of overwork behind him. During this illness he was cared for by a Quaker couple at Reading. Later he recalled that in his 'great sufferings and travails [he] was burdened and almost choked with the hypocrisy and treachery, and falseness . . . and the hardening' he detected in the people in power (N p.254). Gradually, after some ten weeks, Fox came to regain his confidence that, however great the antagonism, it 'would be turned down, and that life would rise over it.' With that realisation he

letter of comfort

'came to have ease; and the Light, and Power and Spirit shined over all' (N p.335). His physical strength returned more slowly, for when he returned to London 'his body and face were swelled' so that enemies ridiculed him for looking fat, as if from luxurious living (N p.356).

In this year, 1659, it seemed that anything was possible, with the return of members who had once been purged from Parliament, and attempts to force further change, or to prevent it, by different armed uprisings. Many Quakers thought the moment had come for them to become Justices, enter political life, or even the militia, to help complete the transformation of the country, which they thought had been frustrated after the first enthusiasms of the Civil War. Burrough put this hope bluntly: 'We look for a New Earth, as well as for a new Heaven' (Reay p.87). After toleration, the ending of the state church and of the universities, they wanted to reform the law, and of course to abolish tithes. Quakers rode around the northern counties and collected the huge total of 15,000 signatures on one anti-tithes petition, and another with 7000, from Quaker women alone. However, they had misjudged the outlook of those who still held power, for these activities succeeded only in provoking an anti-Quaker phobia like those of the past against the Papists, with another fierce campaign to discredit and destroy them. Even men ready for some toleration decided that it should exclude 'the Quakers and some others, whose principles, they said, tended to the destruction of civil society' (Reay p.86). This hostility was led by the clergy, fearful still for their status and tithes. Scares flared up in many places, like the alarm which woke up Tiverton one July night, that the Quakers, Fifth Monarchists, and Anabaptists had come 'not only to cut the throats of the Godly in that town, but the throats of all the Godly in the nation that night' (Reay p.92).

Fox summed it up: 'About this time great stirs were in the nation, the minds of people being unsettled, and much plotting and contriving there was by the several factions' (N p.356). He was anxious about the damage to his cause. 'And a great care being upon me lest any young or raw people, that might sometimes come amongst us, should be drawn into that snare, I was moved to give forth the following . . . warning:

All Friends everywhere, keep out of plots and bustling . . . this I charge you, which is the word of the Lord to you, Live in peace, in Christ . . . and therein seek the peace of all men, and no man's hurt . . .' (N p.357)

Nevertheless 'some foolish rash spirits that came amongst us were going to take up arms, but I was moved of the Lord to forewarn them and forbid them, and they left it.' This was not the end of it, for one brief government, the Committee of Public Safety, actually invited Quakers 'to take up arms, and great places and commands offered', all of which they refused, asserting 'both by word and writing, that [their] weapons and armour were not carnal but spiritual' (N p.358). Fox repeated this with even more urgency in another letter, 'To all Friends everywhere', and left London for further tours to encourage Friends and to answer opponents, first round the home counties, and then right across the south into Cornwall.

In early 1660, whilst General Monck was in control of the government, the authorities tried even harder to suppress Quaker meetings, many of which were savaged by mobs, one of which, at Harwich, threatened them with 'The King is now coming, who will hang or banish you all' (Reay p.99). Fox himself rode slowly northwards, completing what he called his third 'time I had been most part about the nation,' often in danger, although sometimes able to pacify Justices or priests. In April he once more reached his Swarthmoor haven, now in the sole control of Margaret Fell, after Judge Fell's death in 1658. He was not to have peace for long. Within a month, on 25th May, Charles II was brought back to England, and at once some of Fox's enemies took the opportunity now open to them. With a warrant from Major Porter, the Constable of Lancaster Castle, a party of constables came to Swarthmoor, arrested Fox and carried him off to Lancaster, making the furore to be expected at the capture of a dangerous rebel. It was a sign of the new times when one man in the escort exclaimed that he would willingly have 'served Judge Fell so, if he had a warrant for him, and if he had been alive.' Fox, as he was led along, 'sang praises to the Lord in his triumphing power' (N p.377).

Chapter Eight

RESTORATION AND REACTION

New Problems

In 1641 a Royalist pamphleteer had defined true liberty as knowing 'by a certain law that our wives, our servants, our goods are
our own' (Hill p.347). For nearly twenty years all of those confident certainties had been under attack. Out of the confusion
had come no fresh order, but only the fear of an even greater
upset if radicals like the Quakers should gain control, as one
women Friend expected, with her proclaiming that God had
'come to turn the world upside down' (Reay p.82). Fox's own
long and lively pamphlet, *The Lamb's Officer, with the Lamb's Message*, set out like the charges in a court case, turned the practices
of the clergy into offences for which they deserved a heavy sentence. When confronted with writings of this sort their rage and
fear were easy to understand.

King Charles was brought back, less for his own sake than
as a sort of catalyst to allow the gentry to enjoy their authority,
whilst the justices and clergy imposed order on the common
people. It was a futile hope. The Revolution had failed through
jangling amongst people with too many stiff and incompatible
principles, but the coming years were to bring a chaos of self-
centred fears, greeds and prejudices. The authorities felt insec-
ure, but did not know from which direction to expect trouble.
On the one side they feared republicans, old army men,
Quakers and Fifth Monarchists, but on the other were the
Papists, supposed to want not only the authority of the Pope but
a dictatorial regime like that being established by Louis XIV in
France. Twenty five years of plot hysteria followed. Plot making,
plot hunting and perjury became major activities.

The once great question of freedom of conscience turned
into a matter of politics. Very little more was heard of blasphemy
or salvation, but much about deference and conformity. If Charles himself had any religious views he kept quiet about them,

145

accepting conversion to Catholicism only on his deathbed, when it was too late to dethrone him for it. Probably, between indifference and a vaguely humane outlook, he preferred toleration, so long as it did not upset social discipline and might help Catholics. On the other hand the country gentlemen elected in 1661 to his first Parliament were determined that dissidents should have no relief. Charles tried to negotiate a settlement that would have allowed some freedom, even to the awkward sectaries like Baptists and Quakers. As Fox remarked, 'the King was willing that one sort of the dissenting people should have their liberty and that we might have it as soon as any, because they were sensible of our sufferings in the former power's days.' (N p.393)

Whilst Charles had been waiting to hear whether the Convention Parliament would invite him back he had tried to win support by issuing a manifesto, called the *Declaration of Breda*, in which he had offered terms to please everybody: restoration of property to Royalists but without injury to Parliamentarians, back pay to the army but no new taxes, and freedom of conscience to dissenters provided they kept the peace. This last offer was of course welcomed, but even from the beginning anyone might see how easily it could be frustrated. Fox and the Quakers were soon caught up in a struggle merely to survive and had to face the changes in outlook which this enforced.

Fox followed up his earlier cautions to Friends with a further paper, from his Lancaster prison, 'for the staying the minds of any such as might be hurried or troubled about the change of Government'. He advised them to 'be still in the Light of the Lamb, and he shall fight for you' (Ell. p.225). Yet his enemies remained convinced that Quakers, holding great rallies and mysteriously communicating with each other all over the country, must be plotting some armed rising. And if they were not, their anti-social obstinacy fully justified a campaign against them. Even from across the Atlantic, the Massachusetts authorities, when they sent Charles a Loyal Address, defended their brutality to Quakers, calling them, 'open enemies to the government itself as established [by] any but men of their own principles' (QAC p.92). Presbyterians who had endured much hardship to set up a colony according to their own principles could see no reason why Quakers, who were free to go to other areas, should persist in disturbing it.

All this hostility is easy to understand, and was even, from the authorities' point of view, justified, for Fox was indeed asking people to live in a completely new way, following the leadings of Christ, learned as they waited together in worship as equals, without the old familiar chain of command from superior to inferior. Twenty years later, various chances combined to give Quakers the opportunity to attempt their own 'holy experiment' of the new society in the American settlement of Pennsylvania. For the present, under the new pressures against them, no longer able to hope for a rapid change in society, Fox and most Friends came to think that they should defend themselves by developing the skills needed to deal with politicians and lawyers. The faith and courage of martyrs had to go along with the use of legal procedures and the arts of the lobbyist.

First Lancaster Imprisonment

After Major Porter had arrested him at Swarthmoor in May 1660 Fox wrote to him with more blunt truth than discretion.

> Seeing that he appeared so zealous for the King and thought to ingratiate himself into the King's favour by imprisoning me . . . I asked him whose great buck-horns were those in his house . . . and where had he that wainscot that he ceiled his house withal? Had he it not from Hornby Castle that was the King's? (N p.383)

Taunts like this would not get Fox out of prison, even though they showed that he kept well up with worldly gossip.

Once in custody, Fox knew that he had to resign himself to long months of discomfort and confusion. The gaolers, confident of Porter's backing, kept him 'a close prisoner . . . in the dark house . . . and many times would not let [him] have meat but under the door.' (N p.378). Some surviving cells open only on to a subterranean corridor with one small window, and each gets scanty light and air through a grated opening over the heavy door. Even these vents have shutters which a malicious gaoler could easily swing across, putting the victim into stifling

Lancaster Castle: prison cells

and disorientating darkness. To hamper Fox's defence Porter refused to let him see the mittimus, or warrant. When two of his friends coaxed the gaoler to show it to them they found it alleged that he 'with others of our fanatic opinions had of late endeavoured to raise insurrections in this part of the country', and that it ordered the gaoler 'to keep [him] in safe custody till [he] should be released by order from the King and Parliament' (N p.379).

Margaret Fell, and Fox himself, at once began the campaign for his release. Fox told Charles of his earlier imprisonments by those 'that have been against the King's father and him,' and that he had no reason to oppose Charles, 'he having done no harm against me'. He frequently used this line of defence, but nobody listened to it. Margaret sent out a letter to 'all magistrates', listing the irregularities in the detention of Fox, and adding 'I am concerned in the thing, inasmuch as he was apprehended in my house; and if he be guilty I am so too' (N p.383). Her own enemies were quite ready to see in this both sedition and scandal. She next made the long ride down to London, where she and other Friends peppered the King with requests. Many people were then reminding Charles of his debts for past help. Ann Curtis, the Reading Friend in whose house Fox had stayed during his breakdown the previous year, got an interview with the King and asked for Fox's release in compensation for the death of her own father, Sheriff of Bristol, hanged in 1643, 'near his own door' for supporting Charles I. Charles agreed, but hostile clerks raised quibbles, so that Margaret had to keep up the pressure.

When the Lancaster Assizes came on, Fox's case was waiting for transfer to London, and he was therefore left in his cell, able only 'to speak out of the gaol window' to the people who came to see this notorious prisoner. Next, as often, the situation veered towards farce. How was he to be got to London? Fox remarked that, if he were as dangerous as the charge said, 'a troop or two of horse' should be paid to guard him on the journey. The Justices blenched at such an expense, and even at the lesser cost of sending a gaoler and a couple of bailiffs with him. He refused bail, even with 'leave to go up with some of my own friends' (N p.387), arguing as usual that by accepting a bail condition or paying the gaoler's fees he would be admitting that the imprisonment was lawful. He agreed however that if they released him without conditions he and his Friends would carry the warrant to London and present it to the Court by the due day, 'if the Lord did permit'. On September 24th, after four months in custody, the officials showed that the charge was absurd by letting him have his way.

He first doubled north to Swarthmoor and then spent the next three weeks riding to London, with many meetings on the way. At the end of October, after further legal wrangles, the charges were dropped, leaving Fox for the moment free, in a London now strangely different. When he reached Charing Cross he noticed 'multitudes of people gathered together to the burning of the entrails of them that had been the old King's judges, that had been hanged, drawn, and quartered.' (N p.386). Charles had insisted on the execution of the dozen 'regicides', although several, including Cromwell and Judge Fell's friend, Judge Bradshaw, had frustrated him by having already died. Their embalmed bodies were exhumed, formally hanged, and the heads later set up with the rest on spikes round the city, where they stayed for years as grim reminders of the uncertainties of power. Other republicans were imprisoned in the Tower, amongst them the Sir Henry Vane with whom Fox had discussed the prospects before the Republic collapsed. No one seemed troubled by these barbarities. Vane himself refused to make his peace with the King and was later beheaded.

Peace Testimony

Although the Justices went on rounding up Quakers, their problems then were slight beside those which hit them after an incompetent Fifth Monarchy outbreak in January 1661. Several dozen men, with their leader Venner, ran out of a meeting shouting 'King Jesus and their heads upon the gates.' They expected the Londoners to join them, but none did. The authorities soon recovered from their panic, and disposed of the conspirators, but the incident confirmed their terror of sectaries and Quakers. Who could be sure that they were not lying when they claimed that the reign of Jesus was to be entirely non-violent and spiritual? After all, some had been in the army, and if they had been dismissed it was rather for refusing oaths or insubordinate behaviour about hats and titles than for unwillingness to fight for their cause. Fox was arrested again, with the night-time knocking at the door and the rush up the stairs that so many people have heard in our own century. On that night the soldiers were frustrated, for from another room appeared Esquire Richard Marsh, recognized as one of the Royal Household staff, a friend of Fox, who undertook to bring him to Whitehall, where, after much argument, during which he gave his occupation as 'preacher of righteousness', he was released. He continued his work for the hundreds of Friends who had been imprisoned, often just missing soldiers who would have arrested him.

The anxieties of these weeks led Fox and Hubberthorne to

draw up a declaration affirming that Quakers could never use or support violence.

> Our principle is, and our practices have always been, to seek peace . . . and to follow after righteousness and the knowledge of God, seeking the good and welfare, and doing that which tends to the peace of all . . . All bloody principles and practices [= plots] we do utterly deny; with all outward wars and strife and fightings with outward weapons, for any end or under any pretence whatever . . . For this we can say to all the world: we have wronged no man's persons or possessions, we have used no force nor violence against any man; we have been found in no plots, nor guilty of sedition. And when we have been wronged, we have not sought to revenge ourselves, we have not made resistance against authority, but wherein we could not obey for conscience' sake we have suffered even the most of any people in the nation. (N p.398 - 403)

peace testimony

Despite what was said here, the conviction that Quakers should have no part in fighting had not come quickly or easily. Many of Fox's companions had served in the republican army, and some Quakers still thought they could fight if the cause were just.

With almost more urgency, another charge had to be answered, that although Quakers might say they would not fight, 'if the Spirit do move [them] then [they] will change [their] principle, and . . . buy a sword and fight for the Kingdom of Christ', like the Fifth Monarchists. The long-running problem of consistency in personal guidance had to be settled. If opponents could claim that a Quaker was free to change his views, all his declarations were worthless. The statement therefore went on,

> . . . The Spirit of Christ, by which we are guided, is not changeable, so as once to command us from a thing as evil, and again to move us unto it . . .

Fox ended with a long-term aim which had little appeal to his readers.

> Secondly, we do earnestly desire and wait, that by the Word of God's power, and its effectual operation in the hearts of men, the Kingdoms of the world may become the Kingdoms of the Lord, . . . whereby all people out of all different judgements

and professions [= religious outlooks] might be brought into
love and unity with God, and with one another. . . and might
all come to witness the Prophet's words, 'Nation shall not lift
up sword against nation . . .' (Ell. p.233 - 6)

The first copies were confiscated at the printers, but Friends
were able to get it out at a further attempt. This 'Declaration of
1660' (January 1661, by our calendar), although by no means the
first in which Fox and others had disclaimed violence, has come
to be acknowledged as the first official statement of the Quaker
peace testimony. Its origin as an urgent and almost desperate
attempt to clear Quakers of supporting armed rebellion has long
ago been forgotten. Few in those days were thinking of international war. The authorities paid very little attention to such
declarations, but the Venner group at their trial cleared Quakers
of any share in their plot and for the moment the harassment
eased.

The Problem of Oaths

From the beginning the Quaker refusal to take oaths had caused
them trouble. Fox held that people should speak truthfully to
everybody at all times. Oaths were therefore needless; they
were clearly against the teaching of Jesus, and in practice widespread perjury showed them to be futile. Yet every step in civic
or legal life had to be confirmed by an oath and the Quaker refusal to swear had many unexpected consequences. Taking office
as mayor, or even as parish constable; getting probate for a will;
speaking in court as witness, complainant or prisoner: all began
with an oath, and without it the Quaker could neither function
nor be heard. William Edmondson, for example, a friend of Fox,
had trouble after his convincement about getting a cargo
through the Irish customs because he could not swear to its liab-
ility for duty. These difficulties became much more serious in the
new conditions after the Restoration, when tolerance about
oath-taking disappeared. Justices and Judges knew that if no
other charge were handy the oath of allegiance could be 'tendered' to a Quaker prisoner. He would then refuse, and offer his
reasons to hostile ears.

The Judges at Howgill's trial in 1663 put the situation
plainly.

All sects under pretext of conscience did violate the laws and hatched rebellions . . . not that I have anything to charge you with, but seeing the Oath of Allegiance was tendered to you at the last Assizes, and you refused to take it, such persons [are looked upon as] enemies to the King and Government.

At the next Assizes a fresh Judge, before sentencing Howgill, said,

The Law requires an oath; and I cannot alter it; do you think that the law must be changed for you, or only for a few? If this be suffered, the administration of justice [will be] hindered, no action can be tried, no evidence given for the King . . . your principles are altogether inconsistent with the law and government. I pray you shew me which way we shall proceed . . . (Howgill's *Works*. Introduction.)

The Judge's language might be moderate, but the chasm in outlook was complete, and oaths of allegiance went on being tendered for the rest of the reign. Much later on, at least in minor and administrative matters, law clerks took to saving themselves trouble by entering 'Jurat' [he swears] on their forms whenever they heard some sort of affirmation from a Quaker. Friends often let it pass. In the long run the consequences of not being able to take oaths over legal arrangements, along with the drain on an estate from fines, caused great difficulties, especially for Quakers who were landowners, and contributed in the end to a weakening of the movement, for heirs were inclined to leave the Quaker stand to younger relatives, who had less to lose, but less influence.

Religious Persecution and Quaker Response

Much of the difficulty over a religious settlement after the Restoration came because the Presbyterians hoped for a place in some broadly inclusive state church, but could not agree with the Anglicans. These also wanted a single authorised church, but run only by bishops and using their own approved liturgy. Richard Baxter, one of the Presbyterian leaders active in the Conferences on the subject, admitted that he opposed any toleration which would allow 'Papists and sectaries' to go their own way.

(Baxter p.151 - 2). He was ready to hold to this even if it led to persecution for himself. After two years of bickering the only winners were the Anglicans, for Parliament gave them everything: authoritarian bishops unchecked by synods or elders, a Prayer Book and liturgy based on that of Queen Elizabeth (and of Laud); an Act ordering all clergy to use it, and a succession of Acts intended to make any other kind of meeting or preaching impossible. Collectively known as the Clarendon Code, from the name of Charles's chief minister, they came more from the prejudices of the members of Parliament. The once dominant Presbyterians were forced out of the established church and found themselves amongst the very dissenters they had denounced and suppressed.

For ten years the Quakers and the Baptists had been the main sufferers under persecution. Now Presbyterians and Congregationalists were to be tested to find out whether they would stand firm. Over the first two years of the reign about two thousand clergy were turned out of their livings because they would not accept the bishops and the 1662 liturgy. Amongst them Fox's old opponents, Stephens of Fenny Drayton and Lampitt of Ulverston. The laity encouraged their pastors to accept fines or prison for preaching without a licence, but changed their attitude quickly when a fresh law imposed penalties simply for attending a 'conventicle'. One Act imposed a small fine for a first offence, but banishment to America for a third. When the Conventicle Act banned meetings of more than five people in addition to the family of a house, some of the clergy went around preaching to very small house meetings. Sometimes groups would have bread and cheese in the room and if the constables came would pretend that they had met for a meal. Many felt if they paid up once they had done enough for their testimony and were free to avoid further trouble by such subterfuges. Fox teased them over what he thought were their tricks and bendings. Over the years many dissenters were imprisoned or impoverished, but where the numbers have been examined they usually show that the Quakers suffered worst. In the City itself, for example, in the nine months from August 1664, five Presbyterians were committed, five Independents, three Baptists and 791 Quakers (Hutton p.210). In two successive Sundays alone, four hundred Quakers were arrested at the Bull and Mouth Meeting House (Barbour p.224).

In the following years, as Parliament frustrated toleration, Charles used his prerogative to issue pardons and to release or excuse many individuals. Parliament objected to this use of prerogative powers in practice, even though it accepted they were theoretically inherent in his kingship. When he tried to rule without Parliament the recurrent bankruptcies of his administration forced him to recall it for the sake of its grudging grants. The fortunes of Fox and the Quakers swung about erratically under the endless infighting amongst the people intriguing for power.

Fox wanted Friends to meet persecution head on, in the serene confidence that if they were faithful and persistent the power of the spirit would break it. During any local crackdown he wanted every Friend to appear at the public meeting place. This could be anywhere, - house, barn, workshop, orchard or open space, - for most dissenters only began to use special buildings after a short-lived concession in 1672. Fox repeatedly urged Friends to keep up their meetings, even if only the small children were free to attend, and, when a building had been nailed up or knocked down, to stand on the rubble or out in the open. Even when all Friends were in custody they could still hold the meeting, - in prison. Prosecutions and penalties were never consistent, for too much depended on political scares or the phobias of the Justices. In the successive bouts of hysteria most ordinary Quakers were beaten up, or impoverished by fines and distraints, or by being kept in prison and unable to earn their living. A few reached their third conviction for attending meeting and were sentenced to transportation, though hardly any actually left the country. Shipmasters refused to carry them, sometimes out of sympathy, but more often because they were thought to be Jonahs. Some hundreds died of prison hardships and diseases. When they themselves were free, Fox and his companions put all their effort into relieving distress and encouraging Friends to look forward to their eventual success.

Quakers had thought of their efforts to bring about a new society as the 'Lamb's War', and had looked forward to the 'victory of the Lamb'. The more intense campaign to destroy them could be said to give a different force to this image. The many casualties, like those in any war, were usually young. Of Fox's early companions, for example, Hubberthorne died in London's Newgate gaol in 1662 at thirty four, Burrough in the same place and the same year at twenty eight. Howgill lived a little longer, for it took five years in Appleby Gaol to kill him, in 1668, at fifty. Audland died of T.B. in 1664, through overwork. One of the few casualties of a different kind was Anthony Pearson, the influential Durham Justice, an active worker and writer during the 1650's whom Fox had often visited. Under pressure to clear himself of supporting plots and to safeguard his property, he wrote a rather abject letter to the King renouncing his youthful errors, and became a conformist for the remaining seven years of his life.

An unanswerable speculation of history is how Quakerism would have fared if some of those who died had survived, for they were clearly people of ability and promise. One, for example, who had shown this promise most strongly was James Parnell, who had become, even at nineteen, a respected speaker and a forceful writer. Fox's own survival often seemed unlikely, and we may ask what would have happened if he also had been a casualty. Yet by good fortune and stamina he was one who came through, reaching the age of forty six in 1670, and perhaps by then beginning to feel isolated without his early companions, the men from the north country who had encouraged him with their devotion and their own efforts.

Quaker constancy won them some reluctant admiration. Richard Baxter, although he detested Quaker views, acknowledged that other dissenters benefited from their stand.

> The fanatics called Quakers did greatly relieve the sober people; for they were so zealous, and gloried in their constancy and sufferings, that they assembled openly (at the 'Bull and Mouth') and were dragged away daily to the common jail; and yet deserted not, but the rest came the next day nevertheless, so that the jail at Newgate was filled with them. Abundance of them died in prison ... Thus the Quakers so employed the ... persecutors, that they had the less leisure to look after the meetings of soberer men, which was much to their present ease. (Baxter p.189)

A witness of a different outlook was Pepys. One 'Lord's Day' evening, whilst walking home from Whitehall, listening to a friend telling him, 'that by his microscope of his own making he doth discover that the wings of a moth is made just as the feather of the wings of a bird . . .' he noted that,

> While we were talking, came by several poor creatures, carried by Constables for being at a conventicle. They go like lambs, without any resistance. I would to God they would either conform, or be more wise and not be ketched [= caught]. (Pepys p.413. 7th Aug. 1664)

His greater interest in the scientific observation, and his casual assumption that religious fortitude was pointless, fore-shadow a time when Fox would be facing not religious fervour but worldly indifference. Gradually the government and the Anglicans came to realize that harassing dissenters would never get rid of them. If political conditions had been less unstable, some limited toleration might have been got through Parliament at least ten years before the actual *Toleration Act* of 1689.

Trouble amongst Friends

Persecution was not the only problem. The stresses of the time led to disagreements between Friends themselves. In the early days they had been averse to any arrangements which could seem to restrict the free leading of the Spirit and some were now unhappy at what seemed to them creeping signs of human organisation. Their spokesman was the eccentric traveller and minister John Perrot. He rejected any pre-arrangement, even the fixing of times for meetings, as an interference with the working of the Spirit. One expression of this was that he continued to condemn the custom of removing hats when anyone stood to pray. Fox vigorously opposed Perrot's opinions, as a self-destructive individualism and as encouraging the idea that the leadings of the Spirit were changeable. Fox's views were in the end accepted but Perrot's outlook attracted some of the most sensitive of the newer Friends and for a time a damaging failure of unity seemed possible.

Apart from writing about the problem, Fox set off round the country, partly to explain the dangers he saw in Perrot's ideas, but mainly to encourage Friends, despite all their anxieties and hardships, to keep their faith firm and pure. Having no point to make by imprisonment he recalled gleefully when soldiers searching for him were unlucky. In September 1662, however, he and his companions were arrested at Swannington, near Leicester, and searched for seditious letters or weapons, although nothing worse than a 'comb-case' was found on Fox. In Leicester prison his asking for straw to lie on in the yard, because the dungeon was already overcrowded with Friends, led to the gaoler's assessment of their social standing, 'we did not look like men that would lie on straw' (N p.432). Fox then got a room in which to receive the many Friends likely to seek him out by offering payment to the real power, the gaoler's lame wife, who sat on her chair and 'beat her husband with her crutch if he came within reach'. At the Assizes, a month later, the usual arguments included Fox's comments on the absurdity of imprisoning as a traitor someone who had been detained in that very prison eight years before as a suspected Royalist. After Friends had been found guilty, and returned to the prison, the gaoler unexpectedly announced,

> Gentlemen, it is the Court's pleasure that you should all be set at liberty, except those for tithes; and there are fees due to me, you know, but I shall leave it to you to give me what you will. (N p.435)

Consistency was never to be expected. Each Friend continued his service from where it had been interrupted.

Fox was soon back in London, and then off westward to Cornwall, despite the usual troubles, such as the 'captain with his company of musketeers coming to the meeting with matches lit' (N p.438). After he had met the Lowers and 'cleared [himself] of Cornwall' he moved up to Cullompton where, as in some other places, the Friends had hit on a strangely modern form of passive resistance. Where the warrants ordered that the Friends should be 'carried' to prison they were refusing to walk, so that the constables had to hire horses and carts, into which they had to lift each Friend. The ploy was the more successful because some moderate Justices would not press charges and the constables had to ferry the prisoners around from one to another at their own expense. That, said Fox, 'broke the neck of their persecution there for that time' (N p.448). Fox travelled on, through Wales, then across into Yorkshire, where his party met Margaret Fell and her daughters, busy on a long tour of their own. They soon parted, and Fox continued northwards, at last crossing the Pennines to Swarthmoor. Here, in January 1664, after yet another plot, the Northern or Kaber Rigg, in which a few Quakers were implicated, he heard that a warrant was out for him. He decided:

> I could have gone away overnight, for I had not appointed any meeting, and I had cleared myself of the north and the Lord's power was over all; but I considered, there being a noise of a plot in the north, if I should go away they might fall upon poor Friends, so if I gave up myself to be taken I should choke them and Friends should escape the better. (N p.457)

Imprisonment at Lancaster and Scarborough

The next day an officer arrived to arrest him, with a sword as his warrant, and took him to Holker Hall, near Cartmel. The Justices began with a contemptuous digression about a book Fox had initiated, *The Battledore*, intended to show, from a survey of ancient languages, that the Quaker usage of singular and plural pronouns was historically valid. When they moved on to the Oath of Allegiance, Fox asked whether one Justice on the bench had taken it. If he had done so, as a known Papist, the man would have condemned himself as a perjurer. It was of course all futile, for there is evidence that Justices took care to avoid putting difficult questions to their fellow gentry, and they had already made up their minds about Fox. He was soon back in Lancaster Castle, committed at the Assizes in January 1664 to wait in custody until the next sitting, at the end of August. There, after a vigorous debate, with much cut and thrust and some home truths, the jury found him guilty of refusing the oath.

By this time Margaret Fell had herself been arrested for holding illegal meetings at Swarthmoor, and was on trial along with Fox, now also for 'refusing the oath.' She was sentenced at the same time, and began what proved to be a four years' imprisonment, a little less wretched in its conditions, but just as threatening, for she had been 'praemunired'. This was a mediaeval penalty designed to restrict the power of the Papacy. The Royalists revived it, but used it mostly as a convenient catch-all against people like leading Quakers. It amounted to outlawry, with banishment or imprisonment at the king's pleasure, and confiscation of property. It was used in a cat and mouse way to intimidate victims with threats and successive imprisonments. In the two years, 1663 and 1664, over eighty Quakers were praemunired, of whom three lost property (Hutton p.170). The next day Fox forced the judge to admit that the indictment was invalid, but when he asked to be compensated for false imprisonment the Judge put the oath again. Fox refused; the case was deferred to the next Assizes, and he was left in a'close prison',

> . . . a smoky tower where the smoke of other rooms came up and stood as a dew upon the walls, where it rained in also upon my bed and the smoke was so thick as I could scarcely see a candle sometimes . . . and in the cold season my shift would be as wet as muck with the rain. (N p.485)

By the next Assizes in March 1665 Fox had spent a whole winter in those conditions. His own account shows the assurance that kept him going.

> I grew, through smothering in a cold and smoky prison, very weak; but the Lord's power was over all, and supported me through all, and enabled me to do service for him, and for his Truth and people, as the place would admit (N p.487)

He did somehow contrive to keep on writing, with controversial pamphlets, a fresh statement condemning the extortionate penalties Friends were suffering for refusing tithes, and even perhaps some draft material for the first version of his *Journal*.

The authorities next decided to transfer him to Scarborough Castle, because of its greater isolation. The officers, said Fox, 'fetched me out of the castle when I was not able to go [= walk] or stand.' (N p.488). Nevertheless he was hurried off eastwards, although he was almost too weak to stay on the horse's back, especially when a young gaoler whipped it 'to make it skip and leap'. In another of his many references to smell he noted that his clothes 'smelt so much of smoke that they were loathsome to [him]'.

The conditions at Scarborough were even worse than at Lancaster. One cell had a hearth which filled the room with fumes. Another had no hearth at all, and an open window facing the sea, so that his bed was soaked and he had to bale water from the floor with his plate. Yet Fox was still able to crack one of his ironical jokes. When the Papist governor came into his room, and could not find the way out because of the smoke, Fox said it was 'his purgatory, where they had put me into.' He had to hire a non-Friend to bring his food, because no Quaker was allowed near him, and even this woman sometimes had to fight the soldiers to hold on to what she was bringing. He was too weak to eat, recalling that 'a threepenny loaf served me three weeks' and he drank only 'water with wormwood steeped in it'.

Only after reaching Scarborough was he able to discover that he too had been praemunired. Though he had little property to lose, this sentence meant that he could expect to stay in prison until his death, which in those conditions seemed likely to come soon. Fox busied himself as best he could with writing or talking, and slowly won some sympathy from his gaolers. At last his friends in London, with some help from Esquire Marsh, succeeded in getting an order of release from Charles. Fox's friend and fellow minister John Whitehead hurried north with it, and on Sept 1st 1666, Fox was free, with the Governor's discharge certificate in his pocket, as a sort of passport. The soldiers, who had begun by tormenting him, sent him off with their compliment: 'he is a stiff as a tree and as pure as a bell, for we could never stir him' (N p.502).

Soon after his release from Scarborough Fox admitted that,

I was so weak with lying about three years in cruel and hard imprisonments, my joints and my body were so stiff and benumbed that I could hardly get on my horse. Neither could I well bend my knees, nor hardly endure fire nor eat warm meat: I had been so long kept from it. (N p.510)

Yet this crippling, from which he never recovered, did not keep him still, for he went at once from prison to a 'large General Meeting, and all was quiet.' From there he continued south, renewing his friendships, joining in meetings and, incidentally, visiting his relations. During the Plague year, 1665, he had been isolated in Scarborough, and he now returned to London in the autumn of 1666 just after the ruin of the Great Fire, in which of course Quakers shared, losing the main meeting place, the 'Bull and Mouth'.

Margaret Fell remained a prisoner until June 1668, although not in isolation like Fox, for her daughters took turns to stay near her, and she had two brief periods of freedom. One, in 1665, allowed her to revisit Swarthmoor, and the next, in 1667, to ride south to a Quaker General Meeting in Cheshire and there to meet Fox. Though her prison room was cold and exposed she too wrote a great deal, including a pamphlet called *Women's Speaking Justified*, in which she demonstrated that the Bible authorised women to preach and speak in meetings.

Private Lives and Marriages

Fox and his friends had their attention so much on life in the spirit that they thought their outward affairs of little interest and tease us by their reticence. It is easy to forget they had livings to earn, homes to keep up and families to care for. Yet in 1661, Fox had commented,

> It was dangerous for sober people to stir abroad for several weeks, and hardly could either men or women go up and down the streets to buy provisions for their families without being abused. (Ell. p.231)

Fortunately many Friends were tremendous letter writers, who eased every separation by sharing domestic news, as the Fell sisters did about the herbal medicine one should be taking for her 'jaundice', about buying dress fabric, about black as the fashionable colour, and so on. Their interest in herbs would please Fox, who is known to have possessed a famous book on herbal remedies, Culpepper's *The English Physician Enlarged*.

This was an age when reputations, property and liveli-

A copy of the Marriage certificate of Margaret Fell and George Fox

These are to signify unto all whome this may Concerne, That on the Eighteenth day of the Eighth Month, in the yeare one Thousand Sixhundred, sixty nine, George Fox and Margarett Fell Propounded their intentions of Cominge together in the honourable Marriage, in the Covenant of God, in our mens Meetinge, at Broade Meade within the City of Bristoll (havinge before made mention of such their intentions to severall Friends) on the behalfe of which, there were severall Testimonies given, both by the Children, & Relations of the said Margarett then present, and severall others, in the power of the Lord, both of men and women, declaringe their satisfaction and Approbation of their declared intention of Marriage; — And likewise at Another Meetinge, both of men & women, at the place aforesaide, on the Twenty first day of the Month and yeare aforesaide, The saide George Fox and Margarett Fell did againe publish their intentions of Cominge together in the honourable Marriage, in the Covenant of God, unto which againe, there were many Livinge Testimonyes borne by Relations and friends then present, both of men and women; And the same intention of Marriage beinge againe published by Dennis Hollister at our Publicke Meetinge place aforesaide, on the two and twentyeth day of the Month and yeare aforesaide, and then againe a publicke Testimony was given to the same, that it was of God, who had brought it to passe; — And for the full accomplishment, of the aforesaide proposal, and approved intention, at a Publicke Meetinge, both of Men & women Friends appointed on purpose for the same thinge, at the place aforesaide, and on the [illegible] day of the Month and yeare aforesaide; Accordinge to the Law & ordinance of God, and the example & [illegible] order of his people mentioned in the Scriptures of truth, who tooke each other before witnesses, and the Elders of the people, as Laban appointed A Meetinge, at the Marriage of Jacob, and a Publick Meetinge was appointed on purpose, when Boaz and Ruth tooke each other, and also as it was in Canaan where Christ and his disciples went to A Marriage &c: The saide George Fox did solemnly in the presence of God, and us his people declare That hee tooke the saide Margarett Fell, in the Everlastinge power, & covenant of God which is from Everlastinge to Everlastinge, & in the honourable Marriage to be his Bride and his wife: And likewise the saide Margarett did solemnly declare that in the Everlastinge power of the Mighty God & in the unalterable word, & in the presence of God, his Angells and us his holy Assembly, shee tooke the saide George Fox to be her husbande, unto which marriage many Livinge Testimonyes were borne, in the sence of the power and presence of the Livinge God manifested in the saide Assembly; of which wee whose names are here subscribed, are witnesses.

John Rous	William Tayler	Margrett Rous	Jane Rogers
William Yeamans	Thomas Callowhill	Isabell Yeamans	Elizabeth Milner
Thomas Lower	Erasmus Dole	Mary Lower	Elizabeth Stewar
Alex: Roberts	John Wear	Sarah Fell	Mary Wathfilde
George Whiteheade	Nicho: Jordan	Susan: Fell	Margarett Thomas
Edw: Pyott	Charles Harvord	Rachell Fell	Joyce Warren
Charles Lloyd	David Symmons		Ann Speed
	[illegible]		Sarah Moone
			Mary North
			Magdelin Love
			[illegible]
			[illegible]

hoods depended on marriages, and when almost everyone married at least once. Fox's followers soon found themselves with a problem over their own marriages. By rejecting human priests they seemed to have left themselves no legal way of contracting and recording them. For Fox a marriage was a compact between two people, modelled on that first one in Paradise. He held that Friends 'married none', but that the couple themselves made the marriage by declaring their commitment to each other in the presence of Christ, the invisible eternal priest. Yet he was quite clear that marriage had a public aspect, and as far back as 1653, 'when Truth was little spread over the nation', had written about the need for public notices of marriages and for the declarations to be witnessed at a meeting for worship by at least twelve people. He expected that their Minute, with all their signatures, would serve as a certificate for public and legal purposes. By 1661, perhaps because nobody wanted uncertainties over the all-important matters of property, a judge ruled that Quaker marriages were valid, in part for Fox's own reason, that the first marriage in history, that of of Adam and Eve, had been made by the couple themselves without a priest. Yet weary arguments went on when clergy or jealous relatives refused to accept the Quaker certificates.

Fox's passion for spiritual purity did not prevent his recognizing that human life includes mundane needs and weaknesses. In 1667, for example, he wanted couples to consult

> . . . the Men's and Women's Meetings . . . For many had gone together in marriage contrary to their relations' minds; and some young, raw people that came among us, had mixed with the world; and widows had married, that had not made provision for their children by their former husbands. (Ell. p.315)

This advice suggests that in a movement that had expanded so rapidly in difficult conditions strains and uncertainties were showing up, and that unless Friends took care over them the movement might be discredited. The high demands Quakers made for honesty, truth, and so on, made enemies watch mercilessly for any slip.

By this time Fox had a more personal reason for thinking about marriage. He had worked closely for so long with Margaret Fell and her daughters that they were almost his own family. He joined in their letter writing, and exchanged affectionate messages even with the younger children. Rachel, the baby, could hardly have remembered Judge Fell, her own father, for when he had died in 1658 she was was barely six. All of them now wrote warmly of Fox as 'dear father', another expression showing that Fox was far from being ill-mannered or eccentric. Their own marriages strengthened the links, for their husbands had all come to Quakerism through him and were very much attached to him. Margaret junior's husband was John Rous, the planter from Barbados, first convinced there by Henry Fell from Swarthmoor. Isabel married William Yeamans, a young Bristol merchant, brother to Fox's nurse and helper, Ann Curtis, and Mary Fell later married Thomas Lower from Cornwall. Whatever risks and hardships were still to come Fox had round him a warm family group. His own name was linked by gossip with Margaret's, and worldly people couldn't understand why the two should share their faith and not the rest of their lives. Justice Fleming showed his attitude when he reported to the Secretary of State in 1664 on his proceedings against Quakers. Margaret was 'Mrs Fell, [Oliver's Judge Fell's widow, and now wife or I know not what to George Fox] . . .' (Ross p.169)

From Movement to Society

After several months in London, towards the end of 1666, winter being no deterrent, Fox began another comprehensive tour of the country, which took up all the next two years, sometimes so exhausting him that he admitted to being 'so exceeding weak I could hardly get off or on my horse's back' (N p.513). The Perrot problem was still troubling Friends. Persecution meant that plans for support had to be ready in advance and people prepared to take on responsibilities whenever they arose. Friends had to be cleared from blame over the actions of people whose behaviour meant that they could no longer be counted as Quakers. In addition, the very increase in the numbers of Quakers required more organisation: for collecting funds and paying expenses, for publications, for legal defence, for helping the travelling ministers if they were prevented from paying their own way, and for the needs of the poor, including those ruined by persecution. These activities were already going on, but Fox felt sure that Friends should now extend them. He was not alone in this, because, in 1666, whilst he was out of action in Scarborough, a group of his companions had met to consider the need, and had sent out a long letter about the value of more systematic arrangements.

Deaths and imprisonments meant that Quakers could no longer rely on the the initiatives and strenuous travelling of individual preachers and counsellors. Local arrangements were more than ever needed. Fox knew that some Friends took this increase in planning as an unwelcome interference with the freedom of spiritual leading, and that it would need careful explanation. He therefore set about persuading Friends all over the country to agree that clusters of local meetings, more or less county by county, should arrange for monthly meetings to deal with all these matters, or, as he put it, 'to take care of God's glory'. (N p.511). 'Substantial Friends, that can give a testimony of your sufferings, and how things are amongst you in every particular meeting', were also to meet quarterly, but

> . . . none that are raw or weak, that are not able to give a testimony of the affairs of the Church and Truth, may go on behalf of the particular Meetings to the Quarterly Meetings, but may be nursed up in your Monthly Meetings, and there fitted for the Lord's service. (Ep. 265, p.290)

This suggests that he was trying to find a way through the perils that beset organisations, from the consequences of inexperience, to letting dominant or exclusive groups gain excessive authority by a failure to keep the meeting open to a succession of new people.

This seemingly dull work of organisation gave Fox a great deal of effort and anxiety, and much writing. He felt clear that this change was not a drift backwards into formality, but that bringing all Friends into the various tasks and opportunities would strengthen the spiritual renewal. As time went on it became clear that Fox had changed his own position amongst Quakers. The regular meetings for business and the gathering experience of the local Friends who came to them provided a permanent structure through which the affairs of Friends could be handled by a succession of people. Fox had transferred responsibility from himself and the pioneers. He was to be an 'elder brother', an adviser and a welcome visitor to meetings that were quite able to carry on without him. These changes, and the restraints on action resulting from persecution, meant however that Quakerism was becoming less of a world-wide call for spiritual transformation and was settling down as a sect or society, with an increasingly clear form and limited aims. Fox acknowledged this as early as 1667, with his remark that 'Friends are become a good savour in the hearts of all people' (Ep. 251).

In this male dominated age Fox had another problem. He had always been clear that women should share as equals in all Quaker activities. To the disgust and contempt of their opponents women had from the beginning travelled and ministered. Fox wanted them to join in all the responsibilities, including those of administration. To further this goal, and to enable them to learn the relevant skills without the interference of men, he asked that a separate series of meetings should be set up, run entirely by women, to deal with practical personal needs, such as those of children. He argued that through them the women would gain the confidence to carry out tasks then usually thought to be beyond their abilities. Even amongst Friends some men objected to these proposals, and it took years for them to be fully accepted.

Chapter Nine

IRELAND, MARRIAGE AND ILLNESS

Interlude

His past hardships, exertions and illness quite failed to slow Fox down, and he made his next ten years even more complicated and strenuous. At first he was helped by some easing of persecution, as Justice Fleming complained to the King's Secretary in 1668.

> Mrs Fell having her discharge from an easy imprisonment doth not a little encourage that rabble of fanatics, and discourage all magistrates from acting against them. I observe it's now become a general policy to comply with the non-conformists. I'm sure it much increases their number ... (Ross p.204)

The embittered Fleming exaggerated, although the uncertainties about the King's views, the changes amongst his ministers, and other complications, such as the Plague, did lead to some relief. In the London area, for example, imprisonments fell from a peak of 1729 in 1664 almost to none for four years, and then rose to another peak of 519 in 1670 (Horle p.284). Yet in many areas Quakers still suffered brutal assaults, as well as the fines and distraints which the authorities and informers realised were more profitable than prison sentences. Quakers who had followed Fox's advice of 1661 that they should 'gently' send to the magistrates a statement of injustices (Ep. 208) soon took up his further recommendation to collect details of cases and forward them to the Quaker office set up in London to work on their behalf.

Another factor affecting people's lives was that, despite all its problems, and a war with the Dutch, the country was becoming more prosperous. Quakers shared in the general improvement, and paradoxically even benefited from their strange principles. In 1667 Fox was able to remind Friends,

168

. . . At first ye know that many could not take so much money in your trade as to buy bread with . . . now they say they will trust you before their own people, knowing that you will not cheat, nor wrong, nor oppress them. For the cry is now . . . 'Where is there a Quaker of such and such a trade?' . . . Friends, who have purchased this through great sufferings, lose not this great favour which God hath given unto you . . . On the other hand, If there be any oppression, or defrauding . . . the world will say, 'The Quakers are not as they were'.

There is some evidence that this new Quaker policy of fixed prices and reliable quality helped to form the trading standards of the next century, and made easier the growth of a modern economic system. Fox then cautioned Friends against other dangerous business practices: running into debt, 'aiming at great things, and making a great show in the world of other's goods.' He went on to warn them that anyone 'going under the name of Quaker', whilst rejecting Meetings as formalities and saying to Friends, 'We will have none of your laws', would hurt what Friends had 'bought, and kept through great sufferings.' (Ep. 251)

In 1668, three months after Margaret was released from Lancaster prison, Mary Fell and Thomas Lower were married at Swarthmoor, and for several years the two lived there or at the nearby Marsh Grange property, Margaret's own family inheritance. In the spring of 1669 she travelled south with Rachel, her fifteen year old youngest daughter, visiting Friends in prison and staying with her married daughters. After leaving Rachel in a school near London, which had just been founded with Fox's encouragement, she spent her time amongst the London meetings. In London she was reunited with Fox, and the two at last decided that the way was clear for them to marry. Yet however pleased they may have been to meet again they stayed together only briefly, because Yorkshire Quakers called for Fox to help them set up more Monthly Meetings, 'for Truth was much spread in that country' (N p.533). Whilst there he met an old acquaintance, 'Justice Hotham, one that had been tender to me at the first', when Fox was just a voluble and enthusiastic unknown. We might wonder what Hotham thought about the way the young man had developed.

Ireland

Despite the problems of the Catholics and the harsh English rule, Irish conditions were then a little easier under a relatively moderate and efficient governor. Quaker ministers, including William Edmondson, now settled in Ireland, where he had bought a farm so that he could join in the protest against tithes, had convinced enough people for some thirty small Meetings to form. These were in towns settled by the English, for 'in this ruinous nation' the countryside 'generally is without inhabitants, but bands of murderers, thieves and robbers' (Q. in Barbour p.87). Fox had taken an interest in Ireland from the beginning, but had so far been able to share his experience with them only through his letters. As early as 1655, for instance, after a visit to Fox in England, Edmondson was given a short message for the new Irish Friends.

> And all my dear Friends, dwell in the life and love, and power and wisdom of God, in unity with one another, and with God: and the peace and wisdom of God fill up all your hearts, that nothing may rule in you, but the life, which stands in the Lord God. (Ell. p.170)

Fox was now eager to consult with them about their progress and give them the encouragement his presence generally brought. From Yorkshire he therefore turned westwards, but risked not getting far because the old enemy, Colonel Kirkby, although 'sick of the gout', was on the rampage again, offering a reward of £40 for his capture. Fox commented simply that the 'Lord's power prevented and stopped him' (N p.536). It does indeed seem strange that so conspicuous a spokesman could defy the laws and be present at innumerable Meetings. Perhaps the King's reputed softness really did make the Justices feel that the trouble of arresting and trying him was not worth while if they would not be able to keep him in custody.

In May 1669 Fox sailed from Liverpool to Dublin with four others, three of whom knew Ireland. His quick awareness of the atmosphere of places and people meant that as soon as he landed he was shaken by an uncomfortable impression that the very earth 'smelt . . . with the corruption and the blood and the massacres and foulness,' (N p.537). This recalls his intense reaction in Lichfield in 1651, although other comments suggest that the hazards of his Irish mission had heightened his old tele-pathic sensitivity to places and people. The secret service had forwarded the news of his coming, and agents reported on his expected route. He was at risk from spies in Meetings, from search parties and from roadblocks. Warrants circulated con-taining full descriptions of him and his clothes, but unfortu-nately for us these have not survived. 'A Scots sheriff in the north' put the official view that, 'If they could but take that old Jesuit, they would quickly knock all the others down'. He responded to the danger by travelling around with the sort of provocative daring we expect only in adventure fiction. Irish Friends were endlessly apprehensive for him, bringing him warnings, and trying to persuade him to dodge the danger spots.

At Cork, for example, when Friends 'asked him to go the backside of the town, he said nay, his way was through the streets.' To deter him they told him these had been made so slip-pery by the cattle market that 'his horse could not stand'. How-ever, with one Friend as a guide he rode straight on, past the very door of the mayor, who exclaimed, 'There goes George Fox', but did nothing. This ride through Cork followed a per-ception that he would be able to 'ride over' a dark, ugly visaged man. The Cork mayor, he believed, 'had no power' (N p.539). He seems to have felt able to judge how far he could challenge the authorities and get away before they reacted. One descrip-tion of him failed in its purpose. A priest who had, in Fox's Civil War slang, 'left his twattling tub' [pulpit], and become a Justice, sent a bailiff with the description, and a warrant, to the house where Friends had gathered. From the garden Fox thought he saw on the hillside 'three shades of trees, but at last I perceived they were three black coats who were peeping'. After Friends had gone, the unfortunate bailiff reported to his masters, as they waited contentedly for the Quakers to 'preach themselves hungry', that 'there was no such person as was prescribed in the warrant, for he had looked over all the meeting' (N p.544).

Sometimes he kept out of the way, once telling a Friend that he 'thought to reserve himself for a Province Meeting where all met together.' (N p.242). He could also enjoy giving the slip to

Impressions of George Fox's seal (inset shows actual size)

the people who were on the watch for him. Told of one expected search he exclaimed,

> Let the Devil do his worst, this town is blessed. But neverthe-
> less be ready in the morning by two of the clock, for I shall stay
> for none of you! For this many times was our usual hour,
> though we were up till eleven. (N p.546)

Towards the end of the tour he remarked,

> I felt their rage so against me that I felt my body as cut into
> pieces and yet I was well . . . Jesuits, Protestants [= Anglican]
> and Presbyterian priests joined all in a rage against me, but the
> power of the Lord God was over them all. (N p.546)

The danger not only excited Fox to the bravado of challenging the Justices but gave his comments a sharper edge than
usual. The frequent Catholic masses were a new experience and
so riled him that he needlessly upset some people by the tone of

his references to them. In his own meetings the tensions led to exceptional fervour. 'We had a brave meeting in the power of God. Oh, the brokenness and the life that flowed!' (N p.545). 'And a mighty convincement there was that day.' 'When the justice-priest questioned some sober people, and threatened them in a rage', they replied that 'they would go every day if they could hear George Fox.' (N p.544).

Edmondson wrote later that Fox's visit,

> . . . settled men's and women's meetings so that faithful men and women should take care in the government of church affairs among our own Society, which were and are of service. I was much eased by it, as I told G.F. at that time, for I had a great concern in those things, which had lain heavy upon my spirit for several years before. This gave every faithful Friend a share of the burden.' (Edmondson p.51)

This assessment by a hard-working but rather pedestrian Friend shows how Fox's proposals appeared to others, and incidentally illustrates the coming transition to an ongoing society after the apocalyptic and proselytising hopes of the first twenty years.

After a clockwise circuit round the country, with few place-names mentioned, Fox got back to Dublin, where 'there was no small joy amongst Friends . . . because my name had made such a noise in the nation . . . and Friends had a tender fear . . . and would fain have had me out of the City.' (N p.547). Yet only after several farewell meetings were his party able to get their 'horses and things' on board, escorted to the ship by a crowd of Friends very unwilling to lose him. His final comment was that they had 'a gallant spirit in them, worthy to be visited.' (N p.549). The atmosphere of the country was slow to leave him: 'I felt the power of darkness twenty miles afterwards as I was at sea.' (N p.548). Dublin Friends then had to cope with an irritating attempt to discredit him, for when the captain of the ship returned to Dublin he started a story that Fox had 'stayed all night in Liverpool drinking'. Two Friends who had been with him had to get the man to retract, and 'repent of his slander'. Slurs of this 'tabloid press' sort came up regularly and each was laboriously investigated.

When no one had any grasp of the old and complex problems of Ireland Fox could hardly be expected to make sense of them through one short visit. However, he did react, at least with advice, to the unscrupulous taking of land for the benefit of newcomers.

> . . . This is to all you that have bought any Irish land, keep to the equal measure and just weight in all things both inwardly and outwardly, so that justice . . . may be among you . . . by which they may know the just and true God in all his works. (Ep. 272)

Although he sometimes seemed rather indifferent to current political movements as irrelevant to the 'gospel order', he was quick to recognize injustice at the personal level, for that was where he believed it began.

Marriage

For years Fox's enemies had been making unsavoury hints about his friendship with Margaret, and Friends themselves had wondered whether the two would marry. In reality the separations of imprisonment alone would have made this difficult. The Fell property was another deterrent. Most of it, including Swarthmoor Hall, seems to have been left by the Judge either to Margaret or to the girls. The position was complicated by the actions of her hostile son George and the family's efforts to avoid losing the whole estate by confiscation whilst Margaret was under the praemunire, which had not been cancelled despite her release. The details are complicated and not entirely known. The facts are that the daughters kept the use and management of the Hall and estate, although deaths and marriages brought about more changes. Margaret herself went on living there, and Fox stayed there when he could.

Fox was extremely anxious that he should never be suspected of wanting to marry a woman for her property, although many people thought he must be eccentric or even immoral to take anyone past childbearing age, and then refuse the wealth which was her one attraction. In society generally this was the time when high seriousness was giving way to promiscuity, both amongst the courtiers of Whitehall, where Quakers tried to get the King's ear and signature, and amongst middle-class amorists like Pepys. Yet Fox kept to his view that although marriages had a practical and financial side they were above all sacred, the expression of perfection in human relationships. It could be said that he thought of marriage as a continuous sacrament.

All his energy had been spent helping people to find a true way of worship and life. Margaret and he had worked together in Quakerism from the beginning, and were very close to each other. Possibly Margaret had been 'in love' with him from their first encounter. He felt that their marriage should be seen as in some way an emblem of the unity of the whole movement, or even as a token of its unity with the divine order. For him, Quaker meetings, abroad as much as in his own country, made together a single body of worshippers, and he felt that he belonged to each of them. He was therefore not content that only one Meeting should be involved in his marriage but wrote to all, so that they could share in it. Some more mundane Friends were rather taken aback by this view of his marriage as typifying not only the unity of the couple but of the whole movement. Some of his enemies thought his ideas ridiculous.

When at last they had taken their decision, Margaret went to stay with her daughter Isabel Yeamans in Bristol. The other daughters and their husbands were assembled. Fox had 'cleared himself' of Ireland and of another round of visits to Meetings. The couple went through the whole procedure which Friends had just introduced, as if they were a family unknown among Friends. They appeared at the Men's and Women's Meetings; they asked for statements from the daughters that they were provided for. The reply from the family suggested that they may have thought Fox was rather overdoing his scruples, for they said 'she had doubled' their inheritance, 'and would not have me to speak of those things.' He answered, 'I was plain and would have all things done plainly, for I sought not any outward advantage for myself.' (N p.554) On 27th October, 1669, in Broadmead Meeting House in Bristol, the wedding took place, attended by as many Friends from around the country as could get there. Over ninety signed the Certificate. Fox at this point in his life was aged forty five, and Margaret fifty five. For twenty two years they continued to share their work, meeting for short periods when they could, at Swarthmoor, or in the south at the homes of the daughters. The tone of their letters suggests warm affection and a tender care for each other's welfare.

Persecution Renewed

Ten days later they were off again, together for a little way, and then separating, as Margaret headed north and Fox went up to London, for more visiting and more writing. He had always been anxious that Quakers should take action against poverty and unemployment, and during this winter put out a long advice to the newly established Monthly Meetings. He wanted them to make lists of their 'poor, widows, or others that have children fit to set forth apprentices'. Most youngsters got their start in life through apprenticeships, which needed references and money. Fox thought that all Meetings should follow the example of those that were already collecting information about 'masters that be fit for them, and for such trades as their parents desire, or you desire, or the children are most inclinable for.' (N p.556). He saw in this a way to start young people in useful careers and later to have the resources to care for their parents in ill-health or age. Naturally he expected that this support would encourage the youngsters to 'come to be Friends' when they grew up, and told the Meetings that 'by this in the wisdom of God you will preserve Friends' children in the Truth.' (N. p.556) He seems to have had in mind something approaching organised occupational training, and wanted Meetings to provide funds to pay the apprenticeship premiums for poor children. He thought that any sensible community was bound to deal with these needs. To authorities this was yet another example of the Quakers's pernicious building of a state outside the control of parish and magistrate. Friends saw it both as the bringing of their everyday lives 'under the ordering of the Truth', and as a model for the whole of society. Unfortunately they were not left for long to get on with it.

In December 1669 a long letter from Fox to Margaret spoke of rumours that her son George had been scheming again with the old enemy Kirkby not only to have Swarthmoor but to get 'orders to send thee to Westchester [present-day Chester] and me to Jersey.' (Crosfield p.141). It was likely enough, for dangerous or inconvenient prisoners were sometimes sent to remote places to deter visitors and to keep them out of public view, as Fox had earlier been sent off to Scarborough. Four months later, in April 1670, he heard that Margaret had been 'haled out of her house and carried to Lancaster prison', on the old praemunire. He set up the usual counter barrage, and two of Margaret's daughters, 'by diligent attendance' at Court, got yet another order from the King for her release. However, before she was free, 'a violent storm of persecution coming suddenly on,' the hostile party 'found means to hold her still in prison'. (Ell. p.349) What had begun as a private problem, brought about by individual malice, was caught up in a fresh campaign to make life impossible for all dissenters.

The bishops and their party resented the way many Justices had been ignoring the anti-dissenter laws. They were further alarmed by the number of M.P.s who appeared to support toleration, in the debates after the first Conventicle Act expired in 1669. Archbishop Sheldon of Canterbury began to campaign for a new one, more difficult for Justices with dissenting sympathies to ignore, and succeeded in getting it through Parliament. This 'quintessence of arbitrary malice' (Marvell, Q in SPQ p.67) penalised even Justices who were slow to implement it, and allowed informers who reported an illegal meeting to keep at least a third of the fines. Naturally a collection of shady characters saw this as the way to a good income with little effort. Sheldon wrote to the bishops that,

> . . . within a few months we shall see so great an alteration in the distractions of these times, so that the seduced people returning from their seditious and time-serving teachers to the unity of the Church . . . it will be to the glory of God, the welfare of the Church, the praise of his Majesty's Government, and the happiness of the whole kingdom. (SPQ p.68)

The real result was great suffering for many people, scandalous corruption amongst the informers, and the end of all hopes that unwilling dissenters, such as the Presbyterians, could ever find a place within a national church. Nor did these activities lead to much in the way of devotional depth in the Anglican Church itself. Fox issued a statement 'to soften the magistrates'. By banning meetings of more than five people he said the Act 'would have taken hold of the *twelve* apostles', and he asked, 'Do you think that [Christ] . . . would have obeyed it? (N p.559). He also sent round another message.

> All my dear Friends, Keep in the faith in God above all outward things, and in his power. The same power and God . . . is with you to deliver you as formerly . . . and will be, when [this oppression] is gone. (N p.560)

On the Sunday after the Act came into force, the trainbands, [= militia], were mustered to deal with the rebellion that some had talked themselves into expecting, and the London streets were full of spectators. Fox and the other leading Friends went off to the various Meetings as usual. An informer brought a 'file of musketeers' to Gracechurch Street and had Fox arrested. In an argument with Fox the informer let slip that he was a Papist and, fearing the hostile crowd, thought it safer to disappear before they reached the Lord Mayor. The Mayor chose not to ask Fox awkward questions and dismissed him, along with his companion John Burnyeat. Other Justices were less sympathetic, and very many Friends were soon in prison, but Fox himself was left free and able to go on working for them. In Reading, for example, where all Friends were in custody, they asked him to join them in their Meeting for Worship. He did so, but reluctantly, on the principle that he 'would rather be taken in an open meeting than in prison' (N p.567), evidently so that he could best use any arrest to stir public opinion against the Act. After supper with Friends, Fox set off down the stairs,

> And the gaoler was standing at the door, and Friends were very fearful; so I put my hand in my pocket, which he had an eye unto, and the hope of some silver, that he forgot to question me. So I gave him some silver and bid him be kind and civil to my friends in prison whom I came to visit, and so I passed out . . . but the next that came . . . Isaac Penington, [he] caused to be made a prisoner.' (N p.567)

Just as Fox gave pursuers the slip when he could make no point by being arrested, he could also use, if not bribery, at least a little distraction.

In mid August the Gracechurch Street building was blocked off by soldiers, so that Quakers had to stay in the open street, surrounded by a curious crowd. Two speakers, William Penn and a new Quaker, William Meade, 'draper', a wealthy merchant, still called Captain, from his former rank in the City militia, were arrested. The Justices chose to charge them with a string of offences, including riot. If they had been charged under the Conventicle Act simply with attending a illegal meeting the Justices could have done what they liked, but the more serious 'riot' charge made a jury trial necessary. Juries were then only in court to do what their betters told them so that no one expected this to help the accused. Penn saw an opening. Instead of answering the charges as one offence, he dealt with them separately, and had no difficulty in showing that, whilst he had certainly been speaking in the street, there had been no riot and no weapons. The Recorder bullied his way through the hearing, but the jury unexpectedly gave a verdict of 'Speaking in Gracechurch Street'. Since this was no offence at all the Recorder told them to bring in a verdict that would suit him better. Their response was a 'Not Guilty', which riled him even more: 'You shall not think thus to abuse the court; we will have a verdict by the help of God or you shall starve for it.' As they were led off to prison for the night 'without food, fire or tobacco', as happened quite often, their leader called to Penn that they were going to stick firm. All the next day they did so, despite threats, including a furious shout from the Recorder: 'Certainly it will never be well with us until we have something like the Spanish Inquisition to be in England.' (SPQ p.72). This was a strange indiscreet outburst, for in the anti-Papist scares a few years later men were hanged for less.

The jury persisted in their 'Not Guilty', but Penn and Meade, instead of being discharged, were detained for contempt over their hats. They got out because Admiral Penn, who was dying, had the fines paid so that he could see his son again. The jury fared worse. They spent three months in prison whilst legal arguments went on, before they got bail. The next year an appeal hearing decided that a jury could not be penalised for its verdict. An essential principle of modern English law had been established by two alert Quakers and a jury of obstinate

Londoners. The judge's conduct was typical, for in many trials they twisted the law and bullied the juries to make sure of a conviction. Fox mentioned the case, but without emphasis. In the confusion of many prosecutions he apparently saw it as just another example of persecutors thwarted, and did not realise how much it would come to help everyone to have the fair trial which he thought so important. Perhaps through being out of circulation himself, he apparently also failed to recognize how much had depended on the jury and their foreman Bushell, an old republican.

Further Illness

A few weeks after the affair of Penn and Meade began, Fox was on the way back from visiting Meetings in Kent when he felt such a strange 'weight and oppression' that he could hardly sit on his horse. With his companions' help he managed to take the Thames ferry back into Essex but then collapsed and had to stay in a Friend's house at Stratford. Here he remained for several weeks, feverish and drifting in and out of consciousness, nursed by his step-daughter Margaret Rous and other women Friends. He refused to see a doctor, even a Quaker one. This may well have saved his life, for their blisterings, bleedings, purgings and strange medicines would probably have led only to a painful death. Then to everyone's dismay he asked for his clothes and insisted on being carried twelve miles in a coach to see a sick friend at Enfield. This was so obviously the last whim of a dying man that London Friends heard he was actually dead. However, during a winter spent in an Enfield Friend's house he slowly won his way out of dreams and hallucinations back to strength. These dreams seem to have reflected the distress of the persecution, with priests as man-eaters, an 'ugly, slubbering hound,' perhaps an informer, and Quakers buried 'in a mighty vault top-full of people', so that he had to ask for them to be dug out. At the other extreme he enjoyed wonderful visions of the 'New Jerusalem, which are hard to be uttered'. Because his wife was still in Lancaster prison the Rouses and others did their best to keep her in touch, reporting each slight change in his condition as hopefully as they could. Friends hardly expected that he could recover, and the authorities searching the London Meetings wondered where he had got to.

A letter of February 1671, 'To Friends at Bristol in time of Suffering', shows the stifling effect of the fresh persecution. Travel problems alone proved the need for the more local organisation Fox had been working on.

> Dear Friends . . . and you that have been public men, and formerly did travel [amongst Friends], mind to keep up your testimony . . . so that . . . all may be encouraged . . . to stand faithful to the Lord God and his Power and Truth, that their heads may not sink in the storms . . . Go into your meeting houses as at other times . . . Few travel now the countries. It may be well to visit them, lest any should faint. Stir up one another in that which is good . . . And let your minds be kept above all visible things . . . It's hard for me to give forth in writing . . . because of my bodily weakness, but I was desirous in some measure to ease my mind, that you may stand fast, and faithful to Truth . . . (Ep. 283)

The informers in Bristol were so active that they were ruining Friends. One problem centred on how to safeguard the new meeting houses, set up during the lull in harassment, or afford the huge fine of £20 a week on any owner. Friends responded to the letter by making fresh efforts to get them open again. In Cumbria, however, there was a different difficulty. A few Quaker groups, centred round the rather assertive John Story and his friend John Wilkinson, both from the early centre of Preston Patrick, took to meeting in secret, and resented persuasion to stand firm with Friends generally. For several years the resulting estrangement caused much effort and distress.

Very little got into Fox's writing of what he actually said in his more devotional ministry or prayer. From this time of difficulty and weakness he unexpectedly provided one example.

> O Lord God Almighty, prosper Truth, and preserve justice and equity in the land . . . that mercy and righteouness may flourish . . . Bring down . . . this raping spirit which causeth people to have no esteem of thee, nor of their own souls or bodies, nor of Christianity, modesty, nor humanity. And O Lord, put it into the magistrates' hearts to bring down all this ungodliness, and violence, and cruelty . . . and to put down all these whorehouses and playhouses, which do corrupt

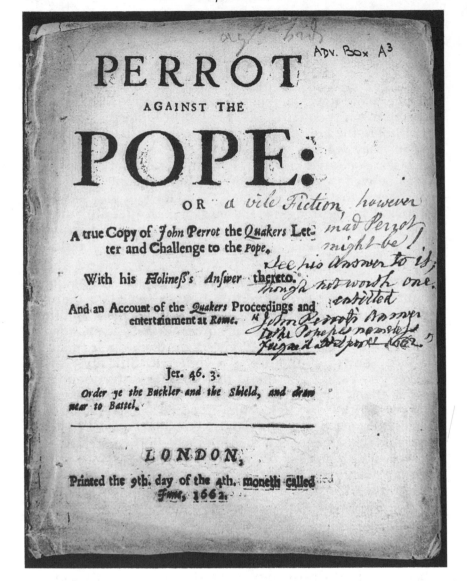

Perrot against the Pope: title page of a work attacking John Perrot

youth and people, and lead them from the Kingdom of God
. . . (N p.577)

If this may be taken as a sample of what he may have 'been
moved to give forth' in Meeting, social justice and sensible living
were evidently as much in his mind during his devotions as in
the rest of his work. The reference to playhouses should probably be taken simply as a not unreasonable comment on the only
ones he knew, the London 'Restoration Theatre'. Entertain-
ments generally were to Quakers not so much an evil as a
needless use of valuable time, better spent on more worthwhile
matters.

The New Project

As Fox convalesced, a new and even more wearing project
began to draw him. But his first problem was to get Margaret out
of prison. He sent, as usual, two women Friends to the King,
although we are never told whether simply due to their being
the people on the spot or as a discreet response to the King's
known liking for women. In early April they got a fresh order,
perhaps the more easily because George Fell had died the previous October. This included a final discharge from the praemunire, by the grant of the estate to two of Margaret's daughters.
Fox then had this taken up to her by John Stubbs, one of his
usual helpers, with a message 'that if she came up to see me she
might come with John Stubbs, for it was upon me to go beyond
the seas into America and Barbados and those countries' (N
p.579). It must have needed great devotion for her to read this
without dismay, for here was a man just getting over a nearly
fatal collapse talking of a journey where the conditions on board
ship would be worse than in prison and the travelling far more
hazardous than in Britain.

Probably to the general relief of his friends, Fox himself had
been taken by coach to stay with the Rouses in their new and
comfortable home in Kingston-on-Thames. His wife came south
and the two had the summer together. From some points of
view they made rather a strange household, for whereas Margaret was ten years older than Fox her daughter Margaret Rous
was only ten years younger. Step-son and step-daughter were

therefore only a little younger than the man they were now calling their 'dear father'. There were even grandchildren, two tod-
dlers, and a boy born to Margaret Rous a month before she had
been caught up in her nursing of Fox the previous October.

By this time the first fury of the persecution had died away
and a 'Yearly Meeting' could be held. Over the years several
gatherings, at least of ministering Friends, had come together.
The one in 1668 had agreed that others should be held yearly, but
persecution interfered. This of 1671 decided that in future years
ministering Friends and representatives from the counties
should come to London each Whitsun Week 'to advise about the
managing of the public affairs of Friends throughout the nation'
(Minutes, in SPQ p.276). The setting up of a regular annual
meeting completed the organisation Fox had spent the past four
years getting Friends to agree on. He was unusually enthusiastic. 'A mighty meeting it was, and the Lord's power was over
all and his glorious everlasting renowned Seed of life was set
over all.' (N p.579). In fact annual meetings only took place regularly from 1678, but the precedent had been made. With this
hopeful meeting over, and Margaret free, he completed the
arrangements for his voyage.

Chapter Ten

FROM BARBADOS TO WORCESTER GAOL

Voyage

On August 13th 1671, at Gravesend, Fox and his party of twelve, with a farewell escort including Penn and Margaret, boarded the *Industry*. This small ketch, probably of less than a hundred tons burden, was packed with fifty passengers, a crew of perhaps twenty, all the provisions and luggage, and perhaps some heavy cargo for ballast. Amongst the twelve, most of them old friends, were John Rous, William Edmondson, and old Elizabeth Hooton, travelling with Fox to help look after him. They were clearly a group with plenty of conversation to ease the boredom and cramped conditons of the voyage. Margaret stayed with Fox as long as she could, until, after an overnight stop at Deal, and a further farewell gathering of Friends, the boat finally set off slowly down the Channel.

Fox was already well informed about American problems. From the fifties onwards, Quaker settlers and 'publishers of Truth' had told him about their difficulties and progress, and had received from him many letters of spiritual counsel and practical advice. For his own journey he seems to have had four motives. Though Quakers always emphasised that the real guide in the religious life was the eternal Christ, everyday stresses made progress hard. The support of Meetings and the advice of more experienced Friends was therefore useful. Fox wanted to share his insights in person with as many of the new American Friends as he could. His second reason was to explain to them the value of the new networks of meetings for church affairs, on which he had just spent so much energy in England, and to help them set these up for their own benefit. Two other reasons related to less happy matters. In the West Indies and in Virginia, John Perrot, who emigrated in 1662, had been active up to his death in 1670, attracting many Friends to his views. In New England, Ranters were causing confusion. In some areas

185

Gravesend

Quakers were being harassed, although after the New England Presbyterians had been deterred from their extermination campaign there was no general persecution. Ten years before, when the difficulties had been worse, Fox assured American Friends,

> And though the oppressors of the earth will not let you have a foot of ground, yet ye have the power of God to stand in. And ye being led by the spirit of God . . . answer that of God in them all. (Ep. 216 and 217)

A final but probably very strong motive was never directly mentioned. Fox had so far spent his life on the move in Britain. Now, with such good reasons, the opportunity to experience travel of a very different kind was an irresistible challenge.

Fox was used to help with his diary, and during this journey, through the pressures of illness and work, most of the record was made by others, some of it in journal letters sent back to Margaret. A young member of the party, John Hull, wrote up a detailed log of the outward voyage. Their boat was barely seaworthy, with a long hole near the keel, 'through which little fish could swim', so that passengers and crew had to work the pumps all the time. Hull thought that the exercise kept them healthy. They were not in convoy and any strange sail might be hostile. When they feared that one vessel might be a Sallee [Arab] slaver the master came to Fox 'to advise with him', though whether for navigation, clairvoyance or prayer is not very clear. After assuring the master that 'the life was over all, and the power was between them and us', Fox more mundanely asked everyone to keep quiet and to put out all candles, and then discussed the best evasive course to steer (N p.586). The danger was real enough, for many Europeans spent time as slaves in Algiers or Moroccan Sallee, whilst waiting for ransom. Later on, English Quakers set up a fund for those who had been captured at sea, and Fox wrote to advise them how to explain themselves to the Moslems.

Everyone on board suffered from the overcrowding. 'It is a very hot time with us, especially in the cabin, being so many crowded together; and when we lay two together we were forced to part' (N p.586). Yet poor food injured them more. Shortage of fresh food led to Hull's obvious relief when they

were able to catch fish or a dolphin, 'which made us good broth'.
He added 'and lovely for variety of colours.' This remark stands
out, as the one comment of its kind, for their other preoccupa-
tions left little energy for aesthetic observation. Illnesses
endangered the party, not only seasickness and food poisoning,
but probably scurvy. Hull was especially worried by the worsen-
ing state of Fox.

> George Fox's legs begin to swell very much and very pimply,
> itching and burning much . . . George Fox . . . has been very
> much out of order , being very much in his bones . . . [He] met
> with such stinking meat, pork and beef, which caused him to
> loathe flesh a long time after. (N p.588)

If he could face them, his likely alternative was biscuit and
beans. At last, on October 3rd, they reached 'Carlisle Bay' in
Barbados.

West Indies

Fox only just survived the journey, and was confined to a
Friend's house for a month, taking hardly anything but water
with a little ginger,

> . . . for, coming weak from London . . . his old pains, and
> former bruises in his joints, all struck up to his heart and
> stomach, so that he became very weak beyond words, which
> was enough to have killed some others. (N p.591)

Fox was made far the worse by reason of the 'filth, dirt, and
unrighteousness of the people, which . . . pressed down the
spirit of God in him as a cart with sheaves.' (N p.596). When he
was able to dictate a letter he uncharacteristically admitted,

> I tired out my body much when amongst you in England. It's
> the power of the Lord that helps me . . . I hope if the Lord
> gives strength . . . I shall work thoroughly and bring things
> that have been out of course into better order . . . I rode twice
> . . . a quarter mile at a time, which tired me and wearied me.'

Naturally a postscript asked that copies 'be sent into the north to
Margaret my wife' and to the others in his family (N p.595).

Many local people were disappointed to see and hear nothing of him.

Apart from defending the Quaker position amongst those who were sceptical or hostile, they had found that Friends themselves had become slack. Perrot had not only taken to elaborate fashionable clothes and a [dress] sword, but had been telling them that attending meetings was not necessary and that they could ignore Fox's advice about such matters as oaths. The newcomers set out to show them the need to see to 'the well-ordering and managing of their affairs'. This apparently included a critical look at their sexual laxities, their financial arrangements, and their treatment of their negroes. Slavery itself was taken for granted. The New Testament raised no doubts about it, and African slaves did not seem very different from the 'indentured servants' from England, the poor people or felons who were virtually slaves during their years of unpaid labour. Fox was content to press for their moral education and humane treatment. His proposal that they should be released after thirty years servitude would at least have prevented slavery from stretching through the generations.

To counter accusations that Quakers not only rejected the Bible but were unitarians, or even atheists, the group put out a paper, 'For the Governor of Barbados, with his Council and Assembly'. In later years a number of Quaker Meetings around the world came to look on this as an acceptable summary of Christian doctrine.

> For your satisfaction, we do now plainly and sincerely declare, that we do own and believe in God, who is the creator of all things both in heaven and in the earth, and preserver of all that he hath made . . . And we do own and believe in Jesus Christ, his beloved and only-begotten Son . . . who was conceived by the Holy Ghost, and born of the Virgin Mary, in whom we have redemption through his blood, even the forgiveness of sins: who is the express image of the invisible God . . . who knew no sin . . . and was crucified for us in the flesh . . . and rose again the third day, by the Power of his Father, for our justification. And we do believe that he ascended into heaven . . .

> This Jesus . . . is our foundation . . . our wisdom and righteousness, justification and redemption . . . It is he alone,

who is the shepherd and bishop of our souls, and our prophet
. . . He rules in our hearts by his law of love and of life, and
makes us free from the law of sin and death . . . for he is the
quickening spirit, the second Adam, the Lord from Heaven
. . . He is our mediator . . . the oath of God, the New Covenant
of Light, Life, Grace and Peace, the author and finisher of our
faith. This Lord Jesus Christ, the Heavenly Man, the Eman-
uel, we all own and believe in . . . And after he was risen from
the dead, the Acts of the Apostles sets forth how the Chief-
Priests and Elders persecuted the disciples of this Jesus, for
preaching Christ and his resurrection. This, we say is that
Lord Jesus Christ, whom we own to be our life and salvation.
(Ell. p.358 - 9).

It is easy to think that of these two paragraphs, the second more
strongly reflects Fox's own experience and language.

From these basic matters he turned abruptly to a quite different charge, the treatment of negroes, with a vigour which
suggests that local hostility was due as much to this as to differences of theology. After admitting that Quakers wanted negroes
treated humanely, he denounced, as 'a most egregrious and
abominable untruth . . . which we do utterly abhor and detest',
that Friends taught the negroes to rebel (N p.604). Interference
with slavery was evidently taken as an intolerable attack on the
basis of the new West Indian sugar plantation economy.

However unlikely it may have seemed when he landed, Fox
recovered so completely that by the end of the year he was riding
round to Meetings with much of his old vigour. After three
months, leaving behind only Stubbs and another, who was
'often very weakly', to continue the work, the party felt free to
move on. On January 8th, 1672, they began the ten day voyage
to Jamaica, their ship still leaking so much that the carpenter
dived over the side to hammer oakum into the hole, and surfaced shouting hopefully that he had made her 'as tight as a dish'
(N p.610).

A brief letter to Margaret, 'My dear Heart', reported from
Jamaica that 'Friends here are generally well, and here is a convincement . . . At the beginning of the next month we shall pass
towards Maryland, if the Lord please' (N p.611). The fifteen
thousand settlers, in an island captured from Spain in 1655 by

William Penn's father, were prosperous, peaceful and fairly tolerant. Many took to Quakerism through Fox's visit, so that Friends were active there for the rest of the century. The party unexpectedly lost Elizabeth Hooton, who died suddenly, 'in peace like a lamb', after her long and strenuous life. Leaving behind someone as usual to continue the work, they took passage to Virginia, choosing a ketch because the fare was ten shillings [fifty pence] cheaper than on a frigate. Their voyage had its considerable dangers and delays, both from calms and gales, so that they took seven weeks to reach Chesapeake Bay, the great inlet which gave access to Virginia and Maryland, about midway along the line of English settlements from Carolina to New England. Another gale nearly wrecked them and, after they had taken on board some local people whose boat had sunk, their own food ran out. They were happy to reach the Patuxent River, a haven used by boats loading tobacco, on the west side of the bay, (south of modern Baltimore).

North American Settlements

John Burnyeat had found during his own visit to Maryland in 1665 that 'the greater part of Friends were led astray by J. Perrot . . . and had ceased meetings and become careless.' (Burnyeat p.33). Returning in 1671 for a further tour, he was pleased to find Friends 'restored to zeal and great openness.' As soon as Fox got to shore he was told of a General Meeting sixty miles away, which Burnyeat had arranged as a final event before he left the colony. Though he admitted to being unwell and weary, Fox hurried there and found the effort worth while, for 'a glorious meeting we had of it', with many of the colony's notables taking part. In the 'men's and women's business meetings' which followed he was able to 'open to Friends the service thereof, and all were satisfied.' (N p.616). It was an important gathering to Quakers, to which the present-day Baltimore Yearly Meeting can be traced back. The party then moved on, to a meeting at which 'many of the world's people' received 'the Truth with gladness and reverence'. Friends who had been 'backsliders' had their enthusiasm or understanding revived, and Fox was able to set up several 'men's and women's meetings' (N p.617). The members of his party then set off in different directions. He

George Fox preaching at Flushing, USA. After an old drawing (c.1800) in the possession of Haverford College Library.

crossed to the east shore of the Bay, to the Choptank River settlement, to another enthusiastic rally (' very great heavenly meeting'). Here he heard that far to the north, at Rhode Island, a 'Half-yearly General Meeting' was due.

His decision to try to take part in it meant a rushed ten day ride, northwards across the Delaware and through the unexplored woods of New Jersey, with much ferrying in canoes and swimming of horses across rivers. A Friend took them over the New York bay to Long Island, where the next day, 'though very weary', Fox rode forty miles to a General Meeting, on May 17th. His presence kept Friends together for nearly a week. Not everything was straightforward, for here too some disliked both the self-discipline and the work of the men's and women's meetings, but he considered that his explanation of these matters 'was of great service to Truth and satisfaction and comfort to

Friends.' (N p.620). The party then moved on across the island for a public meeting, where the townspeople 'were much satisfied . . . and said that if I came to their town I should have their meeting place.' (N p.630).

The party sailed the final hundred miles down Long Island Sound to Rhode Island, 'weary with travelling', but grateful that they had survived the dangers and happy at their friendly welcome. It was a new experience for Fox to be in a place where Quakers were amongst the people in authority, amongst them his host, Nicholas Easton, the Governor. The General Meeting turned into a great rally of Friends from all the neighbouring colonies, an exhilarating experience for them all, for Fox enjoyed their welcome, and they had with them the man they had known only from his writings and the report of others.

> And when it was ended it was hard for Friends to part, for the glorious power of the Lord was over all and his blessed Truth and life flowing amongst them had so knit and united them together that they spent two days in leavetaking . . . (N p.621)

Stubbs reported in a long and breathless letter to Margaret Fox,

> It was a glorious a time as ever I saw since I owned the Truth - some of us went and settled the meeting every day, - and then thy husband came into the Meeting, - the body of the whole island as it were came in to hear, of all sorts high and low - they have no priest on the island so there is no restriction . . . Thy husband stood up every Meeting several hours together . . . all eyes were upon him, and expectations and affections both towards him . . . Words are too narrow and short to demonstrate Truth's prosperity in general in these parts . . . (CJ II p.204-5)

It was not surprising therefore that Edmondson should write to Margaret that he had not seen 'thy dear husband . . . more healthy and cheery than for some years, of which we were all very glad' (N p.627).

One disturbance came from some noisy Ranters, who were, as in England, often confused with Friends. Years later, for example, in 1687, a New York Governor listed them as 'Singing Quakers, Ranting Quakers' (QAC p.234). When Fox arranged a meeting among them he expected trouble, but 'knew that the Lord would give me power over them, and he did, to his praise and glory' (N p.622). Another not impressed by Fox was the founder of the colony, Roger Williams, who had been in London, stirring up controversy about toleration, when the young Fox first reached there. He was far from being satisfied that in his book, *The Great Mistery*, Fox had answered all the objections to Quakerism, and came up with a list of fourteen propositions. For example,

V. Their principles and professions are full of contradictions and hypocrisies.

X. The Popes of Rome do not swell with and exercise a greater pride than the Quaker spirit hath expressed . . . although many humble souls may be captivated amongst them, as in other religions.

XI. The Quakers' Religion is more obstructive and destructive of the conversion and salvation of the souls of people than most of the religions this day extant in the world.

XIII. Their many books and writings are extremely poor, lame, naked, and swelled up with high titles and words of boasting . . . (QAC p.117)

He challenged Fox to a debate, but he had alrady left and others agreed to take his place. A great crowd listened for several days, but, like many such confrontations, as a discussion of principles it was a fiasco. The Quakers said Williams ran on without covering his points. His comments, in his own account of the debate, give a brief glimpse of them. Burnyeat was 'a moderate spirit and an able speaker', and Edmondson a 'stout, portly man of a great voice', who 'would stop my mouth with a very unhandsome clout of a grievous interruption'. (QAC. p.116) The title of his book, *Fox Digged out of his Burrows*, was meant as a sarcastic joke, for Edward *Burrough* had written the Introduction to Fox's own work. Yet, though biased, these Propositions showed that Quakers could upset more than their regular enemies amongst the priests and the establishment. Williams, after all, was both able and moderate.

In June Fox had a meeting, at Providence, about which he 'had a great travail, in having and preserving it quiet, and for the bringing of Truth over them and in them'. He recalled that in the heat of a crowded barn he 'was so hot with sweat as though [he] had been sodden, but all was well' (N p.623). Other members of the party even had a meeting near Boston, where the Presbyterians had hanged Quakers who tried to infiltrate the colony, until Charles II had checked them, and they had to be content with flogging them through each village to the boundary. In the mid 1660s, old Elizabeth Hooton, one of those determined to defy the penalty until the persecutors were shamed out of their cruelty, had suffered ten strokes at each township, and even been left overnight in the woods, apparently in the hope that she would not survive. If Fox appeared sceptical about priests it has to be remembered that many he knew defended their principles, or their authority, by inciting people to sadistic brutality. At another place, where the people wished they had money enough to hire him as pastor, he replied,

> . . . that it was time for me to go away, for then they would not come to their own teacher, [i.e. the Spirit or Light of Christ within them], for hiring had spoiled them, and many [others, into] not improving their own talents.

He reminded them of his principle that Quakers set out to bring 'everyone to the Light of the eternal Christ within them.' (N p.534).

In late July Fox began the return journey south, by coaster to New Jersey and overland to the Delaware, and then through the woods to the eastern shore of the Chesapeake. On the way he found one enemy even he could not resist: when 'we went on shore at night we were not able to stay for the mosquitoes, so we went on the sloop again and put off from the shore and cast anchor and stayed all that night.' (N p.625). At a settlement called Shrewsbury, where 'they are building a meeting house', the first in the new colony of East Jersey, an accident to one of the party led to Fox's strangest venture into medicine, and caused a great stir. Whilst the man was trying out a fresh horse it bolted and threw him, apparently breaking his neck, for his head 'turned like a cloth it was so loose'. Throwing down his 'stick and gloves', Fox got some purchase against a tree and 'wrested his head two or three times with all my strength, and brought it in, and I did perceive his neck began to be stiff, and then he began to rattle, and after to breathe.' (N p.632). When he came to, they sat him by a fire, gave him a warm drink, put him to bed and wrapped up his neck. Next day the man rode, 'pretty well', sixteen miles. The man's feelings were not recorded. It was a desperate venture into bone-setting, and suggests that Fox had not only great confidence but some experience of manipulation.

The incident gives another brief glimpse of Fox the man. Why the gloves in a warm September? Certainly not for fashion. Did he therefore need them for riding, or to protect crippled fingers? And was the stick just for the rough ground or for his rheumatism? A century later an American Friend, visiting descendents of Fox's younger brother John, saw

> . . . the staff, it is said, George Fox used to travel with - a large cane stick about four feet [over a metre] in length, and ivory head - looked as though it might have belonged to a country squire (CJ II p.489)

The American thought it might have come from Judge Fell, but if it were a genuine heirloom it recalls the one that Fox's father threw down in excitement during his son's debate with Priest Stephens.

This dislocated neck was only the most spectacular of the misfortunes for which Fox gave relief by visiting a patient or by laying on of hands. Later in the tour, for example, he helped a depressive,

> . . . a woman who had been many years in trouble and would . . . sit moping two months together and hardly speak or mind any thing. And so I was moved to go to her and tell her that salvation was come to her house, and did speak other words to her and for her; and from that hour she mended and passed up and down with us to meetings, and is well, blessed be the Lord (N p.652)

At another Maryland General Meeting, the thousand or so Friends and others present were especially impressed by Fox's knowledge of the Bible, almost amounting to total recall.

They said they had never heard the Scriptures opened so clearly before, for, said they, 'He hath them at his finger's ends, and as a man should read them in a book and hold it open before him'. (N p.636)

A month later, in November, he set out on the second half of his tour, southwards into Virginia, and then, mostly by boat along the coast, further south to the small Quaker settlements in North Carolina, where his reception was as friendly as on his northward journey. In December he began the return northwards, by way of the Virginian coast, with a remark on the unfamiliar changes of climate. By early January 1673, despite troubles through impassible snow and frozen creeks, he was back at his mid-point on the Patuxent. His many references to cold and heat, or to sleeping in wet and dirty clothes by a fire in the woods, as well as to sweating after speaking, probably reveal that his rheumatism would not let him forget it. One loss at this time cannot have helped him to keep clean or warm. His party stored their heavy luggage with a Friend, whose house was set on fire in this midwinter by a careless 'wench'. Fox's 'great chest was burned . . . and all the clothes in our chests.' (N p.649). It was lucky that this happened so late in their stay.

Fox had now completed two circuits through the settlements, one to the north as far as New England, and the second south into Carolina. The two journeys together form a sort of figure of eight, with the Chesapeake Bay as the centre point. The remaining months of his stay he spent in Maryland, occupied, as soon as the weather relaxed, in what from the Quaker point of view may have been the most productive period of the whole tour, as he took part in many Meetings, helped to set up more, and gave useful advice. People came great distances to meet and hear him and, even if his own happiness and relief at the welcome is discounted, it is clear that those who met him responded to a wisdom and a charisma they had not met before. His many talks with people in authority may not have led them to join with Friends, but cleared away misunderstandings and satisfied them that Quakers need not be treated as rebels, atheists, or ranters.

His year in North America would have been extremely strenuous even in our own time. Yet his party travelled through

untouched forests and waterways, where every one of the hundreds of miles had to be walked or ridden or paddled. Even if he
were uncertain about the animals, the dangers were real,

> . . . through perils of wolves, bears, tigers and lions; and . . .
> rattlesnakes and other venomous creatures; through great
> swamps, and bogs . . . where no way was . . . where we
> lodged in the nights by fires; and perils over great bays,
> creeks, and rivers in open and small boats and small canoes
> . . . and great perils through the Indian companies . . . by man
> eaters . . . and through the cold . . . in lying in the woods and
> wildernesses . . . until some of our company had their hands
> and fingers benumbed . . . (N p.661)

In one way he showed himself a man of his time: he paid no
attention to the appearance of his surroundings. Getting safe to
camp mattered, not the beauty of the trees, even in autumn.
Once, when they 'were very hard put to it for provisions,' his
companions left him to rest.

> . . . I was sitting on a tree a pretty way off where Friends
> looked to their horses . . . and our guides went to the Indian
> houses to get some victuals, and there came a straggling
> Indian to me, and . . . he began to grope me and . . . said I was
> good blood. And it was upon me to see what he would do, for
> though I was alone I was out of all fear, and at last I lifted up
> my hand to the heaven and down to the earth and told him
> that the great God would burn him. And so another came to
> him and they whispered together and went away, and there
> came an Indian king to me and about 70 people and were very
> civil . . . (CJ II p.445)

Steady nerves were needed, and perhaps, placed as he was in
the unknown, Fox could be allowed a touch of psychological
intimidation.

Yet he did not avoid Indians. All through the tour, near
settlements or in their own villages, he tried to get to know
them. Through interpreters he tried to explain Quaker views,
and even to teach them to worship in the Quaker way. He seems
always to have taken them seriously and treated them with respect. They usually responded with equal courtesy, although

without much change in their views. Up in New England one gave Fox his judgement on Christians, telling him that if the Indians went with the 'professors' [here the Presbyterians] they became worse than they were before, and if they turned 'to the Quakers, which was the best', the 'professors' would 'put them to death and banish them as they did the Quakers, and therefore he thought it best to be as he was.' (N p.624). Nevertheless it is tempting to wonder whether the memory of these favourable contacts helped William Penn in his later dealings with the Indians.

At last, on May 21st, Fox and two others were taken down river, to the *Society of Bristol*, which was to carry them, and probably a cargo of tobacco, to England. This was therefore likely to have been a larger vessel than the *Industry*, and without leaks, because sea water would ruin her costly freight. The voyage was quiet, apart from a storm, which made the Quakers sit up in their beds when it roared like enemy cannon. Though they had chosen not to sail in convoy, the few ships seen fortunately proved not to be hostile, neither Dutch, nor Spanish, nor pirate. On his own return the summer before Rous had been less lucky. 'Some hours before we expected to see land, we fell into the hands of a Dutch privateer, who took us and carried us to Spain, where we continued about 17 days, and at last came away in a vessel I bought for our transportation . . .' (Ross p.242). Twenty five years later, another crossing ended in the disappearance of the ship and Rous's own death at sea. With such risks, when Fox's party reached Bristol on June 28th, he might well say, 'Blessings and praises and thanks be to the Lord for ever and ever' (N p.660).

Home

Whilst Fox had been away the fortunes of Quakers had gone almost a full circle. In March 1672 Charles had issued a Declaration of Indulgence. This was an attempt to use his royal prerogative to override Parliament and allow some freedom to dissenters, including Quakers, although he was chiefly trying to help Catholics. Friends, led by George Whitehead, got the King to agree that all Quakers in prison should be released, and after six months of negotiation, the Great Pardon, with its list of

nearly five hundred names, had the Great Seal on it, and could
be carried round the country, or shown to Sheriffs when they
came to London. The move benefited other imprisoned dissenters, who first thought of asking for a separate pardon, but
then realised that they might be caught with a change of policy
before it was ready, and accepted the offer of Friends to include
their names on the Quaker list. One notable prisoner freed in
this way was John Bunyan, after his twelve years in gaol for
refusing an undertaking to give up preaching.

Caution was well justified, for the war Charles had started
against the Dutch went badly and his secret paymaster Louis
XIV did not give him enough subsidy. To get money he had to
recall Parliament, and this compelled him in March 1673 to
revoke the Indulgence, both as unconstitutional and as giving
too much toleration. Two Bills were introduced into Parliament,
one to allow toleration, on much the same conditions as the later
Act of 1689, and the other to make an oath, unambiguously
rejecting Catholic doctrines and endorsing those of the Anglicans, a condition for holding any public office. The first was
rejected; the second became the *Test Act*, which, with its successors, excluded not only Catholics but dissenters from public life.
No immediate burst of persecution followed, but newly opened
meeting houses became illegal again, and opponents who chose
to cause trouble felt free to act. These reactionary changes happened whilst Fox was on his way home, and the news must have
deeply disappointed him.

On his first evening ashore Fox wrote to Margaret,

Dear Heart, This day we came to Bristol again near night, from
the seas; glory to the Lord God over all for ever, who was our
convoy, and steered our course; the God of the whole earth, of
the seas and winds, who made the clouds his chariots beyond
all words . . .
I intend (if the Lord will) to stay a while thisaway; it may be till
the fair. So no more, but my love to all Friends, G.F.

After the weeks of buffeting and helplessness in the frail ship his
relief led him to a little psalm of rejoicing, with the contemporary
touch of God as 'convoy'. The fair was a month ahead, and gave
time for all his family and friends to gather, from Margaret, with

two of her daughters and Thomas Lower, to Rous, Penn, and many others from London. Quakers often met at fairs, which conveniently brought people together for both private and business purposes. This Bristol reunion of Friends was evidently a very happy time, with Meetings 'when many deep and precious things were opened'. Filled with confidence, he was able to exclaim: 'And we can challenge all the world: Who hath anything to say against our Way, our Saviour, our prophet, leader and counseller?' Yet old difficulties soon surfaced.

More Friction between Friends

Any growth can lead to strain or resentments, as people face the clash between their old attitudes and their new principles. The harsh conditions made tensions even more likely. As Fox returned to England, although the difficulties over the 'disintegrating tendencies of Perrot's negative mysticism' (SPQ. p.294) were dying down, in part through the work of the new business meetings, a fresh grievance was developing. In spite of their value in helping Friends made poor, or in other trouble through persecution, some saw these meetings as a centralising move, which might even lead to authoritarian synods like those of the Presbyterians. One statement drawn up for a conference on the problem directly attacked Fox.

> We are not satisfied that George Fox hath of late been guided by the Spirit of Truth in all such matters relating to the Truth wherein of late he hath concerned himself; neither are we satisfied that those who have of late looked upon him as a man worthy of double honour and owned him in all such matters, have had therein a spiritual deserving . . . (PWP p.521)

During the efforts to achieve a reconciliation several lists of the complaints were made. They included such points as these: the objectors saw no use for Women's (business) meetings, especially if, for example, *men* were expected to put their marriage plans to them; they disliked business meetings open to all Friends; they thought that Friends should be dealt with gently who had paid tithes, or met in secret to avoid fines under the (second) Conventicle Act, in order 'not to make things easy for any informer that thirsteth after our estates'. They therefore objected to any public rebuking of those who had bent under persecution, even if this weakening had made things harder for the many Friends who did resist. A minor complaint, which nevertheless shows what sometimes went on in Meetings, was about 'groaning, singing or sounding' whilst anyone was speaking or praying (SPQ p.298)).

This unhappy dispute dragged on through the decade. Although it was called the Wilkinson - Story separation, or the affair of the 'two Johns', from their shared first name, a Bristol Friend, William Rogers, also had a great deal to say. The efforts to restore understanding and unity cost many of the leading Friends much distress and work. Fortunately these were successful and by the next decade only a few kept up their grievance. Fox himself, perhaps because he had been accused of provoking the trouble, usually stayed in the background, and expected Margaret to do the same.

Worcester Gaol and a Legal Tangle

When he had 'finished his service' in Bristol, Fox set off for London, on the way having a meeting with some of his critics, at which he believed 'occasion was offered to answer their objections and to open the services of women in and for the Church.' This was something about which he had no reservations. In his early life there had been his mother. Later on Margaret and her daughters had shown how capable women could be, as they coped with legal problems for themselves and for Quakers, administered Quaker funds, and ran their own estates with great efficiency. The prejudice against women had little logic, for many Friends had reason to respect the women who managed their families' farms and workshops, often for years, whilst their husbands were in gaol or away as travelling ministers.

Fox met Margaret and Rachel again at Kingston, and then moved on to London, for more controversial writing, more public meetings, and more help to Friends in prison. A fresh ground for resentment had now arisen. Fox's 'testimony' that the 'heathens' and Papists' holy days' were not mentioned by the 'true Christians' of the New Testament, and that in the life of the 'spirit of Truth' all days were equal, led Quakers to ignore the customary anniversaries. When the increasing number of

Quaker shopkeepers kept their shops open whilst others were closed the aversion to seeing another man get an advantage in trade sharpened religious or social dislike. In the careful logic with which Quakers turned their principles into action they sometimes failed to notice how other people might be affected, or even injured.

Fox then set out for the north with Margaret and others, including Thomas Lower. They moved by easy stages, staying with old friends on the way, including William and Gulielma Penn, in their large house at Rickmansworth. Fox had began to have premonitions of prison, although he kept silent and did not alter the route. Although he treated these impressions as second sight, it was always likely that his mere arrival in a county would provoke some Justice to have him arrested. Nevertheless his party travelled on, reaching Armscott in Worcestershire, where Friends had been holding enthusiastic meetings, allegedly of up to four hundred people. Fox took part in one, and was afterwards relaxing with friends in his host's parlour, when the local Justice, Henry Parker, arrived, arrested both Fox and Lower and sent them to Worcester Gaol.

When this interruption came on December 17th, 1673, Fox and Margaret were intending to finish the journey separately, the women directly north to Swarthmoor with Lower as escort, whilst Fox turned across country to visit his mother, who was believed to be nearing death, and then back to London. His letter to Margaret at Swarthmoor suggests that she had disagreed with his persistence about their route.

> Dear Heart, Thou seemedst to be a little grieved, when I was speaking of prisons and when I was taken thou began to fall upon me with blaming of me, and I told thee I was to bear it, and why couldst thou not be content with the will of God. (HJC Narr. Pap. p.112)

Perhaps she thought he had done enough and should have 'felt freedom' to avoid capture in order to rest and regain health at Swarthmoor.

Parker had very flimsy grounds for his charges: that the coming to the parish of teachers 'from remote parts of the kingdom . . . tends to the prejudice of the reformed and established

religion and may prove prejudicial to the public peace'; that Fox
had spoken at a meeting of over two hundred people, and that
Fox and Lower were vagrants. The defendants easily refuted all
these: there was no evidence of civil unrest; they had not been
seen at a meeting; and their home addresses were in the very
warrant. Not all the Justices agreed with Parker's action and sent
a message that if they 'spoke little and did not provoke' the
Justices, they could expect to be freed at the January Sessions.
Fox said he behaved there like a lamb! However, when Parker
saw that they might escape he whispered to the Chairman, who
said,

> You, Mr Fox, are a famous man, and all this may be true . . .
> but that we may be better satisfied, will you take the Oath of
> Allegiance?

As always, Fox refused, gave his reasons and offered an affirmation, but the damage was done and the Justices ordered the
gaoler to take him to prison.

They then discharged Lower, so that he had no need to use
a letter from the King, obtained by his brother Richard, a distinguished doctor and royal physician, which would have assured
his release. He refused to go, insisting that his business was to
'wait upon' his father in prison (Ell. p.392). Parker then came out
with what may well have underlain the whole trouble. The parish priest had complained to him that because of the great
Quaker meetings at Armscott 'he had lost the greatest part of his
parishioners . . . and hath scarce any auditors left.' Lower
replied,

> I have heard that the priest . . . comes . . . but once or twice a
> year to gather up his tithes, [so] that it was but charity in my
> father to visit such a forlorn and forsaken flock.

The resulting laughter surprised him. He had not realised that
this was 'notoriously known to be true', or that the very priest
was in the room and hearing it all (Ell. p.393).

Then began a year's legal wrangle. The problem was less
one of how to keep Fox in custody than of how to untie the legal
knots so that he could be free. The first move was to get him
away from Parker, by obtaining a writ of *Habeas Corpus* from the

King's Bench Court in London. When this came through, after Fox had been a month in custody, the Undersheriff showed the absurdity of the charge by actually making Lower his deputy to escort Fox. They travelled by stage coach because Fox was not strong enough to ride, and Lower had been unable to find a private coach. Fox commented that 'the ways were very deep and the waters out' (N p.681). The easy way out would have been to have the case quashed by finding some error in the writ, and Fox was told this might be done. But Parker had also come to London, to play on the plot phobias of the four Judges with a story that at Armscott Fox had been meeting many people 'out of several parts of the nation, and that we had a plot or design in hand; and that Lower stayed . . . long after he was set at liberty, to carry on our design' (Ell. p.395). He asked that the case should be returned to Worcester. In his letter to Margaret, Fox drily turned some London Friends, who mistakenly thought they could get Parker's sympathy, into countrymen struggling unsuccessfully to control an unruly bullock.

> . . . And here you may see R.C. and Ellis Hookes was lugging at the tail, and plucked me into the ditch, who had such a confidence in deceitful Parker. (HJC Narr Pap. p.116)

Fox told them that they might as well tender him the Oath and praemunire him themselves as send him to have it done at Worcester. Their only concession was that he might make his own way back. At the end of March he 'went down leisurely (for I was not able to abide hasty and hard travel)'. In Worcester the Assize Judge was Turner, who had once praemunired him and Margaret in Lancaster, but this time, despite interference from Parker, he merely returned the case full circle back to the Quarter Sessions. Fox 'had the liberty of the town for my health's sake' (N p.687), until these were due at the end of April. When he was of course found guilty of refusing the Oath he used another delaying tactic by 'traversing', or getting an adjournment till the next Sessions. Because bail implied guilt he refused it, although in a striking expression of local sympathy the gaoler's son had offered to be his surety. Yet only two hours later he was released, 'through the moderation of some of the Justices'. Fox then went to London, and took part in the Quaker Yearly Meeting in May.

Some Friends now got a fresh *Habeas Corpus* writ, but again the
the case was returned to Worcester, putting Fox to the effort of
another journey. At the July Sessions, when the jury queried the
charge, the Judge put pressure on them to give a guilty verdict so
that he could praemunire Fox. Somebody later told him the
Judge had said he should lie in prison and rot. This was so real a
prospect that it accounts for the vigour and the complexity of the
campaign for his release.

He now looked likely to be in prison for a long time, and
Margaret rode down to stay near him in Worcester. Because of
his poor health, he was soon allowed to lodge outside the
prison, on an order grudgingly signed by Parker. Release now
depended on the favour of the King, and Friends began to prepare appeals, though even they got into a muddle. In September
one of his friends, Thomas Moore, wrote to Fox that others 'had
got thither before me (out of true love to thee)' and had accepted
from his minister, Lord Arlington, a promise of release, but only
on conditions which he knew Fox would never accept. The next
day he 'went to the King . . . to destroy what was done by
Friends before and put the business of thy release on a new and
more firm bottom. The King told me he was glad to see me,' [and
that he should return the next day]. When Moore reported to
Fox three weeks later he had a long tale of interviews, contradict-
ory conditions, and the 'King's having forgotten what he had
done . . . a day or two before.' (CJ II p.302)

One stumbling block was that, despite his poor health, Fox
was still refusing the easy way out, a pardon, because of its
implied guilt. Quakers must have seemed a puzzling people, for
two years earlier Whitehead had been quite ready to accept that
term in his negotiations about the Great Pardon, even checking
his companion when he had made difficulties, and assuring the
King:

> It is not for us to . . . dictate to the King and his Council what
> methods to take for our Friends' discharge; they know best
> their own methods in point of law; we seek the end thereof,
> the effectual discharge of our suffering Friends. (Whitehead
> p.352)

Perhaps Whitehead wished that Fox might be a little less uncompromising, for the difficulties multiplied, especially as they had to prevent the King from realising that Fox would turn down the royal but fickle clemency. Friends also hesitated to have Fox again before the King's Bench, fearing that a sentence of prae-munire from that Court would be harder to overturn.

However, in January 1675, Fox was brought back to London on a fresh *Habeas Corpus* writ. His new Counsel, an able lawyer who came often to act for Quakers, put forward two arguments, the routine one about technical errors in the documents, and a much more daring challenge to the praemunire legislation itself, that the earlier act which allowed imprisonment had expired, without being renewed in later Acts. The Judges, thoroughly disconcerted at the prospect of numerous similiar appeals, adjourned overnight whilst they read up the matter, and the next day got rid of the problem by using errors in the writs to withdrew the charges against Fox. Once more his obstinacy, at the risk of his health or life had successfully won him freedom without compromise. During this fourteen months imprison-ment Fox was actually in gaol, in several stints, for little over half the time. Gaolers and officials treated him as well as they could, so that he suffered less from cold and neglect. Moreover, he had first Lower, and then Margaret, to support him. In London, Friends, who by now had considerable expertise, and the all-important contacts, were working for him, so that he and Mar-garet had been spared some of the burden.

From prison he sent out, to all Friends, one of his most moving and personal letters, 'Given forth in the time of his sick-ness in Worcester Prison'. In this he defended himself against the accusations of pride, and pointed out the value to Quaker work and witness of the meetings and arrangements he had been advocating.

And therefore it concerns all, that profess themselves to be ministers, to be humble, else they are no learners of Christ, not to be harsh nor high-minded, but walk as examples . . . And you have known the manner of my life, the best part of thirty years . . . I sought not myself, I sought you and his glory that sent me; and when I turned you to him, that is able to save you, I left you to him. And my travels hath been great, in hungers and colds, when there was few . . . that I often lay in woods and commons in the night . . . and prisons have been made my home a great part of my time, and in danger of my life, and in jeopardy daily. And amongst you I have made myself of no reputation, to keep the Truth in reputation, as you all very well know it . . . And so I passed through very great sufferings in my body, as you have been sensible. And few at the first took care for the establishing Men and Women's Meetings, though they were generally owned [= accepted] when they understood them; but the everlasting God . . . sent me forth . . . first to declare his everlasting Gospel, and then, after people had received the Gospel . . . to go through the nation, to advise them to set up the Men's Meetings and the Women's . . . (Ep. 308)

Chapter Eleven

PRIVATE LIFE AND POLITICS

Private Matters

Fox and his wife kept up a sort of amicable contest: she was always trying to help him and he was determined to stay clear of her fortune. The letter in which he referred to her displeasure at his Worcester detention went on to mention 'the three pound thou didst send up to me in love.' He promptly turned it into a present of equal value for her.

> I did speak to a Friend to send thee as much Spanish black cloth as will make thee a gown and it did cost us a pretty deal of money. (N p.681)

He ended with a dismissive comment on a very different matter.

> I hear of a ship of Thomas Edmondson's that is cast away, which I had a part in, but let it go . . .

This gives another clue to his worldly standing. Shipowners liked to reduce their risks by dividing them amongst investors, who paid from a half to a sixty-fourth of the cost of buying vessels and fitting them out for voyages. These shares or 'parts' became a favourite form of investment, because, unlike partnerships, their risk was limited. A single share seems to have cost about fifty pounds. Successful trading voyages could bring very high rates of return, but the risks, with about 5% of vessels wrecked every year, meant that sometimes everything was lost. Fox was not deterred. According to a list of his property in 1685 he had shares in two ships, for which he had paid £38. 7s. 6d. [£38.37p] and £85 (CJ II p.354).

The relationship between two such strong personalities as Fox and Margaret had its moments of tension. When she tried to help over some aspect of the Women's Meeting problem, he evidently thought that her intervention might be seen as high-handed, and said so.

. . . I desire you may be wise and if you do leave Westmorland [in Cumbria] Women's Meetings to themselves awhile and let their spirits cool, Life will arise over all. (HJC. Narr Pap. p.118)

Although he would not take her money he felt free to question her use of it. During the Worcester dispute he wrote from London about some complication over the cost of a new 'meeting place'. In some interlocking transaction the Friend trying to raise the money had apparently lent £100 to Margaret, which Fox felt obliged to repay.

Because I put you to borrow of her I could not but in conscience see her paid . . . and here is her bond with the seals off . . . so come no more in debt in London. (N p.694)

A month later, perhaps after a reply from Margaret or Sarah, he softened his views on the Westmorland affair, but not on the borrowing.

Dear Heart, to whom is my love . . . if thou findeth it lieth upon thee thou may go over to the women's meeting . . . I would not have you . . . borrow money in the country for me to pay me . . . But I would have you to pay them at London that which you have promised there, or anywhere else, according to your time and word . . . I was at Kingston two nights, and [the Rouses] are well. And next 5th day I set forward to Worcester. So in haste, my love to you all, for I am fitting for my journey, (HJC p.121)

The incident suggests that Fox himself was in a position to put up the £100, which by contemporary values was a large amount of capital.

Fox was always eager that all Friends, not only his wife, should neither borrow nor spend beyond their resources. Yet the affairs of one prominent associate, William Penn himself, might well have troubled him at this time. Penn suffered through fines, and gave generously to needy Friends, but his own papers show that he both neglected his accounts and lived extravagantly, at times spending twice his income. At this period he kept himself solvent only by selling part of his wife's property. Fox was often at his home, but there seems to be no record of any caution given to him, although one might have been justified, for Penn's generosity, hard work, and flow of ideas were apparently not backed by comparable skills over money or administration, at least of his own affairs.

Swarthmoor Retreat

Lower, already with his family at Marsh Grange, wrote at the news of 'my father's full and honourable discharge',

> And now we are in hopes of seeing our dear father and thee return into these parts . . . not daring to desire or invite him . . . but only to express how glad we should be of such a blessing if the Lord see it meet and make his way clear. (CJ II p.307)

Sarah Fell concentrated on practical matters, her other sisters' movements, and then a list of provisions to be sent up to Swarthmoor:

> We desire to know as soon as thou can, when we may expect you with our dear father . . . And thou shouldst buy us a cask of wine, of what sort thou judgest father would like best . . . also some anchovies, some olives . . . some oranges and lemons, and what else you should think fit. (Ross p.256)

She evidently intended to give Fox a taste of luxury.

But they had to wait. From Worcester, Fox went slowly to London, rested with the Rouses at Kingston, 'for I was very weak', attended Yearly Meeting, lobbied Parliament and began to hope that some relief might be allowed, at least about affirmations instead of oaths. When the session was broken up and they 'had done nothing for Friends or against Friends' he 'was clear of his service for the Lord at London and so . . . I took coach towards the north with Margaret and her daughter Susan, for I was not able to travel on horseback.' (N p.706). It was something of a triumphal progress, with frequent stops and greetings from Friends who came to see him on the way. Most of the Swarthmoor household met him at Lancaster, of unhappy memories, and they all rode back home over the Sands, arriving on June 25th, 1675.

Fox settled at Swarthmoor for nearly two years, the longest rest in his life. In the eyes of the local gentry he had become 'master' of Swarthmoor, to whom some respect was now due, and one of the strangest incidents was a courtesy visit from Colonel Kirkby, to 'bid me welcome into the country'. Later on Kirkby sent threats to break up the Meeting at Swarthmoor, but the constables 'did not come to disturb us'. Fox spent much of his time sorting and labelling the stacks of letters, epistles, pamphlets and the like which had been accumulating in the house, confident that out of his work would grow something deserving record. In Worcester he and Lower had begun the text which underlies his printed *Journal*, and his main effort was to complete the dictating of this. Although Lower did most of the work, here as in Worcester, some twenty other handwritings can be counted. Many Friends made the difficult journey, 'from London, and out of Scotland and divers other parts of the nation, and from beyond seas' (N p.708) to talk about Quaker work, 'the affairs of Truth' as they called them. Fortunately, along with this activity Fox, in this first long period of quiet and comfort with the people who called him their 'dear father', did rest enough to regain much of his energy.

One chance means that more is known about life at Swarthmoor at about the time of Fox's long stay there than about almost any family of the period. Sarah Fell acted as manager and accountant, not only of the household but of the estate, and even of their iron works up the valley at Force Forge. She kept a very full ledger, and this has survived, with its details of every receipt and scrap of spending. Fox had some share in their business, for in 1683 he had at least £144 invested in the forge. (Ross p.271).

His presence naturally left traces in Sarah's book, including: 'carriage of a box to father with writing paper in', 'for bringing some writing paper from Lancaster for father', 'Some silk laces for father', 'glue and tobacco pipes for father', 'carriage of a salmon from Lancaster for father', 'ink and pipes for him', 'paseboard for father', 'tin plate for father', 'three sheepskins for father', '1 pd of juniper berries for father ', '2 almanacks for father', 'Recd of father for a pr of Stokens for mother whch he sd he would buy', 'some writing paper from Lancaster for father', 'box from Lancaster with ff H book [Francis Howgill] in for father', 'for bringing some red herrings from Lancaster for father', 'tobacco pipes for father', 'skin of parchment for father', 'pr of stockings for father', 'Pd for bringing some red herrings and 2 books from Lancaster for father'. (S.F. passim) His heavy correspondence shows up in the payments for letters 'to father', far more than for anyone else. Paper seems to have been costly enough for everyone to be charged separately when the carrier brought it up from Lancaster. The 'clay pipes' suggest that despite his early objections Fox had taken to tobacco, no doubt, as often then, for health or relief of pain.

Another visitor lets us see how his friends thought of Fox, and gives a further anecdote of a healing through him. As John Banks, an old friend from Pardshaw near Cockermouth, returned from visiting Irish Friends his shoulder became painful and he lost the use of his arm. At last, when doctors brought him no relief,

> . . . in my bed, I saw in a vision that I was with dear George Fox, and I thought I said unto him, my faith is such, that if thou seest it in thy way to lay thy hand upon my shoulder, my arm and hand shall be made whole throughout.

After several days' hesitation Banks decided that it was a 'true vision', and went down to the weekly meeting at Swarthmoor. 'And some time after the meeting I called him aside into the hall, and [told him my story], shewing him my arm and hand. In a little while, we walking together silent, he turned about and looked upon me, lifting up his hand, and laid it upon my shoulder, and said, 'The Lord strengthen thee within and without'. And so we parted and I went to Thomas Lower of Marsh Grange . . . and when I was set down to supper in his house, immediately before I was ware, my arm was lifted up to do its office . . . And the next time that George Fox and I met, he readily said, 'John, thou mended, thou mended . . . Well, give God the glory'' (Banks J. p.110 - 112).

There are few such indications of Fox's manner when relaxed and at home. He may well have wished that his own arthritis would go away as quickly as his friend's shoulder trouble.

Return to Work

Several of Sarah Fell's entries show Fox on the move again: 'male pillion and three girths for father, and mending his saddle', 'for shoeing father's horse', 'cord for one of father's boxes sent to London', '2 boxes of father's to London'. Whilst the carrier took his heavy luggage he set out on March 26th, 1677, escorted by Margaret, Rachel and others. His movements for the rest of his life were recorded by the helper he nearly always had with him, but local colour or decided judgements come only in his own occasional contributions. This employment of assistants, of whom the first was Edward Haistwell, a Swarthmoor lad of nineteen, suggests that Fox was sufficiently crippled or weak always to need a companion. Another sign that he found travel tiring is that the day's journey was usually only a few miles.

He parted from Margaret near Sedbergh, after 'a large meeting in a barn', and more of the long discussions with 'Friends who at that time were not at unity with Friends of the Quarterly Meeting.' (SJ p.226). He then took two months to reach London, by way of York and his first territories, including a night at Skegby, and another in Nottingham, with the Friend who had been the sympathetic Sheriff there during his detention, when he 'first declared Truth in that town'. Often he spoke at large meetings, and Friends travelled long distances to intercept him for discussions. When he reached Hendon, 'William Meade, not knowing of Gff being there, greatly rejoiced to see him', and Thomas Rudyard, the sympathetic lawyer who had become a permanent counsel to Friends, came out from London to him. Then Meade took him, with Penn, Whitehead, and their wives, in his coach to his house at Highgate. After more committees and discussions in the City, Margaret Rous carried her step-father off by boat to Putney, and then by horse to her house at Kingston.

Amongst the many who came to him at this time were two Scotsmen, George Keith and Robert Barclay. Keith worked with Fox and others for over fifteen years but then returned to his earlier theological ideas and attacked Quakers. Robert Barclay, a landowner and a protegé of Keith, was just turning from Latin into English his defence of Quakerism, *An Apology for the True Christian Divinity.* He gave it the analytical form and logical precision expected by Scottish theologians and hoped that it would force them to recognize Quakerism as intellectually valid even by their own rules. The result was a work very different from

One of the many satirical pictures of alleged Quaker Meetings

anything written by Fox or the older publishers of Truth, whose strength to stand up to persecution had grown from inner personal experience, rather than from arguments, however sound. The primacy of experience still underlay Fox's teaching, according to Haistwell's report of his remark in a friendly discussion a few months later, with two leading priests in Holland,

> They should never know God and Christ, and his law and gospel, by studying, nor by philosophy, but by revelation, and stillness in their minds by the spirit of God. (SJ p.251)

Holland

For a century English and Dutch dissenters had been in contact, so that naturally associates of Fox had worked over there from the beginning. Yet the large and active Quaker groups in Holland, and the smaller ones further afield in Germany were the only ones he himself had never visited. Knowing the uncertainties, Fox 'put his books, epistles and things concerning Truth's account in order' and in mid August, 1677, crossed to Rotterdam, with a party which included Penn, Barclay, Keith, and his step-daughter Isabel Yeamans. His host was a scholar and leading merchant of the city, Benjamin Furly, an English Quaker who nearly twenty years earlier had provided Fox with the linguistic information for his *Battledore* about the right use of singular and plural pronouns.

When the members of the party separated Fox and his group made their way across to Hamburg. He would have liked to reach the few Quakers struggling in Poland, but the journey was too risky and he had to be content with sending a message of encouragement and sympathy to his 'suffering Friends in Dantzick' [Gdansk]. His own enterprise was dangerous enough, for they passed through areas which for years had been caught up in the costly and complicated struggles of the continental powers. At the many checkpoints they faced the unpredictable outcome of interrogations by soldiers. Cities still had gates, and when the party arrived after these had been shut they had to sleep out. Even the travelling had its dangers.

We hired a boy to guide us, the waters being out . . . and I drove the waggon through, and then we came to a bridge, part of which the horses broke, and one of the horses fell into the water, and the waggon remained on the part of the bridge that was left . . . (SJ p.245)

Fox wrote this himself, whilst Haistwell was ill. Pain and weakness had evidently not taken away all his old decisiveness and his enjoyment of risk.

They saw the destruction of war, at Oldenburg, for example, where it was 'a lamentable sight to see such a great city burned down, and but few houses standing' (S.J. p.242 - 6). Unfortunately, in his letter to the city, Fox once more reflected the outlook of his time by tempering sympathy with the suggestion that their own materialistic ways might have contributed to their troubles. His 'epistle to the ambassadors that were treating for peace at Nimegen' was more constructive. This was chiefly an appeal that 'there may be no more imprisonment and persecution among the Christians, for matters of tender conscience.' (Ell. p.631). It was not a cause with much attraction to the masters of the diplomats bickering over a truce in the interminable European war, nor were they likely to take any notice of an English Protestant dissident. Fox thought this expedition into the Continent profitable, for he had many conferences and public meetings, besides talks with priests and influential public men. The party's return crossing in mid-October almost ended in disaster. Their leaky and barely seaworthy boat was caught in so severe a gale that they were at sea for three days, pumping furiously all the time, and only just survived. The course of history often seems to be made up of near misses. Fox's work was almost over, but would the story of America have been different if Penn had been drowned, five years before his ventures there?

London Problems

After this escape Fox settled down to his busy round in London, with Haistwell noting 'G.ff spent the forenoon writing about Truth's affairs', or 'passed to Wm Penn at his lodging (where they writ letters into Germany', or 'took coach, and with several other Friends passed to Shacklewell where they had a meeting touching the school for young women' (SJ p.259), or 'his book in answer to Roger Williams was examined and prepared ready for the press' (SJ p.261). This was a compilation called *A New England Firebrand Quenched,* whose five hundred pages should have been enough to quench any reader. When he went to visit Friends in prison at Chelmsford, London Friends rejoiced at his safe return, for they all knew how easily he could have become one of the prisoners. Whitehead, on a similar errand, was detained at Norwich and spent over a year in the wretched gaol there. The notes after any public gathering, 'all was peaceable' or, with more emphasis, 'the glory of the Lord surrounded the meeting and all was peaceable', remind us that they lived always with the risk of assault or arrest.

During a visit in March 1678 to Bristol and its discontented Friends, Fox bought for Margaret 'as much scarlet as would make thee a mantle which thou may line . . .' (HJC p.128). Evidently he knew her taste. Over twenty years later she briskly dismissed the restrictive outlook of the next generation of Quakers.

> Jesus would have all to be saved . . . Let us beware of looking upon ourselves as more holy, than in deed or truth we are . . . Let us stand fast in that liberty wherewith Christ hath made us free . . . and not be entangled again into bondage, in observing proscriptions in outward things, which will not profit nor cleanse the inward man. Poor Friends is mangled in their minds . . . Christ bids us take no thought for what we shall eat, or drink, or put on, but to consider the lilies. But [some Friends] say we must look at no colours, nor make anything that is as changeable colours as the hills are, nor sell them nor wear them; but we must be in one dress and one colour. This is a poor silly Gospel. It is more fit for us to be covered with God's eternal spirit, and clothed with his eternal Light . . . (Ross p.379 - 80)

Neither she nor Fox saw simplicity as deliberate drabness, or the use of an expensive non-fashion, but unfortunately for nearly two hundred years Quakers ignored this sound advice.

After Bristol, Fox moved on to Warwickshire, to the invalid Lady Conway, a scholar and patron of learning, who had turned to Quakerism. Perhaps through her Fox may have met her friend Henry More, the mystical philospher known as one of the Cambridge platonists. He may have been the 'Dr Moor' who had called on Fox the year before in London to 'dispute', or to 'discourse', according to the journal keeper (SJ p.233). Another of her guests, and a friend of Fox, was her physician, a Dutchman named van Helmont, who carried on the work of his more distinguished father. Fox was not likely to have had much use for their belief in re-incarnation, but the Helmonts had a theory of herbal medicine which did attract him, for their interest in traditional herbal remedies was in keeping with his own long-standing belief in the unity and harmony of the 'creation', the natural order. His own old Cumbrian friend Thomas Lawson was a very competent botanist. Perhaps Fox had suggested the tuition, recorded by Sarah in July 1674, at about the time Lower was returning to his medical practice.

> To Bro Lower yt he gave Thomas Lawson for coming over hither to instruct him and sisters in the knowledge of herbs . . . 10/- [50p].

Fox soon returned to London and its endless tasks, counselling Friends in private trouble, writing, or conferring 'in the service of Truth', or speaking at large public meetings, 'where many heavenly testimonies were borne to the Truth and G.ff's was taken down in characters and afterwards writ out' (SJ p.271), another reference to shorthand. Political activity, whether lobbying of the doubtful or conference with the sympathetic, was becoming more necessary, and probably many of Haistwell's brief notes: 'many Friends came to see him', or 'W.P. and several Friends came to see him', were as much related to that as to the incessant legal moves over imprisonments and distraints. Sometimes he went directly to the M.P.s, as when he 'passed down to Westminster Hall, and . . . spoke with some Parliament men' (SJ p.270). The main link with politicians and Court was Penn, although Whitehead often acted as spokesman or negotiator.

Return to Swarthmoor

Young Haistwell's term of service with his 'dear and ever loving master G. ff.' (SJ p.273) ended at midsummer 1678, and in the

> this book is to be printed with th rest of gss in 3
> voulames : 1 : his epeseles & leters & travels & bo
> with out controverce that are on fers
> 2 the ansers & controvences by them sev
> 3 all the bookes of notltes & of this booke if &
> the generall papers to the men & wimens m
> ings by them sevels

A sample of Fox's handwriting

early autumn Fox himself set off back to Swarthmoor. Very little
is known about this stay at his home. Perhaps he simply needed
rest and felt free to return to Margaret and his family in the
north, having decided that he could leave to others the delicate
political negotiations in London. Perhaps he thought, that now,
as he had always wished, his movement was able to carry on
without him. Ellwood, who knew him well, as colleague and
guest, could only say of this stay in the north that he 'had service
amongst Friends' and was 'much taken up in writing books and
papers.' (Ell. p.473). Even in the next spring, 1679, Fox, who
rarely missed Yearly Meeting, contented himself with sending a
letter to the Friends there. This ends with a reminder.

> My dear Friends, the Lord doth require more of you ...
> because he hath committed more to you. He requires the fruits
> of his Spirit, and [Christ] is glorified in your bringing forth ...
> fruits of righteousness, holiness, godliness, virtue, truth and
> purity, so that you may answer that which is of God in all
> people.

Then, even more bluntly, he reminded them of the way of life that should follow from this.

> The world also does expect more from Friends . . . because you profess more. Therefore you should be more just than others, in your words and dealings, and more righteous, holy, and pure in your lives . . . And the Lord God Almighty by his mighty power . . . preserve and keep you all in his power and peaceable holy Truth, in unity and fellowship, with one another, and with the Son and the Father.' (Ell. p.474)

The calm tone of this letter gives no hint of the troubles that were about to break on the country and on the Quakers.

Plots and Crisis

The last period of Fox's life has often been dismissed as if little fresh happened to him or to Quakerism. To those who lived through them the sixteen eighties were years of danger, in which all freedom in the country might have been destroyed. If the decade is looked at from the point of view of Fox and the Quakers it is easy to think that their fortunes mattered most, and that they were the most conspicuous sufferers. It was certainly a time of great distress for them, but to their contemporaries their problems were incidental, and many could be called their own fault for keeping up anti-social practices, which were beginning to seem rather old-fashioned. Politicians had to worry about the future of the country, with an aging King, and his successor known as a Catholic, with an uncertain heiress. Both depended on the seemingly all-powerful King of France, ambitious for power and territory. The future was dangerous and uncertain, with possibilities of rebellions from any side, Catholic or Protestant, royalist despot or parliamentarian. Any upset could bring in the continental powers, with unpredictable results. The outcome remained uncertain till the last minute, and then depended on unforeseeable strings of coincidence and chance. In the crises of his early years Fox had known the people confronting him, understanding their thoughts and able to speak directly to them. In this new struggle the fate of Quakers seemed likely to be settled by people and political motives far beyond their reach.

The great fear was that Charles, or James, Duke of York, his Catholic brother and heir, would try to bring the country back, not to the unassertive faith of the native Catholics, but to the authoritarian version preached by the Jesuits. A further anxiety was that, as absolutist rulers were doing well in Europe, Charles might try to get rid of Parliament, and rely on a standing army, loyal to its paymaster, instead of the militia, with its local ties. Old fears remained, some fed by the still circulating *Foxe's Book of Martyrs*, but increasingly reinforced by new ones, from the experiences of French Protestants, the Huguenots. These were already suffering, before King Louis ended a century of toleration by revoking the Edict of Nantes in 1685, and sent more refugees across the Channel. Rumours of Papist rebellions and assassinations began to swirl around, stirred up by the plausible inventions of an extraordinary and mischievous liar called Titus Oates.

In the autumn of 1678 Oates came out with a string of stories touching on everybody's fears, that the Catholics were preparing to murder Charles, massacre Protestants and introduce an army from abroad. He said, rather surprisingly if his tales had any truth, that James was not involved. However, other evidence soon implicated him, and led to a bitter political campaign to prevent his succeeding Charles, the Exclusion crisis. Oates's accusations led to attacks on Catholics, and to phony trials and executions. For several years Oates profited by the confusion and misery he was causing, until his lies became too outrageous even for the most bigoted and credulous. Unfortunately, even after he had been discredited, the conflicts he had helped to inflame did not end.

Quakers were caught up in the disturbance, through the old suspicions that they were only Jesuits in disguise, although Oates himself seems not to have implicated them. A strange exchange of letters in March 1679 shows the confusion about them. A Northamptonshire rector wrote to Oates.

> Sir, I presume, though utterly unknown, to give you notice, that on Thursday last there was taken up at Northampton, one William Dewsbury, a great pretended apostle of the Quakers, but as I have it from very good hands, you can make him appear to be a Jesuit . . .

Titus Oates himself replied,

> . . . You would do well to discharge him. He is no Jesuit, nor like one. I look on it to be our discretion not to meddle with any common Protestant dissenter in this day. Sir, here is a certificate from some that have known him these twenty years . .
> . . . And pray, did you ever know that there was any such correspondence between Jesuits and Quakers as might render them suspicious . . . ? (JFHS vol. 42 no. 50 p.68)

The letter did not help Dewsbury, who was kept in Warwick gaol until 1685. If Oates had turned his 'revelations' against Quakers, the routine harassments might well have given way to more trials and brutal executions, including that of Fox.

In Parliament, a sort of opposition party was coming together. Penn and Whitehead began work with some of its members to draft a new Toleration Bill, but its main desire was to get an 'Exclusion' bill passed, which would make sure that Catholic James never became King. Charles had no liking for his brother, but detested any interference with the royal prerogative, so that as successive Parliaments brought in 'Exclusion' Bills he dissolved them, and all their projected changes were lost. From 1681 to the end of his life in 1685 Charles seemed to be moving towards the absolutism of the French. Resentful because dissenters had campaigned for his opponents over the Exclusion Bills, he allowed the anti-dissenter laws to be enforced strictly, so that for some five years informers, Anglican priests, and hostile magistrates had a free hand.

The Last Persecution

In the spring of 1680 Fox travelled south again, by way of York, where he 'spent some time with the Friends that were prisoners in the Castle, encouraging them and strengthening them in their testimony' (Ell. p.479). Once in London, all his energies were taken up by the problems of persecution and political uncertainty. Although the family would have liked him to return to Swarthmoor before his health failed he never felt free to do so. After his death Margaret reflected that,

> . . . though the Lord had provided an outward habitation for

him, yet he was not willing to stay at it; because it was so remote and far from London, where his service most lay. (Testimony, in Ell. p.ix)

Margaret herself, much fitter although ten years older, travelled south three times: in the summer of 1681, for the marriage of Sarah to William Meade; in the winter of 1684 - 85 for some unsuccessful lobbying of Charles, and finally in the summer of 1690 to be near Fox.

Local problems kept her in the north, for the Kirkby family were still determined to get rid of Swarthmoor Meeting, and to ruin the family. This soon gained a new member. In the spring of 1683, Rachel, the youngest daughter, married Daniel Abraham, heir to a Manchester merchant, an old friend of Margaret. During the next year, the couple, who made Swarthmoor their home, and Margaret herself, apart from being fined, were briefly imprisoned at Lancaster for non-attendance at church. Like many others, they continued to lose heavily through the distraints of cattle and corn, which sometimes looked very like theft, as a letter from Fox suggested.

Dearly Beloved . . . There is a rumour here that one of the Kirkby's should take one of our fat oxen and kill him for his own table in his own house, which was distrained . . . (HJC Narr. Pap. p.130)

Fox wanted all the details to see whether an appeal was possible. Moreover the Kirkbys charged Margaret as 'Margaret Fell, widow,' (Ross p.320). This convenient insult made her liable to a fine of £20 as a householder instead of 10/- [50p] as a wife. Fox kept up his help, for later on his diarist reported that he 'had business with Rowland Vaughan [a sympathetic lawyer] about distresses made at Swarthmoor' (SJ p.93).

Fox 'spent much time, together with other Friends, in the service of seeking relief for his suffering Friends, attending the Parliament-House day by day, for many weeks together, and watching all opportunities to speak with such members of either House . . . some appeared very courteous, and very willing to help us if they could. But Parliament being then very earnest in examining the Popish Plot . . . our enemies took advantages against us (because they knew we could not swear nor fight), to expose us to those penalties, that were made against Papists' (Ell. p.481). Yet another emphatic declaration from him against plotting ended with an appeal to the M.P.s.

... but as to swearing and fighting, which in tenderness of conscience we cannot do, ye know, that we have suffered these many years for our conscientious refusal thereof. And now the Lord that brought you together, we desire you to relieve us . . . (Ell. p.482)

A contemporary estimate of Quaker sufferings for the years 1660 to 1680 came to about 11,000 imprisonments, and 243 deaths, mostly of prison hardships, apart from fines and distraints (Q Reay p.106). The final years of Charles reign were in proportion amongst the worst. Quakers could never be sure of a safe return from meeting. A raid by informers and constables might lead only to insults, pelting with rubbish, or assault with clubs, but could end in their being dumped in a gaol, with all its filth and disease. Higher living standards made this sort of treatment harder to accept. Yet most Friends stayed firmly with Fox over both meetings and their other testimonies. The contest led to many incidents which went into a sort of Quaker heroic tradition: business meetings, or even marriages, in prison; or the defiant keeping up of weekly worship by children when all the adults were in custody, a stand which in Bristol once led to the children themselves being put in the stocks and caned by a sadistic informer.

Yet in those days oddities or inconsistencies could always be found. Although a Quaker, Penn, for example, was a personal friend of James, known to him through Admiral Penn's work with James in the Navy. This link still gave Penn entry to the Court, if not at that time much influence on events. In addition, another of the King's many debts was to Penn himself, the £16,000 he owed to the Admiral's estate. This sum should perhaps be seen against the £33,300 in suits pending against Quakers during the persecution of 1683, merely in the one county of Suffolk (Barbour p.224). Penn, who was already interested in America through an involvement with New Jersey, had the debt settled by a grant of the adjoining land, between two estuaries and 'as far west as plantable'. Penn, as a Quaker, was against self-advertisement, but had to resign himself to Charles's joke, that the new land should be called *Pennsylvania*. Despite the historic success of the territory's constitution and early government his heavy expenses meant that his sales of land there failed to improve his fortunes, whilst the work and worry of it wore him out. Charles apparently hoped that the troublesome Quakers would all emigrate and relieve England of their uncomfortable criticisms. He was disappointed, for most thought that they should not run away from the trial of persecution. Penn also found time to revise his own notable account of Quaker views, in *No Cross, No Crown*, less systematic than Barclay's but more appealing in style.

By now Quakers had a well organised system for frustrating the persecutors, based on the committee rightly called 'Meeting for Sufferings', which had been set up in the mid seventies. With the help of lawyers, although these did not always give sound advice, all kinds of legal ways were suggested for thwarting the prosecuting informers. Sometimes delaying tactics, such as appeals, could be used, for the informers wanted quick spoils and no unwelcome expenses. Careless clerks made enough mistakes in documents, as always, to give grounds for challenging them. One worry related to a defendant's property, especially anything being held for others. Friends could not make up their minds whether it was legal, much less moral, to reduce the amount left for distraint by arranging to sell or mortgage their goods before a case could be heard. Some Quakers were trustees or agents, and Fox was anxious that their own problems should not lead to loss for others.

> And now, Dear Friends, take care that all your offerings may be . . . of your own . . . You may remember many years ago, in a time of great persecution . . . [when some] Friends who were traders . . . had the concerns of widows . . . and other people's estates in their hands . . . there was especial care taken that all Friends might [lose only] what . . . they had bought and paid for . . . (Ell. p.503).

His name, 'offerings', for the confiscated goods shows that he saw them, not as legal extortions, but as 'sacrifices' willingly made for their cause.

Although the Quaker practices made them most conspicuous, objectionable, and easiest to catch, the laws were intended to suppress all dissenters. Some tried to meet in public, but
most kept their heads down, as they had done before, by dividing congregations, or by using out of the way retreats and
unusual times. A few preachers stayed behind curtains, to prevent informers identifying them, or spoke from horseback,
ready to make a quick getaway. Fox continued unsympathetic to
any deceit, but the huge fines levied, especially on preachers
who did persist, made it easy to understand it. Even Richard
Baxter, the most law-abiding of non-conformists, in spite of his
age and illness, was fined hundreds of pounds, and finally sent
to prison. It is surprising that Fox stayed free, because, like the
other Quaker leaders, he made a point of attending meetings
where trouble was expected. He had, however, one unusual
advantage, which may have helped to keep the informers off
him. If he had been poor his friends could have been made to
pay fines for him, but he was clearly well off, and yet, as no
householder but a mere lodger, he had few belongings worth
distraining.

Several incidents show how unpredictable life could be. At
Kingston, near the Rouses' home, in the March of 1683,

> As I went to the meeting I met the Chief Constable, and he
> was pretty civil and he had set the watchmen to keep us out of
> meeting but they let Friends have two forms to sit upon in the
> highway and we had a very precious meeting in the street.
> (SJ p.77)

Then another rumour, or plot, called the 'Rye House', brought a
change.

> G.ff. went to Kingston in a coach, and the same day the offi-
> cers were very rude and did nip and abuse Friends and drove
> them out of the meeting place. (SJ p.87)

This was in October. Some weeks later in the same area,

> They were very bad to Friends, and put some of the women
> into the ditch and greatly abused the rest of Friends. (SJ p.88)

The 'Rye House' plotters were supposed to be Protestants trying

to assassinate Charles. He conveniently used the story to justify
the execution of several Whig leaders, men with whom Penn
had worked during the Exclusion conflict. In all this confusion
and danger Fox's serene and confident tone stands out.

> Friends and brethren, who have received the peaceable Truth,
> let the fruits of its peaceableness, and of your quiet spirit
> appear in all your meetings, and in all your words and actions;
> for he that inhabits eternity, dwells with an humble heart; and
> he gives grace to the humble, and resisteth the proud. Heaven
> is his throne, and the earth ye walk upon, is his footstool.
> Happy are ye, that see and know him, that is invisible. And
> now, Friends, let all things be done in your meetings, and
> other ways, in love, without strife or vain-glory. For Love ful-
> fils the law, and Love overcomes . . . (Ell. p.512)

One of the worst days for Fox himself came in October,
when the 'constables and people' [here = mob] burst into the
London Savoy meeting, 'like a sea'. His words contrast striki-
ngly with the constable's actions.

> [He] said, 'Come down', and laid hands on me . . . I said,
> 'Thou art a Christian, we are Christians', and he had me by the
> hand and was very fierce to pluck me down, and I spoke to the
> people that the blessings of God might rest upon all, and still
> the constable bid me come down.

Then came an oddly comic moment. 'And I said to him, "Let me
take my hat," and he said, "You may take your hat", and I said,
"How can I take my hat and thou holdest me by the hand?"' (SJ
p.84). Humour of any sort was scarce, but this seems to be
another example of the disconcerting undertone of amused
irony often glimpsed in his writing.

He unsettled the Justice, to whom he was at last led, by
arguing that to 'praise God and confess Christ Jesus' could not
be preaching 'contrary to the liturgy of the Church of England'.
Fox asked the man whether he could in conscience send him to
the infamous Newgate for what he had said in the Meeting.
When an aggressive rogue of an informer annoyed the Justice by
trying to insist on the most profitable charge he let everyone go
till the next morning. The constable then told Fox that the

Justice, after twice putting off writing the mittimus, had sent him a message that he was free till next time. Fox paid the constable the dubious compliment of saying 'that he had the face of a man, and I would not have him to be an informer.' Another passing comment underlines the sly persistence of these men: 'G.F. was at the Meeting of Sufferings, where there was supposed to be an informer watching and gazing at the windows . . .' (SJ p.88). The most ominous remark in Fox's story of his brief detention is the admission that he was 'very weary and in a great sweat.'

Informers and rowdies were not the only hardships. Winters were hard, especially 1683 - 84, which was one of the coldest on record, when coaches used the ice of the Thames as a short cut. When Meeting houses were nailed up or guarded by soldiers Friends had to stand in the freezing street, surrounded by curious or hostile crowds, although perhaps they did not then stay for the full three hours of many indoor meetings. Whitehead, in his journal, mentioned his relief at surviving the winter without even a cold. The weather also upset Fox's movements, for 'the ways being bad', the coach taking him to visit Penn was forced into a ten mile detour.

In the end the informers' very excesses turned the public against them, as incidents like this illustrate. After Fox had spoken at a 'large and peaceable meeting within doors' at Devonshire House, early in 1685, he left, probably to rest. About thirty Friends were arrested by informers and soldiers, who then,

> . . . went to G.W.'s [Whitehead's] house, and said there used to be a meeting there and swore that they would break open the door, but the people came and fell so on the informer that he went away, so the doors were not broken down' (SJ p.103).

At other times Whitehead lost heavily from looting at his grocery store. Sometimes even the officers could be made to admit that they were weary of the work.

As the years went on this destruction of stock and the impoverishment of Friends in business began to make difficulties for others, including their trading associates. Such mundane inconveniences helped the growing feeling that toleration was better than the continued interference with harmless and useful neighbours, or even relatives.

Chapter Twelve

FULLY CLEAR

Changing Times

Early in January 1685, Margaret, in London to lobby the King again, found herself one day facing locked gates at Whitehall. Whilst she waited, words drifted through from officials, that 'he cannot stand' and 'he cannot speak'. She did not then know they were talking about Charles and the stroke from which he died a few days later. The change of King made no immediate difference to the persecution, although Quakers quickly got out an an appeal to James, and Fox spent five hours at a meeting 'with several Friends about drawing up a paper to the King.' For a time conditions were worse, when some Quakers were suspected of supporting the Duke of Monmouth, Charles's illegitimate but Protestant son, who raised an army to unseat James. After its defeat the notorious Judge Jeffreys was sent to deal with the captured rebels. Fox 'had a meeting with several Friends about drawing up certificates to present to the Chief Justice about Friends' clearness in the west from the Rebellion.' (SJ p.115) Apparently about a dozen were implicated, of whom three were hanged (Reay p.110). Jeffreys' brutality and abuse of the law became legendary, although he is said to have shown uncharacteristic moderation in some of his dealings with Quakers.

When James gained control after his brother's unexpected death he wanted to see England, and his other kingdoms of Scotland and Ireland, returned to the Catholic Church, but knew that unlike his model, Louis XIV of France, he could not immediately achieve this. Fears of a Catholic coup remained, even after Oates had been discredited. The Anglican bishops and clergy were determined to keep their dominant position, and some landowners even feared for estates taken long ago from the monasteries. James's first object was to give Catholics freedom of worship and then to have them back in public life and the army, from which they had been kept out by the detailed

230

anti-Catholic declaration required under the *Test Act*. Despite some faint sympathy with dissenters as people who had lived under oppression like the Catholics, they were to him merely heretics, whom he would have liked to get rid of as Louis had done the Huguenots. Yet he dared not favour Catholics alone, and knew that to break the hold which the Anglicans had gained over Parliament and local affairs through the *Test Act*, he needed the help of the dissenters. He began by 'dispensing' some people from the Act, but this was a limited and unpopular action and he wanted a Parliament which would repeal it. Yet dissenters could not refuse liberty simply because it came from the royal will, or prerogative, and had no parliamentary or permanent basis.

Although in 1685 a Justice back in Cumbria told Daniel Abraham that now the Government was settled, 'if you do keep your meetings you must expect the same again,' he was wrong. Margaret herself tried to get an appeal to the new King, which seemed to be refused. Yet she commented, 'However I do suppose they gave the persecutors a private caution, for they troubled us no more' (Fell p.12). This indeed was what began to happen, as James made his wishes known. He began in March 1686 with with his *General Pardon and Release,* and followed it the next year with the *Declaration of Indulgence.* The Pardon led to the emptying of the prisons, and at least 1200 Quakers were freed. One paradoxical effect of the Declaration was a better understanding between Anglicans and Dissenters, as illustrated by the episode of the trial of the seven bishops for refusing to order their clergy to read the Pardon from their pulpits. Bishops who in the past had been little more than royal administrators now claimed the right to act independently for the church. Before their action they obtained the agreement of Dissenting ministers in London, and told the King that it did not come from 'any want of due tenderness towards the Dissenters' (Watt p.259).

The Yearly Meeting of that year was a remarkable gathering, from everyone's delight at seeing 'our ancient, faithful brethren again at liberty in the Lord's work, after their long confinements' (Ell. p.548). The changing times led to people of a different kind being seen openly listening to Fox. Once at Westminster, for example, 'when he spoke a pretty time and afterwards went to prayer . . . many of the world [were] there and several Papists, one or all of which were said to belong to the Pope's nuncio.' (SJ p.156). Fox took part in many committees with Penn and Whitehead, but did not join them when they put their case at Court, another sign perhaps of failing strength. From then onwards almost every meeting he attended is described as 'peacable and within doors', although the informers did not give up willingly. Whitehead collected the evidence of their illegalities for a Commission of Enquiry, and overwhelmed the commissioners with its bulk, so that in the heat of the summer they assured him that he had more than made his case and begged him to stop. It was always the Quaker way to be thorough.

After Monmouth's execution the King seemed secure, for autocratic monarchies were doing well in Europe and he had hopes for his own. His main risk was from William of Orange, the Anglo-Dutch husband of his own Protestant daughter Mary, but he too had many enemies and was under attack from Louis. James was planning to summon a Parliament after carefully rigged elections, and had good hopes of being able to get his way. Unfortunately for him, however, he was a poor manager of men and had no grasp of wider political movements. In three complicated years he alienated everyone, lost all support, panicked, and ran away from the country when William decided to risk an invasion. Even at this point he might have been saved, for William had left enemies behind, and faced the unpredictable weather of the English Channel. Many people of influence who did turn to him waited till they felt sure they would be on the winning side. Everyone's fate depended as much on the intrigues of Louis and his rivals in Europe as on James's absolutist and Catholic aspirations. It was easy to relax when it was all over, and to talk about a glorious, and a bloodless revolution, but everything might have worked out differently.

Whether freedom of worship would have continued if James had acted more discreetly in politics and had survived to carry on his catholicising policy must be doubtful. Yet Quakers had no say in his fall in 1688, and his replacement by the Protestant and more tolerant William. Only Penn worked within Whitehall, using his influence with James, and even at one stage negotiating for him with William. His work got him into trouble, for, although he insisted that he was working only for toleration, his known friendship for James forced him out of public life for three years and nearly led to his losing Pennsylvania. Fox was more than ever involved with politics, spending much time at the 'Friends' chamber near the Parliament house'. Another rather muddled reference, in late October 1690, suggests that in the course of their work Quakers had caught up with the new fashion of the coffee house.

> [Fox] met some Friends appointed to speak with some of the Parliament men concerning Friends at the coffee house where Friends used to be joining to Westminster Hall. (S.J. p.218)

The diaries show that in spite of the time taken by meetings and negotiations about the persecution, Fox tried to keep up his pastoral activities and his writing. His one long journey was in the summer of 1684, a return visit to Holland. It lasted only a month, mainly spent in Amsterdam and Rotterdam, with the usual debates and interviews, including some with prominent people. In the following years he sometimes had dinners with Dutch Friends. Other conferences were with Penn and Friends involved in the troubled affairs of New Jersey. Once he 'had a meeting with the physicians . . .' (SJ p.80). Fox liked to hold discussions with select groups, but we could wish the diarist had mentioned the topic of this one. In 1686, 'he sent for a great doctor that came from Poland, and had discourse with him' (SJ p.129). The sequel was that 'he writ a paper to the King of Poland.' This was an appeal for toleration, thick with references to historical personages who had favoured it, evidently provided by the Polish scholar.

Even with all their troubles, Friends ventured to marry, and Fox took part in a number of weddings. A more frequent pastoral need, however, was the visiting of people who were ill, as when he 'was sent for ten miles into the country to see Mary Wooley that was sick, and she was refreshed with the power of the Lord' (SJ p.82). Some years later he went to 'the gardener's wife who lived at the meeting house, who having broken her leg lay very lame and weak' (SJ p.145). A visit of a different kind was to 'a woman . . . not well in her mind.' (SJ p.92). And what diffi-

Almely Meeting House, Herefordshire

culty lay behind some meetings he had, like those 'about Margaret Drinkell's and her daughter's business.' (SJ p.96), or his 'meeting with a young woman that Friends had trouble with at the Peel'? Naturally he kept up his interest in schools, not only those already functioning but apparently in fresh ones, for in 1686, in the course of a long day, he went 'to Chiswick to see after a house for a women's school.' (SJ p.123). According to Thomas Lawson he also had a scheme for a new school with its own botanical garden as a basis for a detailed study of the characteristics and use of plants (SPQ p.528). In all, a busy life.

A Limited Success

When William's Parliament recognized the change in public opinion by passing its *Toleration Act*, Quakers, even more than other dissenters, needed relief too much to reject it as merely *toleration*, a conditional freedom which left them without many civil rights. Once they had been allowed to make some change to the wording they accepted a sort of credal declaration which it allowed to be put to people. But the Act was granting, not freedom, but merely permission to hold their own meetings, on condition that they were willing to subscribe to this statement. After all that they had suffered, this was enough for gratitude. As the changes came, Fox was still alive, and able to see at least this limited success of the campaign for freedom of worship, which he had begun during the excitements of the Revolution, and kept up through thirty years of repression. When his own record of resistance to any conditional liberty is remembered, he might well have seen toleration as marking the start of a fresh campaign. Could he ever have been content with less than full liberty for the spirit and equal rights in the state? The *Test Act* still kept Dissenters out of civic offices and the Anglican controlled universities. With Fox's passion for education and his sense of public welfare, if he had been fit, it is hard to think that he would have kept quiet for long.

Mosedale Meeting House, Cumbria

Healings and Psychic Awareness

Over the years Fox's visits to someone ill occasionally contributed to an unexpected recovery, and a further instance is mentioned in this period. Told about a Friend in agony with the
'stone', he went to him, and

> desired the Lord to rebuke his infirmity, and as I laid my hands
> upon him the Lord's power went through him . . . and he
> presently fell asleep . . . and the stone came from him like dirt
> . . . the next day he came 25 miles in a coach with me . . . (SJ
> p.78)

Fox, like everyone else, accepted the healing stories in the
Gospels. It followed therefore that, if Quakerism was really a
recovery of the first Christian witness, whatever had formerly
happened could be expected again, even the raising from the
dead. In the early years some people attached to Quakers made
disastrous claims and experiments, with much talk of healings
and miracles. Before long, as Fox realised the harm resulting
from this excitement, he came to put more emphasis on quiet
faithfulness. He responded with caution as well as pleasure to
any improvements in health which could be linked with prayer.
These were perhaps less often dramatic reversals than the
speeding up of a recovery already on the way, as, in the past, of
his own body after a beating up. Many seem to have been of a
functional kind, perhaps related to mental upsets. He seems to
have been especially helpful to those in mental distress, such as
depression.

Fox was not spared health problems in his own family, for
his own step-grandchildren had smallpox, and several died
from it. A fragment of autobiography tells of one such death,
and describes his own overwhelming sense of the unity of the
visible and eternal worlds.

> Hearing that Margaret Rous's child was sick I went to see it,
> and as I stood by it considering its condition I felt the Lord's
> power go through it and the word was the Lord's power was
> come to raise it up or fetch it away, and so I came away fresh in
> the Lord's power and satisfied in myself. And the next day her
> mother came to the town and desired me to go with her to see
> it, and through her tenderness I went, though I was satisfied

in myself. And so I saw that the child was full of the power of the Lord and it rested upon it and rested in it. And at night it died, and after[wards] the spirit of the child appeared to me and there was a mighty substance of a glorious life in that child, and I bid her mother be content, for it was well . . . (HJC Narr. Pap. p.60 and B.of.M. 66b)

Several other stories show this kind of psychic awareness. One, from thirty years earlier, was about two men who had just been hanged, and another concerned his parents, after he had been prevented by the Worcester imprisonment from visiting his dying mother. When the letter about her death reached him, he was grieved, but, 'when my spirit had gotten through I saw her in the resurrection and the life everlastingly with me over all, and father in the flesh also' (B of M. 11b). Everything about Fox shows that he was unusually aware of people's mental states. People who met him, even his opponents, admitted that he had some quality that disconcerted them, including his penetrating and sometimes controlling gaze.

Fox's strong sense of the unity and continuity of life, visible and invisible, meant that he was largely free from the anxieties and grief associated with illness and death. This conviction influenced his dealings with the victims of persecution. Although he campaigned vigorously to get Quakers out of prison, he seems to have thought that imprisonment could not affect anyone's essential life, or spiritual progress. It hurt only the 'outward man', and was a practical nuisance which interfered with people's service and prevented them from maintaining their families. The persecutors were in even more need of help, for their conduct showed them to be in a far worse state of spiritual health. Later generations of Friends, in a more rationialistic period, preferred to ignore these stories, leaving them out of his writings and losing those collected into his *Book of Miracles.* The medical language of Fox's time hardly allows any retrospective diagnoses. We have therefore to be content with noting that Fox and the people around him believed they sometimes saw changes beyond their expectation; that they tried to give truthful accounts of them, and were grateful for the benefits they found. At the present time it may be that increasing knowledge has made us more aware of how much is still unknown, so that we are less confident about being already able to explain every happening.

Fox as Writer and Speaker

When Fox was unable to move around he sent out a stream of leaflets and pamphlets to 'defend Truth'. But his main care was for the letters through which he kept alive his friendship for all who were trying to live, as he tried to do, 'in the Truth', sincere and helpful in their dealings with others, whilst open to a vision of happiness and fulfilment through their 'waiting on the Light of the eternal Christ'. He consoled, he enouraged, he made suggestions, and sometimes told them bluntly where he thought they were going wrong. His feeling for the unity of life leads him to bring together the sublime and the practical, for to him each expressed the other.

A few further, almost random, examples may illustrate this outlook.

> All my dearly beloved Friends . . . The Lord God Almighty, with his holy power and spirit, hath gathered, and kept, and preserved you to this day a people to himself. And now . . . in all your words, in all your business and employments . . . consider beforehand . . . that you may be able to perform and fulfil both your words and promises . . . (Ep. 380)

He assured prisoners in Algiers that, even as slaves, they could still 'live and walk in the everlasting righteousness of Christ Jesus'.

> And now, dear Friends, my desires are, and the desires of Friends here, that you may all walk soberly, honestly, modestly, and civilly, and lovingly and gently and tenderly to all your patroons [Arab masters], and all people . . . that you may reach by your righteous, godly lives, the good in [them] all. (Ep. 391)

'To the suffering Friends of Dantzick', he sent a blunt warning:

> And now, dear Friends, we do hear and understand, that the magistrates have cast you into prison again; and that they

have proferred you your liberty, [if] you would . . . forsake your common meeting-place, or divide yourself into several little Meetings. Truly, Friends, we have had many of these proffers made to us within this twenty or thirty years, but we never durst make such bargains or covenants, to forsake the assembling of ourselves together . . . And the Lord at last . . . [made tender] the hearts of many of our persecutors, and therefore . . . it is good to be faithful. For if [they] should get a little advantage upon you, and get you into weakness, [they would] get more upon you. (Ep. 396)

Within two years, in a further letter, he congratulated them on having come through successfully and on being able to hold their meetings peacefully. In these last years his continuing aversion to any moral temporising comes through as strongly as his deep awe at the mystery of the divine reality.

In his last year he told the London Meeting for Quaker affairs:

The Six Week's Meeting is to see that all their meetings are preserved by the wisdom of God in the unity of the Spirit . . . being ordered by the pure, gentle, heavenly, peaceable wisdom, easy to be entreated, holy and virtuous examples to all other meetings . . . And that all may be careful to speak short and pertinent to matters in a Christian spirit, and despatch business quickly, and keep out of long debates and heats . . . keep that down which is doting about questions and strife of words . . . and likewise not to speak more than one at a time . . . (Ep. 418)

His words here may be old-fashioned, but there is no mistaking the down-to-earth advice. The last letter printed in his Epistles, to some other prisoners of the Arabs, may well be left to represent not only his outlook in religion but this same matter-of-factness.

You may petition the Emperor, or king, and your Patroons . . . that you may have one day in the week to meet together to worship and serve the Great God (that made you) in Spirit and Truth. For you worship no representation, [or] image . . . but the great God, who is Lord over all, both in heaven and earth;

and is manifest by his Spirit in you his people . . . you, poor
captives, who desire their good here, and their eternal happiness hereafter . . .
And you may draw up a paper to this effect, and get it trans-
lated into their language, and send it to [them]. And set your
hands to it with all speed, after the receipt of this. (Ep. 420)

The old drive to get on with the job seemed as keen as at the
beginning.

　　Fox had little interest in abstract argument. He preferred to
support his case by evidence, from history, including the Bible,
or from what he and his readers could see of everyday conduct.
He was above all a speaker, accustomed to large and often noisy
gatherings, where long trains of reasoning would have been
futile. His papers were often built up round short phrases, running in series or set in contrast. For example: 'All who hate this
Light . . .' and then, 'All who love this Light . . .' Sometimes a
phrase runs through a whole paper: 'Now read . . . now mark
. . .', or 'What say you, Guilty, or, Not Guilty?' Or 'The Papists
they cry, Conform. And the Turk, he cries, Conform. And did
not the heathen Emperors cry, Conform? And the Presbyterian,
he cried, Conform. And the Independents . . . So all these cry,
Conform . . . So everyone that gets uppermost, and gets the staff
of authority, commands people . . . But no law of Jesus requires
it, who said, "Freely you have received, freely give."' These rep-
etitions and parallel statements acted as markers, helping listeners their grip on the argument, underlining opponents' weak
points, and leading to the contrasted phrasing of a climax. Often
he interlaced and repeated key words in slightly changing con-
texts. On the page this can appear merely verbose. To the
listener they sounded out at each return to build up reassurance
and emotional impetus, whilst the variations refined and illustrated his meaning. Running through everything were the
rhythms, images and ideas of the Bible, usually in the King
James translation. Occasionally his own expression took off and
can be set out as verse, in the pattern of a psalm. He was thought
to have a special gift for giving words to devotion, his own sense
of the ever-present eternal making it real to his hearers when he
'declared and afterwards went to prayer'.

　　Some of his later sermons survive, transcribed from shorthand. When speaking freely amongst Friends, he used an informal style, which flowed easily and simply, but which is not easily illustrated in brief extracts. In one of these he began with a short prayer.

> Blessed be the Lord God of heaven and earth, who has preserved his people to this day, and hath given us this blessed opportunity, that everyone . . . may feel the . . . power and spirit of life and power and glory.

He then took up a familiar theme, the loss of purity at the beginning of history, and its recovery.

> So here, you see, they did not come to be as Gods, according to the Serpent's word . . . And here came the Lamb to be slain from the foundation of the world (though there's more in that) . . . Everyone must come through this flaming two-edged sword before they can come into the Paradise of God. They must know this sword to cut down the . . . earthly wisdom and to burn it up . . . And this I know by experience, before I went out to declare the Truth . . .

> So Adam and Eve, when they had transgressed . . . they sewed fig leaves together to make them aprons. A sunshine day might dry their aprons to powder. So God found them making aprons; as [in] all the religions in the world in transgression they are stitching or sewing one thing or another to make them a covering . . .

> Now 'Christ is the same today as he was yesterday': can we get any further? Yes: 'and for ever, and to all eternity.' (EQW pp.502 - 512)

And so on, through a range of topics, biblical and practical.

Fox has been dismissed as an ineffective writer. In addition to his oral habits, he often left out explanatory links which would not be needed by people who were with him, or who were used to his ways of thinking. Most of his papers dealt with some immediate problem or dispute, and were more like a politician's campaign speeches and interviews than systematic studies of a subject. They usually began as dictation, and were often intended for reading aloud, as a substitute for a visit from him. A

reader today, used to a more direct style, has to filter out the rep-
etitions and merely topical material, and may fail to recognize
not only the clarity of the underlying concepts, but their simplicity and brevity. Fox always had difficulty, as did Barclay and
others, in dealing with the theologians, for they could not accept
that Quaker experience and thought did not fit within the customary framework. He had so much to say about practical living, that there is a temptation to look for more, even about social
problems which have only arisen since his time. One example of
this would be our preoccupation with the natural world and the
environment. Fox wanted consideration shown to all things,
and nothing to be used wastefully, but the natural balance had
not then been noticeably upset. In England itself it still seemed
safe, and in several continents the human invasion had hardly
started.

Fox's Own Health

Many years earlier Fox had once come upon

> . . . two desperate fellows fighting so that none durst come
> near them, but I was moved in the Lord's power to go to them,
> and when I had loosed their hands, I held one by one hand
> and the other by the other hand, and I showed them the evil of
> their doings, and convinced them . . . (N p.229)

Feats of strength like this subduing of the fighters were distant,
if enjoyable memories. What he had called 'the manner of my
life these thirty years past' caught up with him, and for the last
eight years at least he was clearly an invalid. He was often
'weary' and had to rest. A mile afoot was a long way, and his
companions commented when a coach could not be used, as
once when 'the coach horses tiring, they were forced to go about
half the way on foot'. When he spoke at Quaker public meetings, there was talk of his sweating, and often of his leaving a
hall to rest, or even to lie down. His enemies treated this as the
arrogance of the 'great Quaker', the 'Quaker bishop', who
talked about everyone's waiting for the leading of the Spirit, but
behaved as if there was no more to be said when he had done.
He found himself breathless and unable to stay in the close city
air in summer. Longer and longer periods had to be spent in the

country, at the Meades', out at Gooseyes near Romford, or with some other friend. During these stays he went to few meetings, although people still came to see him, and he was often busy over some fresh writing.

He lived simply, too much so for one visitor to his lodging, who was surprised at his meal of a bit of salt meat and some bread. This suggests that some of his health problems may have come not only from the poor diet of the time but from his own lack of interest in food. Probably his family fed him better. He was called 'burly', but perhaps less through his putting on weight than through the swelling that could go with heart trouble. His breathlessness and his need for frequent rests would be consistent with that problem. His faithful diarist never speaks of doctors and only once of any medical attention, when, in 1685, 'he went to Bridget's at South Street again to be blooded with horse leeches' (SJ p.106). Perhaps he used herbal remedies, in line with his long interest in them, but nobody left a report.

Yet he kept at work, still speaking at meetings and moving round the north London area. In the autumn of 1690 he helped in the discussions about one of his great causes, the bill before Parliament to allow some affirmations instead of oaths. He even lobbied M.P.s himself, 'to get that bill, and another about marriages, so worded that they might not be hurtful to Friends'. Having 'much spent himself in these services', he went away to rest, though not to stop writing. On January 10th, of 1691, he wrote to Irish Friends, to comfort them in their troubles over the Jacobite rebellion, and to pass on to them good news about the welfare of Friends on the continent and over in the American settlements. He was content to think that they were all: 'in unity and peace. The Lord preserve them all out of the world (in which there is trouble), in Christ Jesus, in whom there is Peace, Life, Love, and Unity' (Ell. p.613).

The next day, in the Meeting for Worship, at Gracechurch Street in the City, he 'declared a long time very preciously and audibly and went to prayer' (SJ p.222). That was the end for him, his last preaching and public prayer. On his way to a nearby Friend's house, to lie down for his usual rest, he said that he felt the cold strike to his heart, but added 'I am glad I was here: now I am clear, I am fully clear.' Although he was at first 'pretty cheery', his strength quickly failed, so that he was forced to stay in bed, where he complained of cold, and 'groaned much'. After two days, 'in a heavenly frame of mind', he died quietly, on January 13th, 1691, at the age of sixty six and a half years.

London Friends gave him an impressive, two hour long funeral, with many testimonies, 'given, from a lively remembrance and sense of the blessed ministry of this dear and ancient servant of the Lord' (Ell. p.614). He was buried in the cemetery at Bunhill Fields. Margaret his wife, who had been with him in London from April to July of 1690, was in Swarthmoor at the time. She herself, although then seventy seven, continued an active life for a further eleven years, to her death in April 1702, just before her eighty eighth birthday.

Aftermath

All his affairs were in order. Four years earlier, in 1687, he had transferred a house and field near Swarthmoor to trustees for use as a meeting house, so that the Meeting there would not be dependent on the Hall, if its ownership should change. In Pennsylvania he left to his stepsons the 1250 acres Penn had given him, except for sixteen acres to Philadelphia Friends, for a meeting house, a school house with a botanical garden, a burial place, and a 'close to put Friends' horses in when they come to meeting'. Unfortunately this plan, in which he brought together so many of his interests and sympathies, was never carried out. Swarthmoor was luckier, for it even received his final thoughtful gifts,

> . . . my ebony bed with curtains for Friends to lie on, my great chair, which will serve for Friends to sit on, and my sea case with glass bottles will hold some liquor or drink if any should be faint. (SJ p.353)

All these were no doubt for the benefit of Friends visiting the Meeting from a distance. Was this an echo of needs unmet in the past, or of pleasure at the memory of help received?

His capital, in shares in ships and various loans, added up to about £800. How much he would have been worth today is hard to estimate, even without the complications of our present inflation. Perhaps £80,000 is at least nearer the right value. Some went to his nephew John Fox and the rest in other small legacies. His personal belongings, from his saddle to his 'seal, with the flaming sword' emblem, went to members of the family. His three hundred or so books were to be kept together as a library. His main care was that his stepsons should take the responsibility for editing and printing his writings. He was eager that this should be done carefully, and left money to pay for it.

When Fox murmured that he was 'fully clear' he might well feel he had good reason for some contentment. By physical stamina and resilience of mind he had survived all the efforts of his enemies to destroy him. He had carried his message from Germany to the furthest known west of America, and had left gatherings of his Friends almost everywhere. In his own country a long and vicious campaign to exterminate Quakers had failed. In 1660, when the Stuarts regained power, at least 40,000 people were living and worshipping in the Quaker way. When thirty years of persecution ended in 1690 there appear to have been still about the same number. Human nature on the whole prefers not to run into trouble, and turning Quaker then brought great trouble. That so many people were willing to accept the resulting hardships is a remarkable testimony to the attraction of the Quaker vision of the Christian life. Quakers led the demand for freedom of worship, and it is fair to say that their stand, more even than that of other dissenters, had brought the authorities to realise that toleration had to be granted. It was a kind of success for Fox's efforts, but perhaps a poor consolation for the fact that the longed for transformation of society seemed no nearer.

Fox had faults, but they were not in his integrity, or his moral straightforwardness, for sooner or later the people he encountered, even those who began as enemies, agreed about this. His faults were of a different kind. His own singlemindedness, an uncompromising logic about the right and wrong of an issue, meant that patience did not come easily to him. He could be unsympathetic to human hesitations. He found it hard to understand how anyone who had 'received Truth', could slip back into old ways. When he had come to a conclusion he liked his own way, and he could be tough on people he thought were hypocrites and self-seekers. Not many priests were like the 'vicar of Bray', and those trying conscientiously to do their parish

faults

work and survive on meagre tithes or small glebe holdings hardly deserved his unqualified censure. He failed to work out how some action would appear to others. It took him, and other Friends, nearly twenty years to realise that heckling preachers, or unconventional dramatic exploits, gave opponents grounds for calling them louts and fools. Though he sometimes dealt sharply with his opponents, he usually included some expression of goodwill, and his language was restrained beside what was often written about him and the Quakers.

He was not a tactician. Every wrong had to be set right, so that he attacked on all fronts, without always considering that he might be using up energy or generating illwill over a side issue. The rejection of oaths could certainly be justified, for, quite apart from objections based on the New Testament, their use implied that falsehood was allowed, that truth could sometimes be less than true. The hats and plain speech campaign (though a relevant protest against the extravagance and hypocrisy of the time) may have been taken to an extreme in which its real point was obscured by actions that looked less egalitarian than, in their own way, pointlessly ill-mannered. Did the need to be sure of the truth of one's every word even prevent daily greetings? We now find it hard to see how anyone could have felt so strongly about such matters. Yet Fox, if he were still here, might well ask what irrelevancies we are needlessly fretting over, or what essentials are being neglected.

The early Quaker response to art and music also showed a failure of discrimination. Fox and his Friends turned away from them, for they appeared to take up time and attention needed for more urgent matters, for useful work or reflection. Much of both appeared trivial, or sometimes immoral. Their successors institutionalised this rejection. Yet there appears to have been one exception. Many of these early Quakers wrote verse, which, if not of much merit, usually showed that they knew the accepted styles and could use them with skill. Fox's own young friend Ellwood had been secretary to the poet Milton and later wrote much sub-Miltonic epic verse. He also claimed to have made the thoroughly Quaker comment to his employer: why so much on 'Paradise Lost', and nothing on 'Paradise Found'? This link with Milton invites another speculation. Fox's friends, the

Peningtons, knew Ellwood and were neighbours of Milton, but there is no hint that they all met together. With much in common, and some sharp differences, any conversation between Fox and Milton should have been lively.

In our own time it usually seems to be assumed that everyone is a fraud when looked at closely. From this point of view Fox is a disappointment. The enemies of Quakers wanted to tear him apart, but they could come up only with irrelevant malice. Only in physical breakdowns caused by hardship and work did his confidence in the divine presence and power ever waver. His chief quality from first to last may be described by the curious motto he may have known at Fenny Drayton: 'Joy in pure faith'. He spent all his life trying to help others to experience it and to live by it. His restrained language does not hide his resilience, his exuberance and his sense of adventure. Many Friends wrote about him. All express what seems to be a genuine respect and warmth of affection. Fox kept some provincial accent or mannerisms; he couldn't spell, and he lacked the elegance of expression that had come to be taken for granted by the end of his life. But his total honesty and sincerity were not questioned. His faults came from these very qualities. Those who knew him agreed that he had given his life to his cause with no rancour, and no holding back for self-preservation. They found him unassuming, approachable, and welcoming. To them all he was their dearest friend.

Quakers had stood together and had won through to toleration, but the losses and the huge strains on thousands of ordinary people meant that their impetus was almost gone. A Minute of the 1689 Yearly Meeting already reveals this:

> . . . And walk wisely and circumspectly towards all men, in the peaceable Spirit of Christ Jesus; giving no offence nor occasions to those in outward government . . .

Thirty years later, when Bristol Friends were asked for historical details to complete the record of past persecutions, they were very unwilling for the old story to be revived to 'give occasion [of offence] either to the government in general under whom we enjoy so many favours or the magistrates of this city in particular' (FPT p.xv). This is a far cry from Fox's proclamation of a universal truth and the way of life that should follow from it. Quakers seemed content to exist as a marginalised closed group. As Margaret called the preoccupation with trivialities of dress and manners a 'poor silly Gospel', we may think that Fox himself would have had little use for the timid withdrawals and the watering down of his teaching in the century that followed him.

In the present century Quakers have come out of the shadows, in response to the pressures of war, social change and new experience of religion and human nature. Fox's life was his response to these pressures in that earlier great age of crisis, when the 'world was turned upside down'. In his day political authority and conformity were bound up with questions of church doctrine and organisation. Yet in a secular political dress the same demands and conflicts can still be heard. In personal life this present time seems to be the age of the provisional. Fox expected everyone to be loyal to clearly considered convictions and to behave with unreserved integrity. Have these qualities reached their sell-by date, along with other discarded attitudes? Fox was a gadfly, a public nuisance, one of a long succession of prophets who have wanted to test and purify every aspect of belief and conduct. Their manners and words grow old-fashioned, but should their challenges to accepted ways and standards be therefore written off?

BOOKS QUOTED

Abbreviations

('Q' introducing a reference = quoted in)

B of M *George Fox's Book of Miracles,* edited by Henry J. Cadbury. Cambridge U.P., 1948

BQ *The Beginnings of Quakerism* by W. C. Braithwaite. London: Macmillan, 1912; Cambridge U.P., 2nd edn. 1961 prep. by Henry J. Cadbury, now York: Sessions

CFP *Christian Faith and Practice in the Experience of the Society of Friends.* London Yearly Meeting, 1960

CJ *The Journal of George Fox,* edited from the mss. by Norman Penney. Cambridge U.P., 1911

Ell. *The Journal . . . of George Fox,* edited by Thomas Ellwood. [1694]

Ell. History *The History of the Life of Thomas Ellwood,* London, 1714.

Ep. *A Collection of . . . Epistles, Letters and Testimonies,* by George Fox [1698]

EQW *Early Quaker Writings 1650–1700,* edited by Hugh Barbour and Arthur Roberts. Grand Rapids, Mich., USA: Eerdman, 1973

FPT *The First Publishers of Truth: Early Records of the Introduction of Quakerism into . . . England and Wales,* edited by Norman Penney. London: Headley, 1907

GTD *Gospel Truth Demonstrated in a Collection of Doctrinal Books . . .* by George Fox [1706]

HJC Narr. Pap. *The Narrative Papers of George Fox,* unpublished or uncollected. Edited by Henry J. Cadbury. Richmond, Ind., USA: Friends United Press, 1972

JFHS *Journal* of the Friends Historical Society, London

N *The Journal of George Fox,* revised edition by John L. Nickalls. Cambridge U.P., 1952; London Yearly Meeting, rptd. 1975

PWP *The Papers of William Penn,* edited by Dunn & Dunn. Philadelphia: University of Pennsylvania P., 1981

QAC *The Quakers in the American Colonies* by Rufus M. Jones. London: Macmillan, 1911

SF *The Household Account Book of Sarah Fell,* edited by Norman Penney. Cambridge U.P., 1920

SJ *The Short Journal and Itinerary Journals of George Fox*, edited from the mss. by Norman Penney. Cambridge U.P., 1925

SPQ *The Second Period of Quakerism* by W. C. Braithwaite. London: Macmillan, 1921; Cambridge U.P., 2nd edn. 1961 prep. by Henry J. Cadbury, now York: Sessions

Sw.Mss. *Swarthmore Manuscripts*, the collection of letters and other papers, mostly once at Swarthmoor Hall, now in Friends House Library, London

Other titles

Ashley (Maurice) *Life in Stuart England*. London: Batsford, 1964

Banks (John) *Journal* [1712]

Barbour (Hugh) *The Quakers in Puritan England*. New Haven, Conn., USA: Yale U.P., 1964

Barclay (R.) *The Life of the Religious Societies of the Commonwealth*. [1877]

Baxter (Richard) *Autobiography*. London: Everyman, 1931

Burnyeat (John) *The Truth Exalted in the Writings of that Eminent & Faithful Servant of Christ John Burnyeat*. London, Thos, Northcott, 1691

Bunyan (John) *Grace Abounding*. London: Everyman, 1928

Capp (B. S.) *The Fifth Monarchy Men: a Study in Seventeenth-Century Millenarianism*. London: Faber, 1972

Coward (Barry) *The Stuart Age 1603–1714*. London: Longmans, 1980

Crosfield (Helen G.) *Margaret Fox of Swarthmoor Hall*. London: Headley, 1913

Edmondson (William) *A Journal of the Life* . . . [1715]

Edwards (D. L.) *Christian England from the Reformation to the Eighteenth Century*. London: Collins, 1983

Fell (Margaret) [Works:] *A Brief Collection* [1710]

Fraser (Antonia) *Cromwell, Our Chief of Men*. London: Weidenfeld and Nicolson, 1973

Gardiner (R. S.) *Constitutional Documents of the Puritan Revolution*. Oxford U.P., 1906

Gough (Richard) *The History of Myddle* [1700]. Harmondsworth, Middx: Penguin Books, 1981

Hill (Christopher) *The World Turned Upside Down: Radical Ideas during the English Revolution*. Harmondsworth, Middx: Penguin Books, 1975

Hill (Christopher) *A Turbulent, Seditious and Factious People: John Bunyan and his Church.* Oxford U.P., 1988

Hill (Christopher) *The Intellectual Origins of the English Revolution.* Oxford: Clarendon Press, 1965

Hirst (Derek) *Authority and Conflict in England 1603–1658.* London: Arnold, 1986

Horle (Craig) *Quakers and the English Legal System.* Philadelphia, USA: University of Pennsylvania P., 1988

Howgill (Francis) [Works] *The Dawning of the Gospel Day* [1676]

Hutton (Ronald) *The Restoration: A Political and Religious History of England and Wales 1658–1667.* Oxford U.P., 1985

Morton (A. L.) *The World of the Ranters.* London: Lawrence & Wishart, 1970

Pepys (Samuel) *The Shorter Pepys.* London: Bell & Hyman, 1985

Raistrick (Arthur) *Quakers in Science and Industry.* London: David & Charles, rptd. 1968, now York, Sessions

Reay (Barry) *Quakers & the English Revolution* London: Maurice Temple Smith, 1985.

Richardson (R. C.) *Puritanism in North West England.* Manchester U.P., 1972

Ross (Isabel) *Margaret Fell: Mother of Quakerism.* London: Longmans, 1949; York: Sessions, rptd. 1984

Sewel (William) *The History of the Rise, Increase and Progress of the Christian People called Quakers.* [1722]

Tolmie (M.) *The Triumph of the Saints* Cambridge U.P., 1977

Watkins (Owen) *The Puritan Experience.* London: Routledge & Kegan Paul, 1972

Watt (Michael) *The Dissenters from the Reformation to the French Revolution.* Oxford U.P., 1978

Whitehead (George) *The Christian Progress . . .* [1725]

SOME FURTHER READING

Brinton (Howard) *Friends for Three Hundred Years.* Wallingford, Penn., USA: Pendle Hill Publications, 1952

Gwyn (Douglas) *Apocalypse of the Word: The Life and Message of George Fox* Richmond, Ind., USA: Friends United Press, 1984. (This includes a useful bibliography)

Jones (T. Canby) *The Power of the Lord is Over All: The Pastoral Let-*

ters of George Fox. Richmond, Ind., USA: Friends United Press, 1989

Pickvance (Joseph) *A Reader's Companion to George Fox's Journal* London: Quaker Home Service, 1989

Punshon (John) *Portrait in Grey: A Short History of the Quakers* London: Quaker Home Service, 1984 (This includes a full bibliography)

Punshon (John) *Testimony & Tradition*: Quaker Home Service, London, 1990

No More but My Love: Letters of George Fox selected and edited by Cecil W. Sharman. London: Quaker Home Service, 1980

INDEX OF NAMES & INDEXES

offices of Christ p. 100
peace statement p. 119, 144, 151
letter of comfort p. 142

The Family Tree of George and Margaret Fox

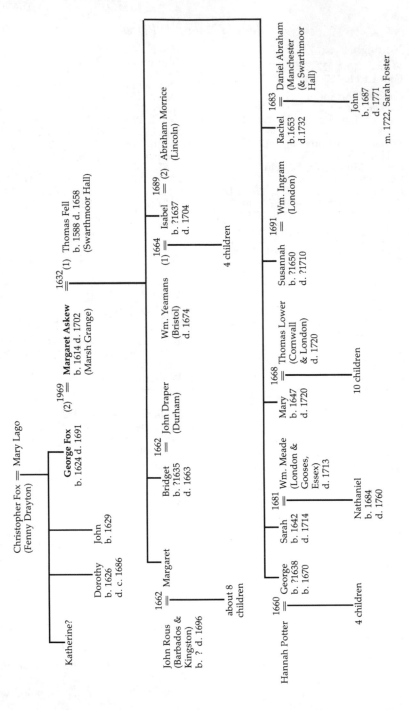

Katherine?

Christopher Fox = Mary Lago
(Fenny Drayton)

Dorothy
b. 1626
d. c. 1686

John
b. 1629

George Fox
b. 1624 d. 1691

1632 (1) Thomas Fell
b. 1588 d. 1658
(Swarthmoor Hall)

(2) 1969 Margaret Askew
b. 1614 d. 1702
(Marsh Grange)

John Rous
(Barbados &
Kingston)
b. ? d. 1696

1662 Margaret

about 8
children

Bridget
b. ?1635
d. 1663

1662 John Draper
(Durham)

Wm. Yeamans
(Bristol)
d. 1674

Isabel
b. ?1637
d. 1704

1664 (1) (2) 1689 Abraham Morrice
(Lincoln)

4 children

Hannah Potter

1660 George
b. ?1638
b. 1670

4 children

Sarah
b. 1642
d. 1714

1681 Wm. Meade
(London &
Gooses,
Essex)
d. 1713

Nathaniel
b. 1684
d. 1760

Mary
b. 1647
d. 1720

1668 Thomas Lower
(Cornwall
& London)
d. 1720

10 children

Susannah
b. ?1650
d. ?1710

1691 Wm. Ingram
(London)

Rachel
b.1653
d.1732

1683 Daniel Abraham
(Manchester
(& Swarthmoor
Hall)

John
b. 1687
d. 1771
m. 1722, Sarah Foster